STOP WORRYING!

THERE *PROBABLY* IS
AN AFTERLIFE

DAILY GRAIL PUBLISHING

Daily Grail Publishing
Brisbane, Australia
publications@dailygrail.com
www.dailygrail.com

Greg Taylor is the owner and editor of the alternative science and history news portal *The Daily Grail* (www.dailygrail.com), and is also the editor of the Fortean anthology series *Darklore*. He lives in Brisbane, Australia.

For

Tonita, Isis, Phoenix and Maya

and

Mum, Leanne and Natalie

CONTENTS

"What is this dying? No one who has done it can tell us what it is like.

Are we mere sparks of sentience that death extinguishes, or fledgeling immortals who fear to leave the nest? Or both, or neither?

We are conceived in mystery, and into mystery we die."

– Olaf Stapledon

PREFACE

Exit Music

The earth is mostly just a boneyard. But pretty in the sunlight.

Larry McMurtry

YOU ARE GOING TO DIE.

Okay, probably not the best way to start a book. Hang in there dear reader – at least things can only get better from this page onwards. I just wanted to be clear regarding our shared mortality, as many of us tend to drift through life trying our best to ignore that rather important fact. It's an understandable reaction to our impending annihilation. But thrusting our heads in the sand will not help us one iota when that day finally rolls around, the advent of perhaps the most significant and special event of our lives: its termination.

How special an event is it? Only an elite club of some 100 billion humans have experienced it thus far.[1] And this year, just 58 million more people will be permitted to join those shades of the departed – around 160,000 people each day (or, to put it another way, since your last breath five people have slipped this mortal coil, their existence upon the Earth – with all its attendant hopes, dreams, joys and loves – apparently extinguished forever).[2] Some of those people will welcome the approach of the grim reaper, expecting union with their god or saviour of choice; others will hand themselves over to death confident in their belief that it is the utter end of them in every sense. But none of them know for sure – and regardless of their belief (or non-belief, if they see it that way), in the back of their mind they probably all know it.

And this book will not change that. For all our ingenuity and the exquisite knowledge-gathering power of science, we have not found the definitive answer to what happens to us after we die. That's in large part due to the fact that the dead don't tend to come forward with information too often, so the data is a bit thin on the ground. But also because research into the question of 'what happens after death' remains a rather taboo topic for some strange reason. As philosopher Michael Grosso has pointed out, "the current U.S. military budget is roughly $350 billion, all dedicated to the technology of death. Contrast this with the funds available to do research on the conscious survival of death. Did I hear an amused snicker?"

That's not to say that there isn't any research being done however. Over the past 150 years, a small percentage of scientists have taken it upon themselves to investigate testimony given by the dying from their deathbeds, by patients who went as close to death as possible before returning to life, and from others who claim to be able to speak with the dead. At risk of ridicule and damage to their reputations within the academic community, these scientists have nevertheless reported on what they have found – and as the following chapters will show, there's no shortage of hints and suggestions that some part of us does continue on after the physical death of our body.

But I want to make clear from the beginning that this book is not about convincing or converting any reader to *a belief* in an afterlife. Belief, as the sagacious Robert Anton Wilson once remarked, "is the death of intelligence". Once we believe in something, we stop questioning that model of reality, and we thus fail to update and modify our worldview and move forward through continued learning. Additionally, as Wilson noted, once locked into only one belief, we are also "destined to become virtually deaf, dumb, and blind" to the beliefs and opinions of others, which is a surefire recipe for inhumanity.

We are, however, human beings, and it's difficult to live life without some sort of model of reality. And that's fine – assemble the facts and evidence that you've come across throughout your life, and construct the best possible model you can to help get you through the day-to-day of life. Just don't *believe* in it all too seriously, and be willing to update that model as you integrate new evidence with it.

As such, I encourage readers to practice skepticism, and doubt everything you read in the pages of this book. Not because I've filled the following pages with any nonsense I could find – far from it, I've endeavoured to discuss the topic using only evidence that I find truly fascinating and worthy of inclusion. But doubt is a necessity when swimming in these waters at the edges of the scientific world – it helps protect you from the sharks interested only in profit, rather than your education, and the desperate flailing of those drowning in their own belief system, keen to bring you down with them. So don't just read this book – follow the references, search the web for discussions of the topic, learn more. My only warning to you is to practice that same doubt when you encounter any other resources – and that includes those created by so-called 'skeptics', many of whom are embedded within their own belief system and wish to impose it upon you. Attaching the label of 'skeptic' to themselves should not grant them an exclusion from your doubt. Form *your own opinion,* based on the best available evidence and criticisms, all the while being as honest with yourself as possible.

The title for this book has its origin in a talk I had with my father a few years ago, when he was in the late stages of Early-Onset Alzheimer's Disease. Some twelve years on from his diagnosis at age 54, Dad could no longer talk, and to most appearances seemed to have only the barest understanding of the world around him. As his brain continued to lose control of his body, muscle spasms and seizures became constants throughout his day, and the most basic movements now seemed Herculean tasks for him. Concerned that he may have been grimly 'holding on' for us, his family, at great personal expense, I told him that while he fought on he had our total support, but that if he wanted to 'let go' then I totally understood and respected that decision. And, as someone who has been interested in the scientific investigation of the possibility of life beyond death for many years now, I also let him know my thoughts on what he might experience if he did desire to let go. Drawing on everything I have read, from scientific studies through to skeptical investigations, I told Dad my opinion at that point in time: that there *probably* is some sort of afterlife. I emphasise the 'probably' for the reasons outlined above: I retain doubt, and the right to revise that opinion as more evidence on these topics is collected. But, given the facts I've come across in my own research – in which I believe I've been as honest as possible with myself – that is the model of reality that seems the most likely to me at this point.

I'm not sure if Dad had the ability to comprehend everything I said in my conversation with him. I do know that when I finished talking, a single tear ran down his cheek – but whether that was a result of our discussion, or just the breeze from a ceiling fan aggravating his eye, I cannot say. I prefer to think the former, that somewhere deep within the besieged fortress of his mind, he understood everything I said.

Dad died the following year. In the pages of this book, I've done my best to share with you the perspectives that informed my talk with him, as I think it's worthwhile information to have when contemplating the fact that you too will one day die.

INTRODUCTION

Ghosts in the Machine?

By far the most usual way of handling phenomena so novel that they would make for a serious rearrangement of our preconceptions is to ignore them altogether, or to abuse those who bear witness for them.

William James

In December 1943, as World War II raged across the European continent, Private George Ritchie lay perilously close to death in a Texas military hospital as he suffered from a severe case of pneumonia. The twenty-year-old had recently completed his basic training, and was booked on the next day's train to Richmond to study as a doctor at the Medical College of Virginia. However, as a fever took hold, the young soldier's body temperature soared above 106 degrees. On the cold winter's night of December 20th, 1943, Private Ritchie left on another, far stranger journey:

I heard a click and a whirr. The whirr went on and on. It was getting louder. The whirr was inside my head and my knees were made of rubber. They were bending and I was falling and all the time the whirr grew louder. I sat up with a start. What time was it? I looked at the bedside table but they'd taken the clock away. In fact, where was any of my stuff? I jumped out of bed in alarm, looking for my clothes. My uniform wasn't on the chair. I turned around, then froze. Someone was lying in that bed.[1]

Private Ritchie didn't stop to think any further, assuming that he had slept through the night and was now late for his Virginia-bound train. He rushed out into the corridor and attempted to gain the attention of an approaching sergeant. However, the sergeant appeared not to see him and brushed past without the slightest acknowledgement.

The young private decided to take matters into his own hands, and dashed down the corridor toward the exit, a pair of swinging metal doors. Suddenly he found himself flying through the air, faster than he'd ever travelled before, as if he'd suddenly taken on the powers of the recently created comic book character Superman. When he finally came to a halt, Private Ritchie realized with amazement that he had traveled to his desired destination, Richmond – "one hundred times faster than any train could". Despite still wearing his army-issue hospital pyjamas, he approached a civilian stranger to ask for some bearings, but to his distress the man didn't appear to see him either. While that fact disturbed Private Ritchie, what followed left him gaping. Reaching out his left hand to tap the man on the shoulder, he found to his astonishment that his hand passed straight through the stranger's body.

At this point, Private George Ritchie realized that he was, in fact, dead:

> And suddenly I remembered the young man I had seen in the bed in that little hospital room. What if that had been … me? Or anyhow, the material, concrete part of myself that in some unexplainable way I'd gotten separated from.

What if the form which I had left lying in the hospital room in Texas was my own? And if it were, how could I get back to it again?[2]

Within an instant of this thought he found himself rushing back to the army hospital, where he desperately searched ward after ward for his physical body. Scanning the faces of sleeping soldiers, Private Ritchie was at wit's end when he finally came across a body covered with a sheet. Noticing the onyx and gold fraternity ring on the middle finger of the cadaver's hand, he was – not surprisingly – only slightly relieved to realize that this corpse was his own body.

Suddenly the room became much brighter, and a 'being of light' appeared to Private Ritchie. Episodes of his life began to play out before him – "everything that had ever happened to me was simply there, in full view, contemporary and current, all seemingly taking place at the same time" – while 'the Light' asked one simple question: "What did you do with your life?" But despite the magnitude and interrogatory phrasing of this question, at no time did Ritchie feel that he was being judged by the being. After this review of his life, the being – whom the newly-dead man guessed was Jesus – then took him on a tour of both earthly and heavenly realms. To Private Ritchie's surprise, the being then gave him orders to return to the land of the living.

If anybody was more surprised at his return to life than George Ritchie, it was probably the army physician who had just signed the young soldier's death certificate. An orderly had noticed some movement as he prepared the corpse for the morgue, and summoned the doctor who quickly administered a shot of adrenaline straight into the dead man's heart. Private Ritchie returned to life with a burning throat and a crushing weight on his chest, a full nine minutes after he had appeared to have taken his last breath.

Death by Science

The resurrection experience of George Ritchie marks a key moment in the modern debate over the existence of 'the afterlife', as it directly inspired the modern fascination with a phenomenon which has become known as the near-death experience (NDE). The young private went on to become Dr George Ritchie, a psychiatrist whose description of the deathly realms made a great impression upon one of his students, one Raymond Moody, when he related it during a philosophy lecture in 1965. A decade later, that same student told the world about not only Dr Ritchie's NDE, but also a great many others when he published his best-selling book *Life after Life*. Going on to sell more than 13 million copies, Moody's book brought the NDE into the public consciousness for the first time, inspiring Hollywood movies such as *Flatliners*, and sparking further scientific investigation of these strange experiences. Today the near-death experience has well and truly established itself in popular culture: as an example, witness how perhaps the most crucial scene in one of the most popular books and films of all time – *Harry Potter and the Deathly Hallows*, where Harry dies and meets up with Professor Dumbledore in an afterlife way-station – is closely modelled on near-death experience accounts.

What was it about Moody's book that made it such a hit with the general public? No doubt the diminishing role of organized religion in many peoples' lives during the 20th century had left a spiritual hole that the NDE filled quite adequately. But it was perhaps something more than this as well. A century previous, before 'near-death experience' became a household word, the public had a similar fascination with Spiritualism – a movement that revolved around the idea that the denizens of the spirit world were still able to communicate with the living, most notably through 'spirit mediums'. What is notable about both of these modern modes of encountering the concept of an afterlife is that they are, by their very nature, experiential. For an extended time in the last 2000 years, with Christianity as the dominant force shaping Western culture, the idea of an afterlife was largely taken as a given, and a simple matter of religious faith. The dead had their place in heaven (or in some unfortunate cases, hell), and humans their place on Earth until they were duly called by their Maker. People were asked simply to put their trust in the authority and truthfulness of the Church and the Bible.

But from the time of the Renaissance, both God and Western civilization's collective ego had begun to take some serious hits. In the 16th century, the heliocentric theory of Nicolaus Copernicus had displaced Earth from the centre of the Universe, by showing that our planet was actually only one of many that revolved around our Sun (previously, the common belief was that the Sun, planets and stars all revolved around the Earth).

In the 17th century, Isaac Newton's formulation of his famous laws of motion suggested to scientists that our Universe was deterministic: one thing followed another based on strict physical laws of cause and effect. There was no divine creator who intervened on behalf of man; at best there could only be a 'Supreme Architect', the equivalent of a watchmaker who designed the cosmos but stepped aside after that point and let it run as it was meant to, obeying the universal laws that Newton had discovered. The implications of a deterministic Universe for human beings were humbling, almost demeaning. Astrophysicist Bernard Haisch explains:

> Unfortunately we ourselves are included in the Universe. And if we think of ourselves as just complex organic machines, then every thought and every action that we think we are consciously and freely choosing is in reality just the consequence of the previous state of the Universe. There is no freedom, there is no true choice, not in the slightest. In this view, we ourselves are no more than wind-up dolls, automatons, executing thoughts

and actions that we inherited from everything that came before us. Every choice we make is illusory from this perspective, because even the atoms and molecules in our brain are just following the positions and motions they inherited. The universe becomes like a giant billiard table whose countless billiard balls (the particles making up matter) are just following the laws of mechanics: the 5-ball hits the 9-ball knocking the 8-ball in the pocket and that explains why I just scratched my head thinking I was doing so of my own free will.[3]

And the hits kept coming. The following century brought the mind-blowing concept of Deep Time, which contradicted the Biblical tale of the Creation. Contrary to the calculations of Bishop James Ussher – who in 1650 had declared the date of Creation to be the night preceding Sunday the 23rd of October, 4004 B.C. – scientists in the nascent field of geology were staggered to find that the history of the Earth should be measured not in thousands, not even in millions, but in billions of years. Suddenly, the human life-span shrank into insignificance. The mathematician John Playfair, upon viewing the geological evidence in June 1788, remarked that "the mind seemed to grow giddy by looking so far into the abyss of time." Even the entire life-span of human civilization itself became lost in time. Mark Twain put things into perspective with these words: "If the Eiffel tower were now representing the world's age, the skin of paint on the pinnacle-knob at its summit would represent man's share of that age".[4] If humans had lost their exalted place in the Universe with the ideas of Copernicus, they had now also lost their place in time.

But in the mid-19th century came the *coup-de-grâce:* Charles Darwin's theory of evolution by means of natural selection. Far from being God's most cherished creation – made in his image no less – humans turned out to be nothing more than monkeys. Insignificant little puppet monkeys, dancing on a pebble in the unfathomable depths of time and space, with their fates already pre-determined by Newton's laws of motion...

In the last century and a half, this diminished view of humanity's significance has become the dominant paradigm within the scientific community. The eminently recognizable theoretical physicist Professor Stephen Hawking has stated plainly his view that "the human race is just a chemical scum on a moderate-sized planet".[5] And not only are we simply "scum", we're scum with no control over our fate: the late Francis Crick – co-discoverer of the structure of DNA – echoed Bernard Haisch's "billiard-ball analogy" of the current scientific consensus on the idea of free will when he noted that "you, your joys and your sorrows, your memories and ambitions, your sense of personal identity and free will, are in fact no more than the behaviour of a vast assembly of nerve cells and their associated molecules".[6]

While scientists such as Hawking, Crick, Richard Dawkins and others certainly don't reject the inherent beauty of life and the cosmos – quite the opposite, in fact, as they believe the scientific discoveries of the last few centuries only enhance the wonder of our Universe – they have asserted, sometimes quite aggressively, that there is no deeper meaning to life, and certainly nothing *after* life for each of us. But what are the implications of these discoveries for the average person?

In his wonderful fictional series *The Hitchhiker's Guide to the Galaxy*, the late Douglas Adams (who was, incidentally, an atheist and a close friend of Richard Dawkins) introduced the 'Total Perspective Vortex' – a machine built by inventor Trin Tragula, who after being constantly nagged by his wife to "Have some sense of proportion!" (sometimes as often as thirty-eight times in a single day), decided to build a machine "just to show her". Into one end, he plugged the whole of reality (in classic Adams fashion, extrapolated from a piece of fairy cake), and into the other he plugged his wife, so that she would be shown in one instant "the whole infinity of creation and herself in relation to it". To his horror, Trin Tragula realized that this single, devastating shock had completely annihilated his wife's brain, but to his satisfaction "he realized that he had proved conclusively that if life is going to exist in a Universe of this size, then one thing it cannot afford to have is a sense of proportion".

The story of the Total Perspective Vortex could very well be an analogy for the last five hundred years of human history. If humanity can be equated with Trin Tragula's wife, then the ground-breaking scientific discoveries during that period have acted somewhat as the Total Perspective Vortex. To avoid having their brain annihilated, many people have unfortunately fled from a sense of proportion by rejecting science outright, retreating into fundamentalist religiosity, or at the very least enveloping themselves in a blissful (to them) shroud of ignorance. A false dichotomy has been created – and somewhat promoted, it must be said, by both fundamentalist preachers and outspoken atheists – where the widespread public view seems to be that you're either with science, or with spirituality, but you can't have a foot in both camps.

Humanity Resurrected

However, what is not as well known is that many prominent scientists – some of the finest minds alive, in fact – actually argue *against* diminishing the cosmic role of human life and consciousness, and feel that there *is* some deeper reason for the presence of both in the Universe. Indeed, many of these thinkers believe that 'mind' – rather than being an accidental by-product of physical processes – may actually be a, perhaps *the*, fundamental part of the cosmos. As theoretical physicist and mathematician Freeman Dyson has noted:

> To me the most astounding fact in the universe is the power of mind which drives my fingers as I write these words.

Somehow, by natural processes still totally mysterious a million butterfly brains working together in a human skull have the power to dream, to calculate, to see and to hear, to speak and to listen, to translate thoughts and feelings into marks on paper which other brains can interpret. Mind, through the long course of biological evolution, has established itself as a moving force in our little corner of the universe. Here on this small planet, *mind has infiltrated matter and has taken control. It appears to me that the tendency of mind to infiltrate and control matter is a law of nature.*[7] [my emphasis]

Respected cosmologist Paul Davies, in his essay "Life, Mind, and Culture as Fundamental Properties of the Universe", argues that the orthodox view about the insignificance of life – as espoused by the likes of Stephen Hawking – is "profoundly wrong". Davies says that "Not only do I believe that life is a key part of the evolution of the universe, I maintain that mind and culture, too, will turn out to be of fundamental significance in the grand story of the cosmos." He explains further:

It is fashionable to downplay the significance of consciousness, perhaps because of its perceived mystical associations. However, this is in my view a serious error. Conscious organisms should not be casually shrugged aside as just another sort of physical system, albeit a peculiar one. The qualities of conscious systems are totally unlike anything else found in nature. Mental entities such as thoughts and feelings are clearly not just "other sorts of things"…some philosophers are prepared to defend the fundamental nature of the mental realm, and to argue that subjective experience cannot be relegated to a sequence of mere epiphenomena attaching to physical processes.[8]

Davies goes on to point out that as intrinsic, physical parts of the Universe ourselves, our capacity for investigation and understanding through scientific and mathematical thinking suggests there is a deep and mysterious link between our consciousness and the greater cosmos. In his eyes, the human mind is no mere illusion or unneeded by-product of the brain. Instead, the arrival of human awareness – and in particular the human *understanding* of nature – seems to be nothing less than a watershed moment in the history of the cosmos:

> Somehow, the universe has engineered not only its own self-awareness, but its own self-comprehension. It is hard to see this astonishing property of (at least some) living organisms as an accidental and incidental by-product of physics, a lucky fluke of biological evolution. Rather, the fact that mind is linked into the deep workings of the cosmos in this manner suggests that there is something truly fundamental and literally cosmic in the emergence of sentience.[9]

The acclaimed American philosopher (and atheist) Thomas Nagel has recently voiced a similar opinion, to the consternation of a number of his fellow academics. "The appearance of reason and language in the course of biological history seems, from the point of view of available forms of explanation, something radically emergent," Nagel states in his 2012 book *Mind and Cosmos*. Echoing the words of Paul Davies, he writes that "each of our lives is a part of the lengthy process of the universe gradually waking up and becoming aware of itself".[10]

The curious fact that human consciousness seems to be a way for the universe to observe itself ties in closely to developments in science over the past century, most notably in the field of quantum physics – the field of science concerned with phenomena at the microscopic scale (atoms and sub-atomic elements). The enigma that emerges at the quantum level is that the act of observation seems to be a crucial part of creating 'reality': until observed, the fundamental building blocks from which physical things are constructed exist only as probabilities, in 'quantum superposition'; it is not until there is a measurement or observation that these particles solidify into something tangible and 'real'. Interpretations of this quantum mystery vary, but every one of them involves consciousness in some way.[11]

The development of this new paradigm of physics in the 20th century undermines both the idea of a deterministic cosmos – as suggested by Newtonian physics – as well as the assumption that consciousness is an accident of biology with no real significance. And yet, respected physicist Henry Stapp notes, despite nearly a century having passed since the Newtonian world view was shown to be "fundamentally incorrect", the notion of mechanical determinism "still dominates the general intellectual milieu".[12] The shadow of the Newtonian worldview is promulgated by those who wish, for whatever reason, to reinforce the view of a deterministic Universe with consciousness as a bizarre epiphenomenon. Stapp points out, as an example, that one of the leading modern philosophers of mind, Daniel Dennett, has said his own 'mundane' viewpoint on consciousness rests on the idea that "a brain was always going to do what it was caused to do by current, local, mechanical circumstances". Yet this statement seems at odds with the current and accepted paradigm of the laws of physics.

Just as Davies, Dyson and Nagel have argued, a number of scientists now suggest, based on the theory of the quantum world, that consciousness may in fact be *a fundamental property* of the cosmos – far from the 'accidental by-product' of a biological brain. The pioneering cosmologist Sir James Jeans made clear his own thoughts about the importance of human consciousness – to him, mind is *the* most important element of the cosmos:

> I incline to the idealistic theory that consciousness is
> fundamental, and that the material universe is derivative
> from consciousness, not consciousness from the material
> universe... In general the universe seems to me to be nearer
> to a great thought than to a great machine. It may well be,
> it seems to me, that each individual consciousness ought to
> be compared to a brain-cell in a universal mind.

But if this radical new view of consciousness is correct, what happens
to it when our body – the physical substrate upon which it appears
to depend – no longer exists? It's an odd question actually, because
your body has never been a permanent thing – it is an illusion. As
cardiologist Pim van Lommel has pointed out, every second some
500,000 cells in your body are broken down and regenerated, and
within two weeks *all* of the molecules and atoms in your body's
cells are replaced. Which raises some interesting questions: "How
can we account for long-term memory", van Lommel asks, "if the
molecular makeup of the cell membrane of neurons is completely
renewed every two weeks and the millions of synapses in the brain
undergo a process of constant adaptation?"[13]

   Our self, our consciousness, persists as a continuity despite
the physical substrate of our body being constantly destroyed and
replaced. So are there any reasons to believe that this 'fundamental
property' continues on in some way after we die?

Facing our Fears

Woody Allen once wrote "It's not that I'm afraid of death. It's just
that I don't want to be there when it happens." His words probably
mirror the thoughts of most human beings. Most especially for
those of us not facing advanced age or a terminal illness, death is
generally perceived as something that happens to someone else,
not us, and is thus best not thought about. We hide the concept

out of sight, using euphemisms such as "passed away" (or with pets, "went to sleep") to disguise the actual event of death. And even when we do contemplate the day that the Reaper will come knocking – the final and perhaps most significant event of our lifetime – many people express their desire to be ignorant of the actual moment, hoping to die in their sleep, or so quickly they are unaware of its happening.

This modern fear of death may well be, more than anything, stark terror in the face of oblivion. For many people today, based on the current orthodox scientific worldview, all our memories, our ambitions, and that central part of us that we identify as 'I', are seen to suddenly disappear forever upon our physical death. However, as we have seen, there are a number of scientists and thinkers who don't agree with the 'orthodox' view of the cosmos. And you may be surprised to learn that there is a substantial amount of evidence that suggests human consciousness lives on, beyond the death of our physical body – and that it truly is a thing apart from the physical Universe.

Though scientists and outspoken atheists often regard belief in an afterlife simply as a natural human reaction to the idea of annihilation, the idea of survival of our consciousness in some discarnate form has been widely held in almost every culture from the beginning of human history – based not on blind faith in some sort of God-like being maintaining a celestial salvatory for souls, as found in Christianity, but instead on direct personal experiences that suggest postmortem survival.[14] We have already seen George Ritchie's own apparent experience with some sort of afterlife state, which certainly convinced *him* of the belief that consciousness survives the body's death. Many millions of people around the world have had this 'direct experience' of some sort of afterlife, courtesy of a near-death experience. Others have had that experience not by going through the dying process themselves, but by communicating with visions or apparitions of those who have passed.[15] And yet others claim to have talked with the deceased through so-called 'psychic mediums'. Such strangeness is not restricted to a certain 'type' of person, normally categorized as "delusional", or more politely "fantasy-prone". Individuals from scientists to heads-of-state to business leaders have been known to have perceptions of a world beyond the veil of death, and interact with those that reside there. And while these experiences do not necessarily prove the existence of an afterlife, these manifold interactions with some sort of 'beyond' are nearly always absolutely convincing to the experiencer themselves, so much so that many precipitate Damascus-road type conversions. This should at least give us pause, and prompt further investigation with a view to finding the truth, as best we can determine it, behind these mysteries. The results may just contain more than a few surprises...

ONE

No One Dies Alone

Death is not extinguishing the light;
it is putting out the lamp because dawn has come.

Rabindrananth Tagore

In October 2011, the death of Apple founder Steve Jobs made news across the world. His premature passing at the age of 56 was yet another reminder to us that, no matter what your age, or the position you hold in life, death is the great leveller. But his death might also offer clues to something more: in her eulogy, Steve Jobs' sister Mona Simpson closed by sharing the technology guru's last spoken communication before his passing. According to Simpson...

> ...Steve's final words, hours earlier, were monosyllables, repeated three times. Before embarking, he'd looked at his sister Patty, then for a long time at his children, then at his life's partner, Laurene, and then over their shoulders past them.
>
> Steve's final words were: OH WOW. OH WOW. OH WOW.[1]

Perhaps Steve Jobs' exclamations were referring to his family, an attempt to transmit his deep feelings of affection and awe for each of them, or maybe he was simply summing up his own amazing life in his final moments of reflection. But Mona Simpson's description of the scene could also be read another way – and is perhaps meant to be, given that just a few sentences earlier she mentioned how her brother had told her "that he was going to a better place". She relates that when exclaiming "OH WOW" three times, he was not looking at his family anymore, but "over their shoulders past them". This scenario is strongly suggestive of a strange experience that sometimes occurs shortly before the time of passing: the so-called "death-bed vision", or "take-away vision", in which the dying person sees apparitions of already-departed loved ones – and also sometimes what appear to be heavenly creatures such as 'angels' – who have apparently come with the express purpose of collecting the individual and guiding them into the afterlife. For example, one recent death-bed account from a palliative carer tells how a lady...

> ...about an hour before she died said, "they're all in the room; they're all in the room". The room was full of people she knew and I can remember feeling quite spooked really and looking over my shoulder and not seeing a thing but she could definitely see the room full of people that she knew.[2]

How often do these experiences occur? A lot more commonly than you might think: in a recent British study, researchers found that almost two-thirds of doctors, nurses and hospice carers reported witnessing 'end-of-life experiences' (ELEs) such as death-bed visions (DBVs) in their patients.[3] The survey, headed by neuropsychiatrist Dr. Peter Fenwick, concluded that such experiences were a common element of the dying process, and additionally that they were often "healing experiences" for both the dying and their families.

Peter Fenwick (pronounced 'Fennick') would only have been mildly surprised by the data though, as he has been studying end-of-life experiences for more than three decades now, during which time he has collected hundreds of cases and has authored a number of books on the phenomenon with his wife Elizabeth; he may just be the closest thing there is to an expert on the topic. With his rangy 78-year-old frame (that seems to be perpetually dressed in a suit a half-size too big), a shock of silvery hair flowing from the back of his mostly bald head, and a genial, cut-glass English accent, Fenwick would also not look out of place as a teacher at Hogwarts School of Witchcraft and Wizardry. But his approach to end-of-life experiences is solidly grounded in science – even though, as he and fellow researchers Hilary Lovelace and Sue Brayne point out, the current view of mainstream science "is that ELEs, particularly deathbed visions, have no intrinsic value, and are either confusional or drug induced". That view, however, seems to be profoundly wrong: the vast majority of the carers interviewed in their study "agreed that ELEs were not due to confusional states resulting from either medication or the toxic processes involved in dying", and "usually occurred in clear consciousness". What's more, carers considered end-of-life experiences "to be profoundly subjective and meaningful events" that often "helped the individual to let go of life and lessened the fear of dying". Far from being of no value, end-of-life experiences such as death-bed visions were seen as important 'spiritual' events, imbued with personal meaning, and which took patients beyond the distress of dying.

An Irish study in 2009 of 40 carers revealed very similar numbers to Peter Fenwick's British study, with around two-thirds of respondents having witnessed end-of-life experiences in their patients.[4] A larger scale study in the U.S. with 525 respondents found that more than half of them reported instances of a dying person seeing or hearing deceased loved ones.[5] And a small study in Australia that surveyed just five palliative care nurses found that all five reported witnessing at least four 'paranormal' experiences while tending dying patients, most common of which were death-bed visions.[6]

But to be clear on a point about death-bed visions made above: as Peter Fenwick's study explicitly noted, carers aren't referring to feverish visions under the influence of drugs, or dementia-induced hallucinations – in fact, research has found that patients were *less* likely to have death-bed visions if they were medicated with drugs, or suffering from an illness which affected their normal state of consciousness.[7] In their own survey, researchers Karlis Osis and Erlendur Haraldsson found that 80 percent of those who had experienced a death-bed vision were not under the influence of drugs when it occurred. And for one doctor at least, the issue was resolved with a patient who was reporting frequent visions of giant spiders, along with the occasional report that his (already dead) brother was visiting him. The physician substituted another pain reliever for the morphine that the patient was on, and the giant spider hallucinations immediately stopped. The visions of his brother, however, continued up until his passing, leading the doctor to state that "it appears reasonably certain that death-bed visions are not part of a delirium caused by medical illness or drug toxicity".[8]

In fact, rather than being a feverish hallucination, patients recount death-bed visions calmly and rationally to family or carers, usually exhibiting no fear or confusion about what they have seen. Indeed, during their final days the terminally ill are often said to be almost living in two worlds, swapping nonchalantly between chatting with palliative carers and family physically present in the room, and interacting with visions of previously deceased individuals who appear to be – in some way – there to help them through the dying process. And perhaps guiding them on to the afterlife world: over and over again in these stories, the dominant theme is that the 'here-and-now' is suddenly not of any importance to the dying person; their focus now lies with the next world and those who have come to take them there. For instance, in Italy a wife ran to her dying husband's side only to be told by him that her mother – who had died 3 years previously – "is helping me to break out of this disgusting body. There is so much light here, so much peace".[9]

Death-bed visions are certainly not just a recent phenomenon – they have been recognised and written about for centuries across the world, from indigenous cultures[10] to modern Western society. For example, in 1878 we find testimony from a doctor concerning the prevalence of death-bed visions that could just as easily apply to the Jobs family in 2011: "There is scarcely a family in the land", the doctor wrote, "some one of whose members has not died with a glorious expression on the features, or exclamation on the lips, which, to the standers by, was a token of beatific vision".[11] In the same era, the author Frances Cobbe similarly wrote that "in almost every family or circle, a question will elicit recollections of death-bed scenes, wherein, with singular recurrence, appears one very significant incident, namely, that the dying person, precisely at the moment of death, and when the power of speech was lost, or nearly lost, seemed to see something".[12] Cobbe noted that over and over again, the experience is described "almost in the same words by persons who have never heard of similar occurrences, and who suppose their own experience to be unique". Certainly, Cobbe's description of such scenes correlates with Mona Simpson's account of Steve Jobs' final moments:

> It is invariably explained that the dying person is lying quietly, when suddenly, in the very act of expiring, he looks up, sometimes starts up in bed, and gazes on what appears to be vacancy with an expression of astonishment, sometimes developing instantly into joy, and sometimes cut short in the first emotion of solemn wonder and awe. If the dying man were to see some utterly unexpected but instantly recognized vision, causing him a great surprise or rapturous joy, his face could not better reveal the fact.[13]

It is this commonality between experiences that is so suggestive that we are viewing an important phenomenon here. And an example from Cobbe's book should suffice to show that very little has changed in the experience over this substantial amount of time. It gave me goosebumps the first time I read it:

> I was watching one night beside a poor man dying of consumption. His case was hopeless, but there was no appearance of the end being very near. He was in full possession of his senses, able to talk with a strong voice, and not in the least drowsy. He had slept through the day, and was so wakeful that I had been conversing with him on ordinary subjects to while away the long hours. Suddenly, while we were thus talking quietly together, he became silent, and fixed his eyes on one particular spot in the room, which was entirely vacant, even of furniture. At the same time, a look of the greatest delight changed the whole expression of his face, and, after a moment of what seemed to be intense scrutiny of some object invisible to me, he said to me in a joyous tone, "There is Jim". Jim was a little son whom he had lost the year before, and whom I had known well; but the dying man had a son still living, named John, for whom we had sent, and I concluded it was of John he was speaking, and that he thought he heard him arriving. So I answered, "No. John has not been able to come". The man turned to me impatiently, and said: "I do not mean John, I know he is not here: it is Jim, my little lame Jim. Surely, you remember him?" "Yes", I said, "I remember dear little Jim who died last year quite well". "Don't you see him, then? There he is", said the man, pointing to the vacant space on which his eyes were fixed; and, when I did not answer, he repeated almost fretfully, "Don't you see him standing there?"

I answered that I could not see him, though I felt perfectly convinced that something was visible to the sick man, which I could not perceive. When I gave him this answer, he seemed quite amazed, and turned round to look at me with a glance almost of indignation. As his eyes met mine, I saw that a film seemed to pass over them, the light of intelligence died away, he gave a gentle sigh and expired. He did not live five minutes from the time he first said, "There is Jim", although there had been no sign of approaching death previous to that moment.[14]

The title of Cobbe's book in which the above account is found, *The Peak in Darien*, was inspired by John Keats' sonnet "On First Looking into Chapman's Homer", referring to the moment in the poem when the Spanish conquistador Hernán Cortés and his men climbed a mountain in the Darién province of Panama and were met with the grand and unexpected vista of the Pacific Ocean stretching into the distance as far as the eye could see. Cobbe made the analogy that certain death-bed visions might similarly give us a glimpse into the grand and unexpected vista of the afterlife realms, with the experiencer beholding from their own peak "an ocean yet hidden from our view".[15]

The final days of another technology guru illustrate Cobbe's analogy well: eighty years to the month before Steve Jobs passed away the great American inventor and businessman Thomas Edison had his own death-bed vision. According to the testimony of Dr. Hubert S. Howe, who was Edison's personal physician during his final illness in October 1931, the famous inventor suddenly opened his eyes and gazed into space, his face illuminated with a smile. "It is very beautiful over there!", Edison exclaimed, leading Dr. Howe to wonder if Edison had "climbed the heights which lead into Eternity and caught a glimpse beyond the veil which obstructs our earthly vision?"[16] Dr. Howe was moved to ask, in what appears some frustration, "Must this question always remain hidden in the mystery of death?"

Another interesting facet of death-bed visions is that they seem to occur regardless of age – if they are just a 'trick of the brain', then we would have to consider it somehow, and for some strange reason, hardwired into our biological make-up. The brilliant *fin de siècle* physicist Sir William Barrett, in researching the phenomenon, was impressed by not only the commonality of the description of the experience in those of a younger age, but also that their dying visions did not agree with what might be expected by them from their religious upbringing.

Barrett also recounted the case of a schoolgirl, Hattie Pratt, who passed away from diptheria in the early 1900s, whose death-bed vision once again shows how the dying seem to straddle the boundary between the living and the dead. As the family gathered around during her final hours, gazing upon her "dear features, as the light of life gradually went out, and the ashy pallor of death settled over them", another family member apparently appeared to help young Hattie on her way to the next world. I feel compelled to quote it at length:

> Although her throat was so choked up with diphtheritic membrane that her voice was very thick, and it required close attention to catch all of her words, her mind seemed unusually clear and rational.

> She knew she was passing away, and was telling our mother how to dispose of her little personal belongings among her close friends and playmates, when she suddenly raised her eyes as though gazing at the ceiling toward the farther side of the room, and after looking steadily and apparently listening for a short time, slightly bowed her head, and said, "Yes, Grandma, I am coming, only wait just a little while, please". Our father asked her,

"Hattie, do you see your grandma?" Seemingly surprised at the question she promptly answered, "Yes, Papa, can't you see her? She is right there waiting for me". At the same time she pointed toward the ceiling in the direction in which she had been gazing. Again addressing the vision she evidently had of her grandmother, she scowled a little impatiently and said, "Yes, Grandma, I'm coming, but wait a minute, please". She then turned once more to her mother, and finished telling her what of her personal treasures to give to different ones of her acquaintances. At last giving her attention once more to her grandma, who was apparently urging her to come at once, she bade each of us good-bye. Her voice was very feeble and faint, but the look in her eyes as she glanced briefly at each one of us was as lifelike and intelligent as it could be. She then fixed her eyes steadily on her vision but so faintly that we could but just catch her words, said, "Yes, Grandma, I'm coming now". Then without a struggle or evidence of pain of any kind she gazed steadily in the direction she had pointed out to us where she saw her grandma, until the absence of oxygen in her blood-stream, because respiration had ceased, left her hands and face all covered with the pallor of lifeless flesh.

She was so clear-headed, so positive of the vision and presence of her grandma, with whom she talked so naturally, so surprised that the rest of us could not see grandma, the alternation of her attention and conversation between her grandma and father and mother were so distinctly photographed upon the camera of my brain that I have never since been able to question the evidence of the continuance of distinct recognizable life after death.[17]

Peak-in-Darien Experiences

While death-bed visions are no doubt an extraordinary experience for those present at a loved one's passing, do they offer any serious evidence that they are a 'real' interaction of some sort with a post-death world, or can they be dismissed simply as an hallucination based on wishful thinking, brought on by a misfiring brain in its death throes? Certain cases suggest, quite incredibly, the former.

In her 1882 book describing death-bed experiences mentioned above, the author Frances Cobbe wrote of an incident "of a very striking character" that occurred in a family with very tight bonds. A dying lady exhibited the usual tell-tale sign of a death-bed vision by suddenly showing emotions of recognition and joy, and began telling how, one after another, three of her brothers who had long been dead had appeared in the room. Then, strangely, a fourth brother appeared to her as dead, despite the fact that he was believed by those present to still be alive and well at his residence in India – the suggestion that he had passed away was enough to cause one person to run from the room in shock. Being the late 19th century, there was no instant way of checking on the brother's health, but sometime later letters were received announcing his death in India at a time before his dying sister appeared to recognize a vision of him at her bedside.[18]

Though Cobbe's analogy of the 'Peak in Darien' was referring to death-bed visions in general, in modern research that phrase is now associated with the particular type of experience "of a very striking character" narrated above – those where the dying person has a vision of a person thought to be alive, but who has actually passed away sometime before they appeared to the dying person. Such experiences do offer some evidence that the vision has some basis in reality, as they seem to display direct knowledge gleaned from an encounter with those in the afterlife realm.

As another example, consider the following death-bed story, related in Chapter 2 of Sir William Barrett's *Death-Bed Visions:*

The Psychical Experiences of the Dying, published in 1926. In the book, Barrett – a British scientist of some renown – investigated the so-called "Peak-in-Darien" experience, and told the story of a woman named 'Mrs B' (also referred to as 'Doris'), who had given birth to a baby despite the fact that she was dying from heart failure herself. This story was passed on to Barrett by his wife, who was the attending obstetrician. He then investigated further and gathered testimony from others present during the incident.

Barrett's interest in the case was due to the fact that, as Mrs. B approached death, she had a vision of her sister – despite her belief that this sister was alive at the time, having not been told by her family (due to her fragile health) that her sister had recently died. As she began to slip away, Mrs. B gripped Lady Barrett's hand tightly and looked up toward the most brightly lit part of the room, while asking the surgeon not to leave her. "Oh, don't let it get dark," she pleaded to those in the room, "it's getting so dark... darker and darker". The woman's husband and mother were sent for immediately, but shortly after this moment Mrs. B's desperation quickly turned to rapture. Looking across to a different part of the room, a radiant smile lit up her face. "Oh, lovely, lovely," she cried. When asked what she could see, she replied "Lovely brightness, wonderful beings". The conviction with which she reported this shook Lady Barrett, who later noted that it was difficult "to describe the sense of reality conveyed by her intense absorption in the vision".

At that moment, Mrs. B focused suddenly on a particular point in the air, and cried joyously "Why, it's Father! Oh, he's so glad I'm coming." A beatific vision then unfolded before her, something of such majestic and heavenly qualities that the new mother felt justified in leaving her new-born baby for it:

Her baby was brought for her to see. She looked at it with interest, and then said, "Do you think I ought to stay for baby's sake?" Then turning towards the vision again, she said, "I can't – I can't stay; if you could see what I do, you would know I can't stay". But she turned to her husband, who had come in, and said, "You won't let baby go to anyone who won't love him, will you?" Then she gently pushed him to one side, saying, "Let me see the lovely brightness".

Lady Barrett had to leave at this point to continue on with her duties, her place at the bedside taken by the Matron, who reported that subsequent to this initial vision, Mrs. B then saw something that shocked those present:

> Mrs. B. said, "Oh, why there's Vida", referring to a sister of whose death three weeks previously she had not been told. Afterwards the mother, who was present at the time, told me, as I have said, that Vida was the name of a dead sister of Mrs. B.'s, of whose illness and death she was quite ignorant, as they had carefully kept this news from Mrs. B. owing to her serious illness.

Mrs. B's mother gave further testimony which made clear that her daughter was perplexed by the fact that her sister Vida had appeared with her dead father:

> She spoke to her father, saying, "I am coming", turning at the same time to look at me, saying, "Oh, he is so near". On looking at the same place again, *she said with rather a puzzled expression*, "He has Vida with him". [my emphasis]

Lady Barrett was at pains to point out that Mrs. B was not simply in a state of delirium at this time, reporting that she seemed to have a dual consciousness of both the otherworldly visitors as well as those physically present in the room. In spite of the 'afterlife' visions she was experiencing, she also retained enough worldliness during her final moments to make arrangements for the care of her new baby. Mrs. B died within the hour.

An earlier, but very similar account, is given by a Mr Hensleigh Wedgwood, brother-in-law of Charles Darwin, writing in the *Spectator* in the 19th century:

> A young girl, a near connection of mine, was dying of consumption. She had lain for some days in a prostrate condition, taking no notice of anything, when she opened her eyes, and looking upwards, said slowly, "Susan – and Jane – and Ellen!" as if recognising the presence of her three sisters, who had previously died of the same disease. Then, after a short pause, "and Edward, too!" she continued – naming a brother then supposed to be alive and well in India – as if surprised at seeing him in the company. She said no more, and sank shortly afterwards. In the course of the post, letters came from India announcing the death of Edward from an accident, a week or two previous to the death of his sister.[19]

Such examples are not restricted to previous centuries however. In their 1993 book *Final Gifts*, hospice nurses Maggie Callanan and Patricia Kelley reported the case of an elderly Chinese lady, terminally ill with cancer, who...

> ...had recurrent visions of her deceased husband calling her to join him. One day, much to her puzzlement, she saw her sister with her husband, and both were calling her to join them. She told the hospice nurse that her sister was still alive in China, and that she hadn't seen her for many years. When the hospice nurse later reported this conversation to the woman's daughter, the daughter stated that the patient's sister had in fact died two days earlier of the same kind of cancer, but that the family had decided not to tell the patient to avoid upsetting or frightening her.

In his 2010 book *Visions, Trips and Crowded Rooms*, David Kessler offers another modern version of the Peak-in-Darien experience. Heather, a medical nurse, was suffering through a terrible time in her life with both of her parents seriously ill: her father Joseph with Alzheimer's Disease, and her mother Mabel diagnosed with pancreatic cancer. Confined to separate facilities, it was all Heather could do to visit both regularly, while continuing with her job and looking after her own children. At 81 years of age, her mother decided not to undergo chemotherapy or other aggressive treatments, serenely noting that after eight decades, it was simply 'her time'. But as her mother's condition worsened, and it became apparent that the end was approaching, Heather began to fret, wondering if she should figure out a way of bringing her father to the facility to spend a final few hours with his wife.

That evening, my family and I sat by my mom, who was still very alert, but her breathing was more audible than usual. She suddenly looked up and said, "Joseph died, Why didn't anyone tell me this?" I jumped in and quickly corrected her: "Mom, Daddy isn't dead. He's still in the nursing home."

Startled by her statement, I suddenly realized that I'd better find a way to get Dad over here. We were afraid that my mom was beginning to lose her faculties, and we wanted her to see her husband while she could still talk to him. "Mom," I said, "we'll see if the nursing home will let us pick up Dad so he can visit." I nodded to my cousin Jackie to call the nursing home to make arrangements for one of us to get him.

"Joseph already came to say good-bye," Mom insisted, "and he told me that I'd be with him soon." We all just looked at each other, acknowledging that my mother was hallucinating. I gently repeated, "Mom, Dad is in the nursing home. We're going to bring him here."

Once again she repeated, "No, he's dead," but this time, she also sat up. "Look, there he is!" She seemed to be gazing past everybody, and then she said, "Joseph, you came back for me." Her eyes filled with tears, and she lay back on the bed.

Just then, a nurse and my cousin motioned for me to come over and talk to them at the nurses' station. I met them just outside the door when Jackie said, "Heather, I don't know how to tell you this. I called the nursing home, and Joseph died about 15 minutes ago. He had a heart attack."

Mom died two days later.

Another account related by Technicolor pioneer Natalie Kalmus involved the final moments of her sister Eleanor's life. The dying woman began having visions of deceased loved ones appearing in the room with her, when suddenly she also saw her cousin Ruth, who was – as far as she knew – still alive, and exclaimed "What's she doing here?" In actuality, Ruth had died unexpectedly a week previous, but Eleanor had not been told due to the delicate nature of her own condition.[20]

The Death Whisperer

Regardless of our own opinion on whether death-bed visions offer evidence of the survival of consciousness after death, for the dying they often bring great meaning and guidance in the final days or weeks before death. According to Australian palliative care physician Michael Barbato, "those who have a death-bed vision are rarely concerned about possible causes". To the dying, Barbato says, such visions help guide them through the final moments of their life. "In nearly all cases they are consumed by joy and wonder, and explanations are irrelevant," Barbato tells me. "The experience is so real they have no doubt of its validity and meaning."

That's not to say that Barbato doesn't have an interest in where these strange experiences originate. In almost a quarter of a century of tending to the dying, he has seen more than his fair share of death-bed strangeness – in fact, his career was in some ways inspired by one such experience in the 1980s. Barbato had been in medical practice for some 15 years at the time it occurred, but had never encountered anything that made him question the idea that consciousness ends with the death of the physical body. But he was mystified when a young man dying from leukaemia roused from the coma he'd be in for days, just as his sister – arriving from the other side of the world – entered the room. He gazed at her, gave her a big smile, and then lapsed back into unconsciousness, dying just a few hours later.

The experience shook Barbato, but many of his physician colleagues dismissed it, even though they couldn't explain it. He began to question both his own and the entire medical profession's attitude towards the dying, and how they should be cared for. His job became more and more tedious for him, and it started impacting his home life as well. He and his wife were already struggling mentally and emotionally after losing their one-month-old daughter Moira to Sudden Infant Death Syndrome (SIDS) some years previous. Barbato decided to take a few days to clear his head and try and divine a way forward in his career, setting off for some camping and bushwalking, only to be turned back home by floodwaters. With his mood getting darker by the hour, he was not impressed to open his letter box and find the latest copy of the *Medical Journal of Australia*. Though reading about the medical profession was the last thing he wanted to do, he flipped it open out of habit

– and in one of those seemingly benign moments that turn out to be life-changing, it fell open on the 'Positions Vacant' section. In the middle of the page, staring back at him, was an advertisement for a job: the Sacred Heart Hospice in Sydney was seeking a Palliative Care Physician. Barbato's heart jumped, and he immediately knew he had found his calling. "Fate, in its own strange way," he recounts, "had played its part".[21]

Since that time, in more than two decades of working with the dying, Barbato has come to realize that strange experiences like the one he encountered with the young leukaemia patient are hardly rare: "When I first heard about death-bed visions I wondered why none of my patients had shared these experiences with me". The key, Barbato found, was simply taking the time to talk (and listen) to his patients about what they were going through. "It was only when I started to ask that the flood gates opened – they were only too willing and happy to share, provided I showed an interest and a willingness to listen".[22]

Once Barbato knew more about these experiences, he realized many had probably been passing him by without him even realising. He offers me an analogy: "When you buy a new car, you are surprised to find how many of these same cars are on the road. The same applies to death-bed visions: once you know about them, you notice them more". Now, he says, hardly a week goes by without him witnessing or hearing about "some mysterious or magical moment surrounding a person's death".

In a small study he carried out in the 1990s, Barbato found that about 20 to 30 percent of patients reported a death-bed vision.[23] But he points out that this is "almost certainly an underestimation" of the number of experiences, as his study only included reports from the patient or next-of-kin. "I, like many, suspect the incidence of death-bed visions increases as death approaches, but loss of consciousness or sheer fatigue get in the way of these visions being shared", Barbato notes. "This number may therefore be the tip of an iceberg, with many, and possibly the majority, of death-bed visions going unnoticed".[24]

This may also be part of the reason why death-bed visions are barely discussed in the public sphere, while other strange experiences related to death, such as the near-death experience (NDE) have a much higher profile. Those who report a near-death experience, Barbato points out, live to tell their story. Those who have a death-bed vision though may not get the opportunity to report their experience, being too sick or unconscious in the lead-up to their death. But even if they do, Barbato says, many in the caring profession label it as delirium and the experience goes unrecognised. "The medical profession (including palliative care) has contributed to the 'poorer-brother' status of death-bed visions [relative to the NDE] by not acknowledging their occurrence," he opines. "When I first submitted an article to an International Palliative Care Journal some 15 years ago on death-bed visions, their reply was 'this is not for us' – code for 'it's too fringy'."

Barbato found further evidence of this deleterious attitude toward reports of death-bed visions during his work with the indigenous people of Central and Northern Australia while they were – as they term it – 'finishing up'. "The Aboriginal health workers, indispensable members of the palliative care team, told me that visions of pre-deceased relatives or 'spirits' are common among their people," he reveals. They believe the job of these spirits is to lead the person to 'the other side'. Within Aboriginal culture, Barbato notes, visions such as these "are accepted as part of the normal process of 'finishing up', and surviving family members are not at all shocked or perturbed by what they are told or witness". Such visions are respected and honoured by Aboriginal people and, Barbato says, play an important role in alerting significant family members "to the need to make the prescribed preparations for 'finishing up': preparations that are not only unique to that culture but also to the dying person and his/her tribe". Barbato found, however, that the dying and those surrounding them are unfortunately reluctant to share the experience with non-Aboriginal people, for fear that their experience will be misunderstood, dismissed or seen through the prism of materialist Western medicine.[25]

These fears and misunderstandings regarding death-bed visions – across cultures – prompted Barbato to write a book to help inform relatives and friends of the dying, health care workers, and experiencers themselves about these strange phenomena that occur near the time of death: how common they are, and how they can be of help in the dying process. The title, *Reflections of a Setting Sun...*

> ...came from a conversation I once had with an elderly Chinese woman who was dying of cancer. Although she spoke little English, Mrs. T and I were able to communicate using her children as interpreters. Among many things, Mrs. T told me about her faith, her culture and her beliefs, all of which were comforting to her at that time. When the subject of deathbed visions arose she became animated and not only indicated her belief in them but she also referred to an old Chinese saying that could be interpreted as, 'the last shining of a dying candle' or the 'transient reviving of the dying'. She did not like either expression and preferred her own metaphorical interpretation, 'reflections of a setting sun'. She wanted me to remember this and asked her daughter to record the saying on paper for me to keep. Mrs. T died at home with her husband and children by her side. Her words have lived on in my mind.[26]

Barbato hopes that by reading his book, more people will be ready and willing to accept, understand and discuss these significant experiences if they occur. "When someone is talking about their death-bed vision", Barbato says, "beliefs and prejudices should be put aside and the focus must be on the person and what the experience means for them. The important message is that when someone is dying, carers, family and friends accompany them on their (the dying person's) journey rather than the reverse". In fact, Barbato wonders why some seem so desperate to even find the cause of death-bed visions. "The problem, if there is one, only resides with those who want answers or explanations."

But, as a physician, doesn't he want to understand why humans have these strange, fulfilling experiences near the time of death? "Of course I am interested in their origin," he confesses. However that interest is "another story" to the one that has been most important to him as a palliative care physician. "The approach I take is to focus only on the experience and what it means for the person rather than question its origin," he explains to me. "We should remember that for those who have a death-bed vision, the experience is very real, personally significant and almost always helps them as they transit from life to death. That, surely, is what really matters".

That's not to say he is anti-science, or scared of what the answer might be. "I have no problem with science searching for a cause", Barbato clarifies. In fact, he is himself quite interested in the scientific exploration of the phenomenon of death-bed visions, and discusses some of the possible explanations in his book *Reflections of a Setting Sun*. But as a carer for the dying, his main focus has always been on what the phenomenon provides to the experiencer: "Even if they can be attributed to some neurological/psychological explanation this should not invalidate the experience or its meaning". He quotes the words of pioneering psychologist William James to summarize his position: "The fruits of these experiences are a great deal more significant than their roots".[27]

It is difficult to argue with Barbato's position. We are, after all, human beings searching for meaning in both life and death. And, when confronted with a dying person who is relating a meaningful death-bed vision of their deceased parents, who have apparently come to guide and accompany them to the next life, how many of us would feel it appropriate to start debating the objective reality of the experience, acting as a 'bean-counter' of the evidence collected thus far?

But then, for every person who has died, others are left behind, often trying to make sense of their loss. And most of us *do*, in some way, weigh the evidence and come to a conclusion about the possibility of an afterlife. So, beyond Peak-in-Darien experiences, is there any other evidence to suggest that the dying continue to survive in some way after the physical death of their body?

Visions of the Living

Arthur James Balfour was a stalwart of British politics at the turn of the 20th century, serving as both Prime Minister of the United Kingdom and later as the Foreign Secretary. His influence is still felt today, via his authoring of the landmark Balfour Declaration of 1917, which supported the establishment of a Jewish homeland in Palestine. Less well-known though is the tale of his final days, in which the former Prime Minister and Foreign Secretary was apparently feted by a diplomatic mission from the 'Undiscovered Country'. With his niece (by marriage) Jean Balfour sitting by his bedside, Arthur lay listening to his favourite music, seemingly content with his lot, despite his impending appointment with death. With the nurse having retired downstairs, and Balfour's sister Eleanor Sidgwick sitting with them in the room, Jean suddenly felt "an odd sort of feeling of expectancy, as though anything might happen"...

> [P]resently I became aware with a sensation of a mighty rushing wind (which was entirely subjective, as nothing around me was even stirred), that the room was full of a radiant, dazzling light. This I felt rather than saw, as a blind person might do, and I started trembling. Now it seemed to me that there were people there too; they had no

concern with me, they were invisible; but I knew that they were clustered about A.J.B.'s [Arthur Balfour's] bed, and that their whole attention was concentrated on him. They seemed to me to be most terribly eager, and very loving and strong; and I recollect feeling a good deal of apprehension because I felt they were there for some purpose, though I did not know what it could be.

I could not stop the trembling, so I was wondering if I ought to go out of the room into the passage for a little while, when it seemed to me that something like a voice within me said, "You are not to go away", and I looked at E.M.S [Eleanor Sidgwick] sitting in the armchair to see if she was aware of anything unusual, but she did not appear to be. The music came to the passage where the words occur: "And in my flesh shall I see God". At that moment my eyes were compelled to look at A.J.B. His face, transfigured with satisfaction and beauty, seemed to express all the glorious vision which both music and words conveyed; and I stared, fully expecting him to die at that moment, and to pass straight into the Heaven that awaited him on all sides. But his face changed, and then he was shaken with the seizure that marked the last phase of his illness, and I was filled with terror and distress. Perhaps my shock was the greater for having just been upon such spiritual heights; and the extraordinary thing was that I was vividly aware that the feeling in the room had not changed, that the radiant joy and light still thrilled around him, and that the agonising spectacle of the poor body's affliction caused no dismay to those unseen ones who watched, but that it was what they had wanted to happen. That was what seemed to me so incredible as I fled for the Nurse; and as I ran immediately afterwards to telephone for the Doctor, I was saying over and over to myself, "It was intended – it was intended".

...Thinking it over afterwards I began to realise that though
to my bodily view it was terrible, to those who see the spirit
it may have been simply a fierce effort to cast off the body
and set free a soul already with them; and since a merciful
unconsciousness accompanies the onset of a stroke we do
not know, and never will know, into what peace and joy his
soul may have receded in that little space...[28]

The experience of Jean Balfour highlights another aspect of death-
bed visions which goes against the theory that they are simply an
hallucinatory artefact of the dying patient's misfiring brain. And
that is, that in some cases, other quite healthy people present in the
room *also* experience the 'veil' to the afterlife being lifted.

For example, there have been numerous cases in which carers
for the dying have described seeing a bright light surrounding
the dying person, exuding what they relate as "a raw feeling
of love".[29] What sort of numbers are we talking? Researcher
Peter Fenwick was amazed to find in a survey that one in every
three palliative carers reported accounts of "a radiant light that
envelops the dying person, and may spread throughout the room
and involve the carer", while in a similar Dutch study, more
than half of all carers reported witnessing this 'light'![30] In the
survey of palliative care nurses in Australia mentioned earlier,
one respondent told how he, another nurse, and the patient's
husband saw a blue-white light leave the body of the patient and
drift toward the ceiling. "As she died we just noticed like an
energy rising from her...sort of a bluey white sort of aura," the
nurse explained. "We looked at each other, and the husband was
on the other side of the bed and he was looking at us... he saw
it as well and he said he thinks that she went to a better place".
As is often the case, this experience was transformative for the
nurse: "It probably changed the way I felt about people dying
and what actually happens after death".[31] In fact the researcher
responsible for the Australian study, Deborah Morris,[32] was

herself originally inspired to investigate death-bed experiences further by her own experience of seeing 'the dying light'. "There was a young man who had died in the room with his family and I saw an aura coming off him," she recounts. "It was like a mist. I didn't tell anybody for years. I've never seen it again".[33]

Family members too have reported strange sights, sounds and feelings, just as Jean Balfour did. Peter Fenwick relates an instance in which a person, at the time of their brother's death, witnessed "odd tiny sparks of bright light" emanating from the body – and what's more, these 'sparks' were also seen by another person in the room.[34] In another case, a carer awoke in the darkness of early morning to the sight of "a flame licking the top of the wall against the ceiling" above her dying father's bed. "I saw a plume of smoke rising, like the vapour that rises from a snuffed-out candle, but on a bigger scale…it was being thrown off by a single blade of phosphorus light", the witness recounted. "It hung above Dad's bed, about 18 inches or so long, and was indescribably beautiful…it seemed to express perfect love and peace". She switched on the light to investigate further, but the light instantly vanished; "the room was the same as always on a November morning, cold and cheerless, with no sound of breathing from Dad's bed. His body was still warm".[35] This sighting of a vapour-like substance leaving the body at the time of death is another element that is often reported:

As he died something which is very hard to describe because it was so unexpected and because I had seen nothing like it left up through his body and out of his head. It resembled distinct delicate waves/lines of smoke (smoke is not the right word but I have not got a comparison) and then disappeared. I was the only one to see it. It left me with such a sense of peace and comfort. I don't think that we were particularly close as my sister and I had been sent off to boarding school at an early age.

I do not believe in God. But as to an afterlife I now really do not know what to think.[36]

Another case involved a carer looking after their mother at home during her final days. The woman told Peter Fenwick that when her mother died she was "holding her in my arms and there was a brother there and a niece and I distinctly heard my father's voice calling her, just at the point of death". The carer tried to rationalize the experience, but couldn't deny its impact: "He may have been in my subconscious but I distinctly heard his voice call her name. That was amazing! It was lovely". Another individual, as she sat beside her mother's death-bed, suddenly experienced a vision of a beautiful garden, in which her already-dead aunt greeted her mother and led her away into this 'other-world'. She was adamant that the vision was not her imagination or a dream, and reported that it brought her great comfort.[37]

Similarly researcher O.O. Burgess recounted the case of a man, 'Mr. G.' who experienced a vision that persisted for some five hours as he watched over his dying wife in May 1902. The man's statement began with what he believed to be important information about his own beliefs and state of mind at the time: "For the benefit of any who may read this paper, I will state that I am not addicted to the use of alcoholic liquors, cocaine, or morphine, being almost strictly temperate; nor am I nervous or imaginative, but considered cold, calm and deliberate, and a disbeliever in what is known as materialization, spiritualism, or the existence of spiritual bodies visible to mortal eyes, and hostile to all such theories". He then went on to outline exactly what he saw:

I happened to look towards the door, when I saw floating through the doorway three separate and distinct clouds in strata. Each cloud appeared to be about four feet in length, from six to eight inches in width, the lower one about two feet from the ground, the others at intervals of about six inches.

My first thought was that some of our friends (and I must ask their pardon for the thought) were standing outside the bedroom smoking, and that the smoke from their cigars was being wafted into the room. With this idea, I started up to rebuke them, when, lo! I discovered there was no one standing by the door, no one in the hallway, no one in the adjoining rooms. Overcome with astonishment I watched the clouds; and slowly, but surely, these clouds approached the bed until they completely enveloped it.

Then, gazing through the mist, I beheld, standing at the head of my dying wife, a woman's figure about three feet in height, transparent, yet like a sheen of brightest gold; a figure so glorious in its appearance that no words can be used fitly to describe it... Two figures in white knelt by my wife's side, apparently leaning towards her; other figures hovered about the bed, more or less distinct.[38]

Mr. G. then noticed a 'cord' extending from his wife's forehead to a nude, white figure hovering above the bed. At times the figure "struggled violently, threw out its arms and legs in an apparent effort to escape". Viewing this scene continually for some five hours, Mr. G. believed himself to be losing his mind. "Interruptions, as speaking to my friends, closing my eyes, turning away my head, failed to destroy the illusion, for whenever I looked towards that death-bed the spiritual vision was there...the sensations were so peculiar and the visions so continuous and vivid that I believed I was insane, and from time to time would say to the physician in charge: 'Doctor, I am going insane'." His doctor, however, made a statement to researchers days later that he could "exclude every possible tendency to any form of chronic mental alienation [and] put aside a temporary acute state of hallucinatory insanity" as the cause of the visions. With the exhalation of his wife's final breath, Mr. G. reported that the clouds and figures immediately disappeared.[39]

Another woman reported that as she watched her mother pass away...

>...Suddenly I was aware that her father was stood at the foot of her bed. My mother was staring at him too and her face was lit up with joy. It was then that I saw her face appeared to be glowing with a gold light. The light began to leave through the top of her head and go towards the ceiling. Looking back to my mother's face I saw that she was no longer breathing.[40]

Similarly, Peter Fenwick was told by one lady that while sitting at her dying husband's bedside there was suddenly "a most brilliant light shining from my husband's chest". The light began to rise toward the ceiling, and she began hearing "the most beautiful music and singing voices", filling her with an overwhelming feeling of joy. At this point, the nurse interrupted with news that her husband had just passed, and the light and the music instantly disappeared, leaving the woman bereft at being left behind, after being shown just the barest of glimpses 'behind the veil'.[41]

As well as the light phenomenon, the 'heavenly music' mentioned in the case above is another anomaly that is widely reported at the death-bed, both by those dying *and* those close to the dying individual, be they carers, friends or family. Perhaps the most famous example is that of the celebrated German writer Wolfgang Goethe:

>On the 22nd day of March, 1832, about 10:00 in the evening, two hours before Goethe's death, a carriage stopped outside the great poet's house. A lady got out and

hastened to enter, asking the servant in a trembling voice, "Is he still alive?" It was Countess V., an enthusiastic admirer of the poet, who always received her with pleasure because of the comforting vivacity of her conversation. While she was going up the stairs she suddenly stopped, listening to something, then she questioned the servant, "What! Music in this house? Good heavens, how can anyone play music here on such a day as this?" The man listened in turn, but he had become pale and trembling, and made no reply. Meanwhile, the Countess had crossed the drawing room and gone into the study, where only she had the privilege of entry. Frau von Goethe, the poet's sister-in-law, went to meet her: The two women fell into each other's arms, bursting into tears. Presently the Countess asked, "Tell me, Ottilie, while I was coming upstairs I heard music in the house. Why? Why? Or was I perhaps mistaken?"

"So you have heard it too?" replied Frau von Goethe. "It's inexplicable! Since dawn yesterday a mysterious music has resounded from time to time, getting into our ears, our hearts, our bones." At this very instant there resounded from above, as if they came from a higher world, sweet and prolonged chords of music which weakened little by little until they faded away.

…The Countess, going back into the drawing room, said, "I don't think I can be mistaken; it must be a quartet playing fragments of music some way off which reach us from time to time."

But Frau von Goethe for her part remarked, "On the contrary, it seemed to me that I was hearing the sound of a piano, clear and close by. This morning I was so sure of it that I sent the servant to implore my neighbours to stop playing the piano, out of consideration for the dying man. But they all said the same thing: that they knew very well what condition the poet was in, and were too much distressed to dream of disturbing his last hours by playing the piano."

Suddenly the music burst out again, delicate and sweet; this time it seemed to arise in the room where they were; only, for one person it seemed to be the sound of an organ, for the other a choral chant, and for the third [this sounds as if Jean, the valet, must have been with them] the notes of a piano.

…[T]he mysterious music went on making itself heard up until the moment when Wolfgang Goethe breathed out his last sigh.[42]

In fact, researcher D. Scott Rogo found so many cases of 'transcendental music' that he filled two books with case examples,[43] many of which were coincident with the time of death. One of those cases features music heard during a death-bed vision, as well as a separate element that was also reported in Jean Balfour's anecdote above: a 'rush of air'. A New York lady was caring at home for her Aunt Selma, who had terminal cancer, when one day, while walking up the stairs to Aunt Selma's room to bring her lunch, she felt "a rush of very warm air". Then, as she approached the door to the bedroom she was "startled to hear faint strains of beautiful music, that came from her room and dwelt lightly in the hall where I was". Upon opening the door, it was immediately obvious to her that Aunt Selma "was seeing something that I could not, even though I did hear the music". As she stood spellbound by the sight before her, Aunt Selma turned to face her, "smiled the most peaceful and happy smile I ever saw", and gently fell back on the pillow, dead.[44]

Another case features an experience of heavenly music occurring alongside a 'Peak in Darien' vision. A lady was on her death-bed, but perfectly composed and making arrangements for after her passing (which occurred the following day). Suddenly she asked the person she was talking with, "Do you hear those voices singing?" When told that they could not hear anything, she remarked "I have heard them several times today and I am sure they are the angels welcoming me to Heaven". But she was also puzzled by one voice amongst the angelic choir that she felt was hauntingly familiar. Then, all of a sudden, she pointed over the head of the one other person in the room, crying "Why, there she is in the corner of the room; it is Julia X [a young lady who had, six or seven years previous, spent a week with the dying lady, singing with her girls]... she is praying; do look, she is going". They turned to look, but saw nothing, and admitted that they simply considered the vision "to be the phantasies of a dying person". However, two days later, on picking up a copy of the *Times*, they were amazed to discover a notice announcing the death of Julia X. Checking with her father for confirmation, they were told that yes, she had recently died, and that "on the day she died she began singing in the morning, and sang and sang until she died".[45]

The list of accounts that include visions of deceased loved ones, *seen by healthy people* while in the company of the dying, is surprisingly long. Sir William Barrett included a case in his book regarding a seventeen-year-old girl who, after a prolonged illness, was in her final days. Her already-widowed mother, facing the second major loss of a loved one, was tending to her when she noticed the girl seemed absorbed in something nearby. Querying her as to what she was so focused on, the girl pointed to the bed-curtains and asked what her mother saw. "I followed the direction of her hand and saw a man's form, completely white, standing out quite clearly against the dark curtain," the mother recalled later. "Having no ideas of spiritism, my emotion was intense, and I closed my eyes not wishing to see any longer". The girl was puzzled by her mother's silence, asking why she didn't reply, but her mother – through fear, or incredulity – was unable to admit to the vision. "I had the weakness to declare to her, 'I see nothing'; but my trembling voice betrayed me doubtless, for the child added with an air of reproach, 'Oh, little mother, I have seen the same thing for the last three days at the same hour; it's my dear father who has come to fetch me'".[46]

Barrett also reported the case of a dying woman who claimed that "her sister had come for her" as she had seen her in the room. During the same evening all three of her nieces had witnessed an apparition of the dying woman's deceased sister walking through the house.[47]

How do we explain such reports from healthy people, when death-bed visions are supposed to be hallucinations of the dying brain? It is of course obvious that people tending to the dying are also under heavy emotional stress – perhaps this can sometimes trigger a shift into some sort of altered state, in which they hallucinate or 'overlay' their own wishes and hopes (that the dying person's spirit lives on) upon the scene before them. But how then do we explain the cases where multiple people are involved, such as the Australian nurse who saw a blue-white aura leaving the body along with two other people? Some sort of trick of the light coinciding with a meaningful moment, perhaps? We find ourselves reaching to impose mundane explanations upon these extraordinarily meaningful moments, when perhaps the obvious answer ('they are what they seem to be') should be given at least equal weight in our consideration.

'Coincidences' at the Time of Death

Most of us, even in this digital age, know what a grandfather clock is – but do you know how they got their name? They were once known as long-case clocks, but in 1876 American songwriter

Henry Clay Work wrote the song that would give birth to the name that we know them by today: "My Grandfather's Clock". The lyrics tell the tale of the passing of a grandfather from the point of view of his grandson, and how a clock that was bought on the day the grandfather was born suddenly stopped at the moment of his death:

> It rang an alarm in the dead of the night,
> An alarm that for years had been dumb.
> And we knew that his spirit was pluming for flight,
> That his hour of departure had come.
> Still the clock kept the time, with a soft and muffled chime,
> As we silently stood by his side.
> But it stopped short, never to go again,
> When the old man died.

It is said that Henry Clay Work wrote this song after hearing a report about two brothers who ran a hotel in the United Kingdom and owned the longcase clock that inspired the song. When the first brother died, the clock began losing time, until, when the second brother died aged 90, the clock stopped working completely.[48] A nice enough anecdote, but this type of 'coincidence' actually seems to be a relatively common occurrence when it comes to people's passing. In Peter Fenwick's recent survey of British palliative carers, 33% related experiences of "synchronistic events" at the moment of death, such as clocks stopping, electronic devices shutting down, lights going on and off, and dogs howling.[49] More than a hundred years before that survey, a 19th century researcher found so many recorded reports of such happenings that he concluded that they "cannot be considered a mere fiction".[50] This is a phenomenon that has been experienced constantly throughout the ages.

These types of coincidences become more puzzling when they extend to dreams and visions of friends and family at the time of their death. Peter and Elizabeth Fenwick, in their book *The Art of Dying*, present a number of 'coincidental' visions by those close to the dying that appear to be visits to say farewell. Their research suggests that many such 'visits' come via sleep: either in dreams, or immediately upon awakening, or in the hypnagogic and hypnopompic states (the drowsy, half-asleep periods that occur as people slip in and out of true sleep, respectively). As such, there is often a certain 'unreal' feel to the visions, though their timing in coincidence with the passing of a loved one ensures that the 'visit' is deeply significant to the experiencer.

Jean Hallsworth's story is an excellent example of this type of 'coincidental' vision at the time of a loved one's passing. Her 74-year-old mother had been taken to hospital on a Thursday after feeling unwell, but her health had picked up the following day, and by Saturday it looked like she would be okay to come home within a few days. But in the early hours of Monday morning, Jean awoke and became aware of the figure of her mother, "very clearly standing in a spotlight in a very dark area". Dressed in her usual attire, she had her hands clasped tightly together, and repeated the words "Don't worry Jean, I'm all right". Her mother faded from sight; Jean turned to the bedside clock and noted that it was 3.20a.m. Upon waking in the morning, she was informed that her mother had passed during the night, at that exact time.[51]

Dr. Michael Barbato relates a similar account in his book *Reflections of a Setting Sun*. He was caring for a young South American man named Albert, who was dying from cancer. Immediately after his death, Albert's wife rang close family members to let them know of his passing, one of whom was his brother in Chile. Albert's brother, however, was already aware that he had died. "Albert appeared to me in a dream several hours ago to say goodbye," he told his brother's shocked wife.[52]

Respected psychologist Dr. Stanley Krippner has told how he developed a personal interest in paranormal topics: "At about the age of 12, while awake", Krippner recalls, "I had a sudden premonition that my uncle had died. And, I was in my room, and heard downstairs the phone ring, and then I heard sobbing and crying, and indeed my cousin had just told my mother, saying that her father – my uncle – had just died. That was quite an alarming experience, I didn't tell anybody about that for years".

These strange 'coincidences' have long been recognized as yet another odd phenomenon linked with the dying process. From its inception in 1882, the British Society for Psychical Research (S.P.R.) set out to explore strange phenomena suggestive of the survival of consciousness in an intelligent and academic manner. Blessed with a membership consisting of many hard-working, respected intellectuals, the S.P.R. invested much time and effort collecting testimony from the the public about any strange experiences they might have had – not only through private inquiries among their own social networks, but also by publishing advertisements in major newspapers and periodicals.[53] The response to their enquiries was overwhelming, with the number of death-related visions alone – including those in which a dying person was 'seen' as they passed away elsewhere (labeled 'crisis apparitions' by the S.P.R.) – reaching 400 within the year. The Society's researchers quickly realized that these 'crisis apparitions' differed substantially from the more commonly known ghost stories, not least due to their lack of 'spook factor': such tales, the group wrote in 1882, were "far more likely to provoke sleep in the course of perusal than to banish it afterwards".[54] Instead, these visions of the dead were overtly ordinary – there was generally no fright involved, and no amazement. Witnesses simply saw someone they knew, who would then mysteriously disappear from view; only after some time had passed (remembering the era in which these were reported) would they find out that these individuals had died around the same time as the vision.

In 1886 the S.P.R. published their detailed report on such accounts as a book, under the title *Phantasms of the Living*. More than 1300 pages long and consisting of over 700 cases, the work involved in compiling the two-volume report was enormous: researchers would follow up each case reported to them, interviewing the witness and seeking to verify the account with testimony from third parties, contemporary written reports and so on. The main researcher and author, Edmund Gurney, would often pen 50 to 60 letters a day; locations had to be visited and witnesses interviewed; cases had to be deliberated upon and categorized. And then, of course, the book had to actually be written.

One 'textbook' case presented in *Phantasms of the Living* was that of Lieutenant-General Albert Fytche, who served as the Chief Commissioner of the British colony of Burma during the 1860s. Arising from bed one morning, Fytche was please to find an old friend had come to visit him. He greeted him warmly and suggested to the friend that they meet on the veranda for a cup of tea, though the man didn't seem to respond in any way. When Fytche went to join him a few minutes later, the friend was nowhere to found. Fytche was shocked to later read in the newspaper that this friend had actually died at the time he had seen him, some 600 miles distant. Here is Lieutenant-General Fytche's direct testimony, as reproduced in *Phantasms of the Living*:

> A remarkable incident occurred to me at Maulmain, which made a deep impression upon my imagination. I saw a ghost with my own eyes in broad daylight, of which I could make an affidavit. I had an old schoolfellow, who was afterwards a college friend, with whom I had lived in the closest intimacy. Years, however, passed without our seeing each other. One morning I had just got out of bed, and was dressing myself, when suddenly my old friend entered the room. I greeted him warmly; told him to call for a cup of tea in the verandah, and promised to be with him immediately. I dressed myself in all haste, and went out into the verandah, but found no one there. I could not believe my eyes. I called to the sentry who was posted at the front

of the house, but he had seen no strange gentleman that morning; the servants also declared that no such person had entered the house. I was certain I had seen my friend. I was not thinking about him at the time, yet I was not taken by surprise, as steamers and other vessels were frequently arriving at Maulmain. A night afterwards news arrived that he had died 600 miles off, about the very time I had seen him at Maulmain.[55]

Obviously, I can't reproduce the vast number of accounts in *Phantasms of the Living* here – for those interested, the book is now in the public domain and can be found online.[56] Suffice to say, however, that the number of such 'coincidences' now collected, from the S.P.R.'s investigations through to accounts given to modern-day researchers such as Peter Fenwick, is voluminous. This is *not* a rare occurrence: in the British survey of palliative carers, a full *half* of respondents said that they were aware of "coincidences, usually reported by friends or family of the person who is dying, who say the dying person has visited them at the time of death"![57] And as if to illustrate this point, when I announced that I was writing this book, a number of readers immediately contacted me wanting to share their own experiences, such as the following account by artist Kevin Wright which conforms very closely to the classic crisis apparitions presented by the S.P.R more than a century ago:

Early in 1995 my father was diagnosed with myelodysplastic syndrome, a rare and fatal condition, similar to leukemia in that it stops the bone marrow from producing white blood cells, which are crucial to proper immune system function. His doctors assured us that, with weekly white cell transfusions, he would likely survive through the holidays and into the following year.

Fast forward to a very hot August of that year. My father had his weekly appointment at the hospital for his transfusion and, because it was a time-consuming process to receive the white cells, my sister decided to go along for company. I was in the basement of my home some 35 miles distant, doing some weight-lifting prior to a jog. As I was in the middle of a standing dumbbell exercise, I suddenly sensed that someone was standing next to me, slightly behind my left shoulder. Stopping the exercise, I turned to look and was startled to discover my father standing beside me. He made no attempt to communicate, and vanished perhaps 5 seconds or so after I viewed him.

The moment was very disorienting, and I struggled to understand what had just happened. So shaken was I that I abandoned the weights after a few minutes, and headed up the stairs to exit and begin my run. After hydrating properly, I made for the door just when the phone rang. It was my sister calling to tell me that our father had passed while right in the hospital, an undetected case of pneumonia shutting down lungs damaged by many decades of cigarette smoking. The medical staff was on him in a minute, but were unable to revive him.

[T]he effect of the crisis apparition has been nothing short of transformative, because it gave me a sense of certainty as regards the survival of consciousness beyond bodily death…and accelerated my disinterest in money or material possessions (save, perhaps, for a very good piano).

But could it be, as many skeptics might argue, that the prosaic explanation for such 'coincidences' – so surprising in isolation – is that we should in fact expect them as random, mundane occurrences in any survey of a large number of people? Edmund

Gurney addressed this question himself by conducting a general census of 5705 people, who were asked whether they had experienced "a vivid impression of seeing or being touched by a human being, or of hearing a voice or sound which suggested a human presence, when no one was there?". With 23 responses in the affirmative – 1 in every 248 people surveyed – Gurney used a little math to extrapolate (using the number of deaths per day in Britain at the time) to find that the probability of any one person in the previous twelve years having a coincidental vision of the dying should be around 1 in 4,000,000. But the *Phantasms* investigation had reached only perhaps 300,000 people with its enquiries, and yet in that same twelve year period Gurney could point to 32 well-attested visual crisis apparitions in his collection.[58]

As for the theory that these accounts were, perhaps, just stories – confections of creative minds – Gurney's response was scathing. "When we submit the theory of deliberate falsification to the cumulative test...there comes a point where the reason rebels", Gurney wrote. The hundreds of accounts collected were from many well-regarded people, and every effort had been made by investigators to corroborate the accounts. Some even featured multiple witnesses! For example, in one case a man and his 5-year-old son simultaneously saw his father's face above them, although his wife did not (though she did acknowledge witnessing their reaction and comments at the time). They learned later that the man's father had died at this time.

And Gurney was further convinced by hearing the stories directly from the witnesses' mouths, noting in a letter to the eminent psychologist (and S.P.R. member) William James that he could not "describe to you the effect on my own mind which my hundreds of personal interviews have had". It was very rare, Gurney wrote, "that a case which seemed genuine and sound on paper has not been *strengthened* by the impression (and often by the details) which conversation and careful cross-questioning added":

> I have again and again and again come away with a real
> feeling of irritation and discontent at having been…the
> only one who had had a chance of getting the impression
> which *deserved* to be got; and which I have almost entirely
> refrained from even trying to express in the book, as it
> seemed to be me undesirable to give testimonials and to
> weary the reader's patience and put his back up by forcing
> on him my view of the character of my witnesses… The
> viva voce account has constantly struck me as just what you
> or I might give of a singular experience, which *did happen,*
> but which was wholly isolated and inexplicable.[59]

Modern researchers of the near-death experience – covered later
in this book – have said a similar thing: that it is only through
hearing the direct testimony of the witness that one truly feels the
convincing nature of such cases. Whether *we* believe that they are
simply coincidences, or alternatively that they are evidence for
the survival of the soul, to those who actually experience these
phenomena, the effect is profound: "For the people concerned the
emotional impact of the experience is so great that it remains a
lasting source of comfort", Peter and Elizabeth Fenwick comment.
"Whether it is dismissed by others as 'simply coincidence' is
irrelevant".[60] And in many cases, they note, even for researchers like
themselves the evidence reaches a point where coincidence "seems
much less reasonable or rational than the alternative explanation".[61]
For example, they cite one case of theirs from a man named Chris
Alcock who…

> …described how in the early 1950s one of his school
> friends, Kit, was a young army officer on active service
> in Korea. One night Kit's mother, a girlfriend of his,
> and Chris's sister, who was also sweet on him, all had
> independent similar dreams in which they saw Kit, who
> appeared looking worried and said "I'm lost" and then

faded away. All three woke up and the experience was so vivid that they all feared the worst. Later they found out that the experience coincided with his death in Korea.

This case, and the one from *Phantasms of the Living* mentioned above (involving a man and his 5-year-old son), provide yet more solid evidence that something truly mysterious is happening here, given that multiple witnesses of an apparition would seem to rule out simple hallucination as the cause. And they do not stand alone: in the mid-20th century, researcher G.N.M. Tyrell identified 130 cases in which crisis apparitions were perceived by two or more people, though he remarked that he had "no doubt that this list is not exhaustive".[62]

Peter and Elizabeth Fenwick's feelings are clear: "To keep on citing 'coincidence' for all the very convincing accounts we have been given," they state, "becomes first a weak and then a frankly implausible explanation". Taking into consideration all the evidence at hand, the Fenwicks have come to the conclusion that "the hypothesis of extended mind manifesting at the time of death is a much more persuasive explanation for most of these experiences than coincidence or expectation".[63]

Terminal Lucidity

Imagine being not only mentally disabled, but being so in 1930s Nazi Germany. That was the terrible lot of 'Käthe', a severely handicapped female patient in an asylum run by Pastor Friedrich Happich. Thankfully, Happich's own thoughts ran at odds with the Nazi regime's attitude that such patients were unworthy of life – instead, he believed that such patients had a "hidden inner life" not visible to the rest of us, and as evidence he recorded some of the "numerous experiences" that he had witnessed in his asylum.[64] Käthe was among the most disabled patients in Happich's asylum:

since her birth, she had never spoken a word; her movements were restricted to uncontrolled spasms; she seemingly took no notice of anything happening around her; and the only sounds she made were animal-like utterances. So, when she became seriously ill with tuberculosis, Pastor Happich was astounded to enter her room during her final hours and find her singing. "We did not believe our eyes and ears," he recounted. "Käthe, who never spoke one word, entirely mentally disabled from birth on, sang the dying songs to herself. Specifically, she sang 'Where does the soul find its home, its peace? Peace, peace, heavenly peace!' over and over again. For half an hour she sang. Then, she quietly died".

Those present reported that the woman's face, previously so lifeless, was "transfigured and spiritualized". With tears in his eyes, the attending physician repeated over and over again to Pastor Happich, "I cannot explain this in medical terms". In his own opinion, "from an anatomical perspective, thinking could not have been possible". The doctor's own testimony agreed with Pastor Happich's: "It is true," he noted, "Käthe sang, very intelligibly...a smile caressed her stultified face, the soul flung off restraints".[65]

The case of Käthe is one of a number of anomalous incidents, reported through the ages and collected in a paper by Dr. Michael Nahm, of what is now known as 'terminal lucidity'. Also sometimes referred to as 'lightening', it describes the appearance of sudden mental clarity in the patient as death approaches. Like the young leukaemia victim that Michael Barbato cared for, it is often characterised by the patient 'emerging' from unconsciousness or a confused state, and suddenly being lucid and engaging. In many cases this sudden brightening of an almost extinguished consciousness offers an opportunity for the dying person to say their goodbyes.

Nahm notes that cases of terminal lucidity have been reported throughout history, with classical scholars such as Hippocrates, Plutarch and Cicero all recording its occurrence.[66] Their view was in accord with Pastor Happich's: that beneath the damaged and dying body and brain, the mind or 'soul' remains intact. It was their belief that during the dying process, the soul was 'freed' somewhat from its material prison, and able to present itself more clearly to those attending the patient.[67]

Over the years, researchers and physicians have recognised two ways that terminal lucidity can manifest. In some cases, the mental clarity of the dying person improves slowly in an inverse relationship with the decline of their physical health. In other, more spectacular cases, the mental clarity appears suddenly and unexpectedly shortly before death, often in patients that are believed to have already 'gone' mentally.

In 1812 Benjamin Rush, author of the first American treatise on mental illness, observed that most 'mad' patients "discover a greater or less degree of reason in the last days or hours of their lives".[68] Meanwhile, around the same time in Britain, physician Andrew Marshal published a number of cases of terminal lucidity in persons with mental illness, including one report that is a perfect illustration of terminal lucidity. Marshal was a passionate investigator of the relationship between brain abnormalities and mental pathologies – he once came to blows with another physician who denied any connection – but this particular case in his collection had a strange and counter-logical coda. It involved an ex-lieutenant of the Royal Navy who suffered from severe memory loss (he couldn't even remember his own name), acted irrationally and had become very violent. After his passing, his autopsy revealed that "his cranium was filled with a straw-coloured water to a degree that it widened parts of the brain, whereas the brain matter itself and the origin of the nerves were uncommonly firm, the olfactory nerves displaying an almost fibrose appearance". And yet on the day before his death, Marshal reported, the man suddenly became rational, asked for a clergyman, and with him "the patient conversed attentively and expressed his hope that God would have mercy on his soul".[69]

In 1885, the prominent French physician Alexandre Brierre de Boismont noted that "in certain diseases, the senses acquire an extraordinary delicacy on the approach of death, when the sick person astonishes those about him by the elevation of his thoughts, and the sudden lucidity of a mind which has been obscured during many long years". A century-old anecdote regarding terminal lucidity also ties in with our earlier mention of 'heavenly music' being heard at the death-bed: Peter Nielsen died from stomach cancer, aged just 53, in the winter of 1914. Cared for at home by his wife and daughter during his final months, he was barely able to eat and was thus emaciated, unable to move and seemed to not comprehend nearby conversations as the end approached. However, he suddenly roused from his death-like state, sat upright with his eyes wide open, and exclaimed joyfully "The angels are singing! How beautiful it is". He paused, perhaps listening to the transcendental choir, before saying happily to those at his bedside, "And I'm coming too!" He then, just as suddenly, calmly lay back down and died.[70]

In 1921 we find an account by G.W. Surya recording the experience of a friend whose brother was a patient at an asylum:

> One day, Surya's friend received a telegram from the director of the asylum saying that his brother wanted to speak to him. He immediately visited his brother and was astonished to find him in a perfectly normal mental state. On leaving again, the director of the asylum decently informed the visitor that his brother's mental clarity is an almost certain sign of his approaching death. Indeed, the patient died within a short time. Subsequently, an autopsy of the brain was performed, to which Surya's friend was allowed to attend. It revealed that the brain was entirely suppurated and that this condition must have been present for a long time. Surya asks: "With what, then, did this brainsick person think intelligibly again during the last days of his life?"[71]

Surprisingly, Surya's story is one of the few recorded examples of terminal lucidity that can be found in the medical literature of the past century. In his research on the topic, Dr. Michael Nahm found 80 references to the phenomenon by 50 different authors, but though many of the reports were by prominent physicians of their time, nearly all predated 1850. This may, however, be more related to the unwillingness of physicians and scientists to discuss these anomalous occurrences in the modern scholarly literature, rather than a lack of cases, as in the recent British survey of palliative carers and physicians one out of every three admitted an experience with a "patient who has been in a deep coma, suddenly becoming alert enough to coherently say goodbye to loved ones at the bedside".[72] And in the similar Irish study, "one of the most frequent experiences" reported by palliative carers (57.5% of respondents) was 'Patients in a deep coma becoming suddenly alert enough to say goodbye to relatives'.[73]

The small-scale Australian survey of palliative carers featured one report of terminal lucidity, that of a patient who had been in a severely weakened state, requiring two people to care for him: "He just started talking, and he sat bolt upright in his bed and this was something very unusual because he was preterminal... he was looking over towards the doorway ... and he was talking to the doorway and I myself felt another presence in the room ... and I said to him 'who are you talking to?' and he said 'Oh, that's my brother'." When the patient finished his 'conversation', he lay back down again, "like he didn't have any strength to hold himself up any longer".[74] Another recent case report from America involved a woman who was dying of congestive heart failure, and thus was on oxygen and in a coma, unable to communicate. Her daughter, waiting by her bedside, was therefore astonished when "she not only sat up in bed but leaped over the bottom rail of the bed, saying 'Jim [her deceased brother], wait for me, don't go...' She was looking at the wall behind where I sat and obviously saw something I did not".[75] And researchers Karlis Osis and Erlendur

Haraldsson in 1977 discussed a meningitis patient who had been "severely disoriented almost to the end", who "cleared up, answered questions, smiled, was slightly elated and just a few minutes before death, came to herself".[76]

Obviously, with the lack of scientifically documented cases in recent years, this is an area that remains controversial. Nevertheless, the large number of experiences of this type reported by carers suggest that it is an area that deserves far more attention. If it can be shown that patients with significant degradation of their brain tissue (for example, in advanced cases of Alzheimer's Disease) become lucid, with memories intact, in their final days, what implications does this have for the relationship between mind and brain? And, in practical terms, what does this say about the 'inner life' that such patients possibly experience throughout their illness, and what changes should we make in our treatment and care with this revelation in mind?

Indeed, the entire subject of anomalous death-bed experiences deserves much more scientific attention than it has received. For almost a century the topic has been ignored, though a number of new studies in recent years bring hope that we might be entering an era where more open investigation of these mysterious phenomena is encouraged, and we could soon better understand the experiences we have as we die – and what they mean for us.

TWO

A Glimpse Behind the Veil

What if you slept?
And what if, in your sleep, you dreamed?
And what if, in your dream, you went to heaven
And there plucked a strange a beautiful flower?
And what if, when you awoke,
You had that flower in your hand?

Samuel Taylor Coleridge

Shortly before Christmas 2011, American teenager Ben Breedlove posted a short video to YouTube that would go on to garner millions of views, despite its simplicity.[1] Accompanied by Gary Jules' wonderful rendition of the Tears for Fears track "Mad World", the video is stark: Breedlove simply sits before the camera and doesn't say a word, instead showing hand-written cards in order to tell his story. "Hello, I'm Ben Breedlove", reads the first, followed by "all my life I've had a heart condition…HCM, short for hypertrophic cardio-myopathy". The handsome 18-year-old goes on to elaborate how, as he has matured, he has become more aware of how dangerous his condition is: "it scares me a lot, and I hate that feeling".

Having introduced himself and his condition, Ben begins detailing the times in his life that he has "cheated death", the first being when he was just four years old. The only thing he remembers from that initial experience was being wheeled down a hall on a stretcher by two nurses, with his mother running alongside, and seeing "a big bright light above me":

> I couldn't make out what it was because it was SO bright. I told my mom, "Look at the bright light!" and pointed up. She said she didn't see anything. There were no lights on in this hall. I couldn't take my eyes off it. And I couldn't help but smile.

At this point in the video, just recalling the memory of the occasion makes Ben break into a wide, radiant grin. "I had no worries at all," reads the next card, "like nothing else in the world mattered, and kept smiling. I can't even describe the peace... how peaceful it was". He leaves little doubt as to how much this vision and feeling impacted upon him: "I will NEVER forget that feeling or that day".

This wouldn't be the only time that Ben Breedlove would cheat death though. In 2007 his heart began giving him trouble again, which led to the permanent implantation of a pacemaker and defibrillator – a point at which his heart problem became a "bigger burden", resulting in an emotional low that came to a head in the summer of 2011 when he went into cardiac arrest during a routine tonsillectomy. Thankfully, the surgeons were able to bring him back to life, and from this point Ben says he simply decided to just stop worrying about things as much.

Within six months, however, Ben would cheat death a third time. On December 6th 2011, he was walking in the school hall when he suddenly felt faint and passed out. He woke to find himself surrounded by EMS personnel...

I couldn't talk or move, I could only watch what they were doing. They put the shock pads on my chest. I heard one of them say "They are ready". And the other guy said "Go!". I passed out again. My heart stopped and I wasn't breathing for 3 MINUTES… I heard them say "He's not breathing, his heart is stopped and he has no pulse". I really thought to myself, this is it, I'm dying.

The next thing that happened, I'm not sure if it was a dream, or vision, but while I was still unconscious I was in this white room. No walls, it just went on and on… There was no sound. But that same peaceful feeling I had when I was 4. I was wearing a really nice suit, and so was my favorite rapper, Kid Cudi. Why he was the only one there with me, I'm still trying to figure out. But I was looking at myself in this mirror that was in front of me. The first thing I thought was 'Damn, we look good!'. I had that same feeling, I couldn't stop smiling. I then looked at myself in the mirror. I was proud of MYSELF. Of my entire life, everything I have done. It was the BEST feeling.

Kid Cudi brought me to a glass desk and put his hand on my shoulder. Right then my favorite song of his came on, 'Mr Rager'. The part where it said, "When will the fantasy END, when will the heaven BEGIN?". And he said "Go now". Right then I woke up and the EMS were doing CPR.

I didn't want to leave that place. I wish I NEVER woke up.

In the final moments of the video, Ben asks "Do you believe in angels or God?", before holding up the final card, with his simple two-word answer: "I do".

I would love to have interviewed Ben about his experience for this book. But I can't, because a week after posting his video to

YouTube, Ben Breedlove's heart gave out for the final time, on Christmas Day, 2011. He was 18 years old.

Ben's older sister Ally, in her eulogy for her brother, made clear how much these experiences meant to him. One night, after his collapse and resuscitation at school on December 6th, Ally was looking around their house at Lake Austin trying to find Ben, and was getting worried because she couldn't find him. She eventually found him sitting out on the dock beside the lake. Concerned, Ally asked Ben if he was okay, and what he was doing out on the dock at night. He told her that "the stillness of the water and the quiet in the middle of the night was the closest feeling he could find to that peace that he felt in his vision". Ally asked Ben to tell her more about his 'dream', and, she says, "he made two things *very* clear to me". He told her that "even though he called it a dream, he was awake, and it was very real, and he told me that when he looked into that mirror, in his words he said 'I knew I was ready for something a lot more important'." After Ben had finished telling Ally about his dream, she asked him if he was happy that he woke up: "He said 'I guess', and then he started crying really hard".[2]

The Saturday following their talk, Ben had collapsed once more, but again had been able to be resuscitated. Being too weak to go to church the following day, the Breedlove family had gathered at home for a personal service, at which his father quoted Philippians 4:7, "And the peace that surpasses all understanding will guard your hearts and minds in Jesus Christ". Looking at Ben, he asked "We don't know what that peace feels like, but you do, don't you?", to which Ben replied simply "Yes". When his father asked if he could describe this feeling of peace to them, Ben answered "It's just like the verse says – you can't describe it, you just have to be there". After the family all took turns to pray for him, Ben then offered his own prayer, for the rest of his family: asking that they wouldn't be scared or sad, and that they would have the same peace that he felt.[3]

Ben Breedlove died just days after this family service. What were these strange experiences that led him to such a feeling of peace and contentedness in his life, and ready for "something a lot more important"? A number of elements of his encounters with death suggest that Ben had what is known as a near-death experience (or NDE).

In his bestselling book *Life after Life,* Raymond Moody recounted the various phenomena that one might expect to encounter during a near-death experience, based on the testimony given to him by hundreds of near-death experiencers. The following passage is an idealised description of the NDE, assembled by Dr Moody from the testimony he collected from those who had flirted with death:

> A man is dying and, as he reaches the point of greatest physical distress, he hears himself pronounced dead by his doctor. He begins to hear an uncomfortable noise, a loud ringing or buzzing, and at the same time feels himself moving very rapidly through a long dark tunnel. After this, he suddenly finds himself outside of his own physical body, but still in the immediate physical environment, and he sees his own body from a distance, as though he is a spectator. He watches the resuscitation attempt from this unusual vantage point and is in a state of emotional upheaval.

After a while, he (I will continue to use Moody's example of a 'man' dying, though consider it interchangeable with 'woman', 'child' and so on) collects himself and becomes more accustomed to his odd condition. He notes that he still has a 'body', but one of a very different nature and with very different powers from the physical body he has left behind. Further things begin to happen. Others come to meet and to help him. He glimpses the spirits of relatives and friends who have already died, and a loving warm spirit of a kind he has never encountered before – a being of light –

appears before him. This being asks him a question, non-verbally, to help him evaluate his life, and sometimes aids him in this task by showing a panoramic, instantaneous playback of the major events in his life. At some point he may find himself approaching some sort of barrier or border, apparently representing the limit between earthly life and the next life. Yet he finds that he must go back to the earth, that the time of his death has not yet come. At this point he resists, for by now he is taken up with his experiences in the afterlife and does not want to return. He is overwhelmed by intense feelings of joy, love and peace. Despite his attitude, though, he somehow reunites with his physical body and lives.

Later, he tries to tell others, but he has trouble doing so. In the first place, he can find no human words adequate to describe these unearthly episodes (the 'ineffability' of the experience). He also finds that many who he initially tells scoff at his story, so he stops telling people about it. Still, the experience affects his life profoundly, especially his views about death and its relationship to life.

Moody's account is fictional – the 'perfect' NDE so to speak; a 'real-world' NDE will usually not include every one of these elements. For instance, a survey of Dutch cardiac arrest patients found that, of those who had at least some memory of the time of their 'death', 24% reported an 'out-of-body experience' (OBE), 31% said they traveled through a tunnel-like structure, 13% underwent a life review, and 56% experienced feelings of peace and/or joy.[4] Still, most recorded NDEs *do* include a number of these elements. For example, George Ritchie's experience, presented in the previous chapter, included a 'whirring' noise at onset, the external viewing of his own body, and an encounter with a being of light who helped evaluate his life. Ben Breedlove had a life evaluation, felt intense joy and peace, encountered a blissful light, was disappointed to have returned to life, and could find no human words to describe his experience (although it's worth noting that his experience was anomalous in its manifestation of a still living person, the rapper Kid Cudi, as guide – a rare occurrence in NDEs). Many other real-world reports exhibit other of these 'recurrent regularities' mentioned by Moody in his 'archetypal NDE'. For example:

> I got up and walked into the hall to go get a drink, and it was at that point, as they found out later, that my appendix ruptured. I became very weak, and I fell down. I began to feel a sort of drifting, a movement of my real being in and out of my body, and to hear beautiful music. I floated on down the hall and out the door onto the screened porch. There, it almost seemed that clouds, a pink mist really, began to gather around me, and then I floated right straight on through the screen, just as though it weren't there, and up into this pure crystal light, and illuminating white light. It was beautiful, and so bright, so radiant, but it didn't hurt my eyes. It's not any kind of light you can describe on Earth. I didn't actually see a person in this light, and yet it has a special identity, it definitely does. It is a light of perfect understanding and perfect love.

> Fifteen years ago when I was fifty-nine I had a heart attack... Then everything became warm and bright and light and beautiful...I was travelling along a tunnel. It was light, light, light. I didn't move my feet, I just 'floated' I suppose. But it was calm and peaceful and just lovely. Gradually there was a brilliant light at the end – really brilliant – and I knew I was going right into the glowing heart of that light, but then I saw a group of people between me and the light. I knew them; my brother, who had died a few years before, was gesticulating delightedly as I approached. Their faces were so happy and welcoming. Then somehow my mother became detached from the group. She shook

her head and waved her hand (rather like a windscreen wiper) and I stopped, and I heard the doctor say, "She's coming around," and I was in my bed and the doctor and my husband were there. My first words to the doctor were, "Why did you bring me back?"

My heart stopped beating. I didn't know at that time that that was exactly what happened to me, but anyway when this happened I had an experience. Well, the first thing that happened – now I am going to describe it just the way I felt – was that I had this ringing noise brrrrnnnnng-brrrrnnnnng-brrrrnnnnng, very rhythmic. Then I was moving through this – you're going to think this is weird – through this long dark place. It seemed like a sewer or something.

NDEs have been reported during a number of life-threatening situations, including cardiac arrest, loss of a large quantity of blood, traumatic brain injury or stroke, near-drowning or asphyxia, and other serious health issues. But they have also manifested during situations where death only *seemed* imminent and the health of the body was not compromised at the time of the NDE, such as in an impending traffic accident or a fall from a great height. One such "fear-death experience"[5] was the case of a woman in a car that went into a spin, who suddenly found herself travelling through a "black tunnel, or funnel" accompanied by a loud roaring sound, and aware of "presences" around her that were debating whether she should be sent back. She then found herself back in her car, *about to crash* into another vehicle.[6] Strangely, therefore, this type of case does not seem to depend on a physiological trigger, such as a dose of drugs or a lack of oxygen.

Near-death experiences happen to people of all ages. They can occur in very young children, even in infants who would seem to not yet have a true concept of what death means for them, nor expectations of what might happen during the experience. Psychiatrists reported one case of a 29-month-old who bit into an electric cord and nearly died. The boy later told his mother that he "went into a room with a nice man. There was a bright light on the ceiling. He wanted to know if I wanted to go home, or come play with him".[7] Doctors at Massachusetts General Hospital reported the case of an 8-month-old who appears to have had an NDE after nearly dying of kidney failure. As soon as she could talk, at age two, she told her parents of having gone into a tunnel and into a bright light. The straightforward language used by young children in describing these fascinating experiences confronts us with a real mystery – why do they so often conform so closely to the archetypal experience as put forward by Moody, despite the child's lack of knowledge about death and the NDE? In any case, you can't help but be entertained by the descriptive accounts given by kids: one child who almost drowned after being trapped in a car which had driven off a bridge recounted his experience by saying that after the car filled up with water, "everything went all blank. Then I died. I went into a huge noodle. It wasn't like a spiral noodle, but it was very straight. When I told my Mom about it, I told her it was a noodle, but it must have been a tunnel, because it had a rainbow in it. Noodles don't have rainbows in them".[8]

The NDE has been found to have a strong transformational effect on experiencers (as compared to others who have also nearly died, but did not have an NDE), making them more intuitive and empathic, and prompting increased involvement with family, interest in self-examination, a decrease in competitiveness with others as well as a decrease in the desire for material possessions, and a heightened appreciation of 'the little things' in life. Near-death experiencers also have a significantly diminished fear of death and much higher degree of belief in life after death. Researchers have also been surprised by the long-lasting nature of these effects, considering their origin in an experience that is usually only minutes in length – one study found these post-NDE effects persisting in experiencers when interviewed 8 years after their NDE.[9]

Despite only coming to public prominence in the last few decades, the near-death experience is not as rare an occurrence as some might think: in recent studies, researchers have found that 11-18% of cardiac arrest survivors have some sort of NDE – roughly 1 in 7![10] Though it may well be the case that the experience has become more prominent during this time period due to the revolution in resuscitation techniques that occurred in the 1960s, allowing many more people to 'die' and then be subsequently brought back to life.

Death Before Life After Life

A number of skeptics of the near-death experience were however quick to suggest that the most important contributor to the sudden wealth of near-death experience reports from the 1980s onwards was perhaps the success of Raymond Moody's *Life After Life* itself, with most subsequent NDEs reported just being 'copycat' effects, brought on by contagion – unconsciously or consciously – due to the massive popularity of Moody's book. Despite his impressive collection of original case reports, skeptics seemed happy to reverse the causality, with Moody's archetypal NDE now allegedly serving as the inspiration for later reports featuring elements such as the tunnel, the past life review, and the being of light. The NDE was explained away as a psychological hiccup brought on by the threat of death, based almost totally on expectations from reading *Life After Life* and other afterlife 'mythologies'.

However, the fact of the matter is that there are many examples of 'pre-Moody' experiences, recorded throughout history and in many different cultures. It seems that this is, quite simply, a phenomenon that has been with us since time immemorial. Take for example the writings of the famous Greek philosopher known to us as Plato (428

– 348 BCE). In a number of his 'dialogues', Plato describes the higher planes of existence in familiar terms. He talks of how the soul of a person separates from the physical body at the time of death, how this soul may find itself crossing a body of water on a 'ship of death', and may then meet and converse with the spirits of deceased family and friends. For Plato, death is akin to awakening from a dream – a state of being in which the formerly imprisoned soul is released into a state of greater awareness and memory.

It is in Book 10 of Plato's classic, *The Republic*, that we find a remarkable narrative which suggests that the near-death experience has been with us throughout history. Here the legendary philosopher recounts the tale of a Greek soldier named Er, apparently killed in battle, but who revived with scant minutes to go before his body was to be immolated in the funeral pyre. After awakening, Er described how his soul had gone out of his body and travelled to the deathly realms, where he had seen souls being judged by a display of their past deeds. However, he had been ordered to return to the land of the living and explain what he had seen to others – a feature of many NDEs.

The Roman historian Plutarch also related, some 2000 years ago, the experience of one Aridaeus of Soli, who "fell from a certain height upon the nape of his neck and died... The third day he was carried away to be buried when he came back to himself and rapidly recovered". Aridaeus told how, having 'died', he felt his spirit body exiting his physical body through his head. His sense of vision now seemed augmented; sharper, and strangely capable of viewing "around in all directions at once". Like George Ritchie, Aridaeus found that he could now "move in all directions easily and quickly". A deceased relative who had died at a young age then appeared before him, showing Aridaeus the inner workings of the afterlife realms. It is interesting to note that upon reviving from this state, Aridaeus transformed himself, becoming more pure of heart and helpful in his community. So much so that he was given a new name, 'Thespesius', meaning 'divine' or 'wonderful'.

The story of Aridaeus could be lifted straight from the pages of Raymond Moody's *Life After Life* – apart from the fact that it was written almost two millennia beforehand! Moody makes special note in his book about how experiencers are changed by their NDEs, often developing a zest for life as well as the dual pursuits of focusing more on personal relationships and questing for knowledge. Most also seem to lose any fear of dying. They too have become 'Thespesius'. For example, in *Life After Life* we find one individual's testimony that they now "try to do things that have more meaning, and that makes my mind and soul feel better. And I try not to be biased, and not to judge people. I want to do things because they are good, not because they are good to me... I feel like this is because of what happened to me, because of the places I went and the things I saw in this experience".

The 360-degree-vision described by Aridaeus is another common point with the reports of modern near-death experiencers. For example, one recent account describes how "I still had a 'body', but...I could see in three dimensions as if I had no body at all...I could see all directions at once".[11] Another experiencer explicitly notes that he "could see 360 degrees around me at the same time". This point appears to offer solid support for the conclusion that Aridaeus's experience was an ancient account of an NDE.

Even seemingly minor points made in Aridaeus's account, such as his spirit leaving through his head, agree with more recent accounts – for example, consider this report from Moody's *Life After Life*:

> I lost control of my car on a curve, and the car left the road and went into the air, and I remember seeing the blue sky and saw that the car was going down into a ditch... At that point, I kind of lost my sense of time, and I lost my physical reality as far as my body is concerned... My being or my self or my spirit, or whatever you would like to label it – I could sort of feel it rise out of me, through

my head. And it wasn't anything that hurt, it was just sort of like a lifting and it being above me... As it went out of my body, it seemed that a large end left first, and the small end last.

Similarly, another 'pre-Moody' NDE – that of a Dr. A.S. Wiltse, as related in Fred Myers' classic 1903 book, *Human Personality and Its Survival of Bodily Death* – also mentions this facet: "I began slowly to retreat from the feet, toward the head, as a rubber cord shortens. I remember reaching the hips and saying to myself, 'Now, there is no life below the hips'. As I emerged from the head, I floated up and down and laterally like a soap bubble".

Aridaeus's NDE is certainly not an isolated case however. There are numerous other examples from many centuries ago. For example, a document written in Tibet during the 8th century – although almost certainly part of a much older oral tradition – describes after-death encounters similar to those outlined by Raymond Moody. In fact, this document provided an actual 'manual' for the journey after death. Known as the *Tibetan Book of the Dead*, this enigmatic work was usually read to either the dying or the recently dead, to assist them in their transition to the afterlife realms. It describes at length numerous stages of the journey from the land of the living to the world of the dead, some of which match elements of the modern NDE remarkably well.

For instance, the *Tibetan Book of the Dead* explains that after the soul of the deceased separates from the physical body, it is likely that roaring, thundering and whistling sounds will be heard. The soul will likely be able to observe the physical surroundings, but will be unable to interact with them. However, the newly dead will also find that travel within this new plane of existence is virtually instantaneous, the journey made simply by desiring to go to a destination – just as young Private Ritchie found. At later stages of the post-death journey, this ancient book describes a meeting with a pure light, and a life review in which all past deeds are replayed in order to summarize the life of the newly deceased. It is worth noting that beyond these experiences, there are many 'deeper' stages of death described in the *Tibetan Book of the Dead*, which no survivor of a near-death experience has ever recalled.

Tibetan tradition is not the only place where we find historical crossovers between religions and the NDE. In her book *The Near Death Experience: Mysticism or Madness*, theologian Judith Cressy points out that a number of the biographies of celebrated mystics tell of an apparent dying, followed by a return to life with a visionary message to pass on. For instance, Cressy highlights the experience of Theresa of Avila:

> I thought I was being carried up to Heaven: the first persons I saw there were my mother and father, and such great things happened in so short a time...I wish I could give a description of at least the smallest part of what I learned, but when I try to discover a way of doing so, I find it impossible, for while the light we see here and that other light are both light, there is no comparison between the two and the brightness of the sun seems quite dull if compared with the other. [Afterwards] I was...left with very little fear of death, of which previously I had been very much afraid.

Here we again see many of the standard elements found in modern NDEs – a death, followed by a meeting with deceased relatives, the ineffability of the experience, a 'light' which is beyond compare, and the post-experience transformation and loss of the fear of dying.

More 'Modern' Examples

Moving through time, in the 18th century we find the detailed account of Admiral Francis Beaufort of the British Royal Navy (creator of the Beaufort Scale for indicating wind force). In 1795

Beaufort was a young sailor recently signed up to the Navy, and was sculling about in a small boat in Portsmouth Harbor when he fell into the water. Not knowing how to swim, he spent a considerable amount of time submerged before he was successfully rescued. Beaufort described what he experienced as he realized he was probably going to die, and it runs counter to everything you might expect that a drowning person would report:

> All hope fled, all exertion had ceased, a calm feeling of the most perfect tranquility superseded the previous tumultuous sensations... Though the senses were thus deadened, not so the mind; its activity seemed to be invigorated in a ratio which defies all description, for thought rose after thought with a rapidity of succession that is not only indescribable, but probably inconceivable, by anyone who has not himself been in a similar situation. The course of these thoughts I can even now in a great measure retrace – the event which had just taken place, the awkwardness that had produced it, the bustle it must have occasioned, the effect it would have on a most affectionate father, and a thousand other circumstances minutely associated with home were the first series of reflections that occurred.

This sharpness of thought and ability to analyse vast amounts of information in a seeming short time are hallmarks of the NDE. However, the next stage of the experience touches on one of the most common aspects – the life review. Beaufort tells how his thoughts then began to take a wider range:

> ...our last cruise, a former voyage and shipwreck, my school, the progress I had made there and the time I had misspent, and even all my boyish pursuits and adventures. Thus traveling backwards, every past incident of my life seemed to glance across my recollection in retrograde succession;

not, however, in mere outline as here stated, but the picture filled up every minute and collateral feature; in short, the whole period of my existence seemed to be placed before me in a kind of panoramic review, and each act of it to be accompanied by a consciousness of right or wrong, or by some reflection on its cause or its consequence; indeed, many trifling events which had been long forgotten, then crossed into my imagination, and with the character of recent familiarity.

Beaufort's exact words – "panoramic review" – crop up regularly in modern descriptions of this part of the experience, almost verbatim. For example, one NDEr notes that during the experience their "whole life so far appeared to be placed before me in a kind of panoramic, three-dimensional review, and each event seem to be accompanied by an awareness of good and evil or by an insight into its cause and effect". Furthermore, they point out, "Throughout, I not only saw everything from my own point of view, but I also knew the thoughts of everybody who'd been involved in these events... It meant that I saw not only what I had done or thought but even how this had affected others".[12] This latter observation (mentioned also in Moody's archetypal NDE) is fascinating: the NDE life review isn't just a 'dump' of memories without purpose; from Admiral Beaufort's NDE, through to modern accounts, the review is accompanied by "a consciousness of right or wrong." Neither is it a guilt trip: Moody quotes one experiencer as viewing "some instances where I had been selfish to my sister, but then just as many times where I had really shown love to her and had shared with her." Resuscitation expert Dr. Sam Parnia mentions another similar instance related to him by a patient in his recent book *Erasing Death*:

I wasn't just watching the events; I was actually reliving them again, while at the same time I was also re-experiencing the actions from other people's points of view. I was them. I was reliving the experience from their point of view and at the same time (and I don't know how this works) I was also experiencing it from a higher reality; the truth of the matter. So what I saw was my own lies and my own self deception to myself, which I had used to convince me that doing certain things was okay because people had deserved it. Then I was experiencing the emotional impact it had on other people. I felt their pain. I felt the shock on them... [But] the judgment came all from myself. It was not from an outside source, but then this being that was with me was also sending me comforting messages – thank goodness! – and one of them was it was alright as I was only human.

The life review is also prominent in one of the first studies to record some of the elements of what would later become known as the near-death experience. In 1892, Albert Heim, a Zurich geology professor, presented his findings from 25 years of research into the experiences of people who survived acute life-threatening situations – notably, climbers who fell during their ascents. He found that 95 percent of his subjects reported a certain, consistent experience:

> There was no anxiety, no trace of despair, no pain; but rather, calm seriousness, profound acceptance, and a dominant mental quickness and sense of surety. Mental activity became enormous, rising to a hundred-fold velocity or intensity. The relationships of events and their probable outcomes were overviewed with objective clarity. No confusion entered at all. Time became greatly expanded... In many cases there followed a sudden review of the individual's entire past; and finally the person falling often heard beautiful music and fell in a superbly blue heaven containing roseate cloudlets.

In his paper "Historical Perspectives on Near-Death Episodes", NDE researcher John Audette also cites the 'pre-Moody' case of another Admiral, the explorer Richard Byrd, described by Byrd himself in his book, *Alone,* published in 1938. It occurred as a result of carbon monoxide poisoning that Byrd suffered during his well-known Antarctic expedition. He recalled that "I saw my whole life pass in review," and also that he "realized how wrong my sense of value had been and how I had failed to see that the simple, homely, unpretentious things of life are the most important" – again, both common elements of the NDE. Byrd told how the struggle "went on interminably in a half-lighted borderland divided by a great wall. Several times I was nearly across the wall into a field flooded with a golden light but each time I slipped back into a spinning darkness."

One of the most fascinating accounts mentioned by Audette is the case of Louis Tucker, a Catholic priest. Tucker described his own near-death experience in his 1943 memoirs, *Clerical Errors,* and it is one of the closest analogues of Moody's 'archetypal NDE' that is likely to be found, despite it happening many decades previous to *Life After Life's* publication. It took place in 1909, when Tucker was suffering the life-threatening effects of a severe case of food poisoning. With the family physician in attendance, Tucker lost consciousness, and was shortly thereafter pronounced dead by the doctor. What followed is worth quoting at length, as Tucker goes into wonderful detail about the experience:

> The unconsciousness was short. The sensation was not quite like anything earthly; the nearest familiar thing to it is passing through a short tunnel on a train… I emerged into a place where people were being met by friends. It was quiet and full of light, and Father was waiting for me. He looked exactly as he had in the last few years of his life and wore the last suit of clothes he had owned…I knew that the clothes Father wore were because they were familiar to me, so that I might feel no strangeness in seeing him, and that

to some lesser extent, his appearance was assumed also; I knew all these things by contagion, because he did.

Soon I discovered that we were not talking, but thinking. I knew dozens of things that we did not mention because he knew them. He thought a question, I an answer, without speaking; the process was practically instantaneous... What he said was in ideas, no words: if I were to go back at all I must go at once...I did not want to go back; not in the least; the idea of self-preservation, the will to live was quite gone...I swung into the blackness again, as a man might swing on a train, thoroughly disgusted that I could not stay, and absolutely certain that it was right for me to go back. That certainty has never wavered.

There was a short interval of confused and hurrying blackness and I came to, to find myself lying on my bed with the doctor bending over telling me that I was safe now and would live... I told him I knew that some time ago, and went to sleep.

It's interesting to note Tucker's analysis of how his father's appearance was "assumed" so that he would "feel no strangeness in seeing him" – a real-life foreshadowing of the scene in the movie *Contact* (based on the science fiction novel by Carl Sagan) in which the spokesman of the alien species takes the form of Ellie's father in order to set her at ease. Also worth pointing out is the aspect of "not talking, but thinking," as this is yet another aspect common to near-death experiences. For instance, Raymond Moody quotes one experiencer as saying "I could see people all around, and I could understand what they were saying. I didn't hear them, audibly, like I'm hearing you. It was more like knowing what they were thinking, exactly what they were thinking, but only in my mind, not in their actual vocabulary". George Ritchie mentions in his own seminal account that "the words were out, in this strange realm where communication took place by thought instead of speech, before I could call them back".

Bringing Science to Bear

So what are we to make of these strange experiences? Are they hallucinations of a malfunctioning brain under threat of death, or a glimpse into some sort of life beyond death? For an expert opinion, I decided to ask Dr. Bruce Greyson, Professor of Psychiatry and Neurobehavioral Sciences at the University of Virginia. When it comes to the NDE, Greyson is an authority – he has been actively researching near-death experiences in an academic setting for more than three decades, is a founder and past-president of the International Association for Near-Death Studies (IANDS), and for over 25 years was the editor of the *Journal of Near-Death Studies.*

Bruce Greyson's academic home, the Division of Perceptual Studies at the University of Virginia – of which he is the Director – is one of the few places in the world where scientists are encouraged to research these strange experiences that hint at the survival of consciousness beyond death. The unit is funded by an endowment from the late Chester Carlson, who made a fortune from inventing the Xerox process. Towards the end of his life, Carlson became interested in Buddhism and reports of reincarnation memories (rather befitting the inventor of the Xerox process!), and so decided to spend some of his wealth investigating the question of life after death in a rational, scientific manner. The Division of Perceptual Studies was founded in the 1960s "with the express purpose of studying scientifically the question of whether we survive bodily death". For most of its life, the Division's research was done in a small 1920s house just off the grounds of the University of Virginia – a place that Greyson describes as "great for thinking and writing, but when trucks drove by the whole house shook, which made it hard to do the EEG readings".[13] In 2009 the Division of Perceptual Studies moved into a new facility, fitted with a state-of-the-art EEG lab with electromagnetic shielding, and currently has seven doctoral level faculty members, two research assistants, and a number of volunteers and students helping out.[14]

But does being part of an afterlife investigation unit require some degree of a belief in survival in the first place? When I ask Bruce Greyson if he was a skeptic or believer in the NDE when he first came to the topic, he is quick to clarify the two levels of 'reality' involved when talking about belief in the NDE. Some rather rabid 'skeptics' of the NDE have suggested that it doesn't exist at all, and that all experiencers fabricate their accounts out of whole cloth. So, says Greyson, "if you mean did I believe people really have such experiences, then I never seriously questioned that, any more than I doubt people who claim that they feel anxious when they speak before large crowds". Continuing with the speaking analogy, Greyson points out that though neither of the two experiences can be corroborated by observers, "both have effects that can be observed and studied". And as a psychiatrist, Greyson's primary concern is with the experiences people have, and the effect of those experiences on their lives. "Once I understood that near-death experiences are fairly common events (reported by 10-20% of people who come close to death) and that they have profound and long-lasting effects on experiencers' attitudes, beliefs, values, and behavior, it became for me a valid area for scientific investigation".

When it comes to whether he thinks the NDE is a glimpse into some sort of an afterlife however, Greyson is more circumspect. "We have a lot of data leading us toward or away from various hypotheses, but we are very far from understanding all the factors that contribute to people having NDEs", he confesses. But Greyson's carefulness in not jumping to conclusions applies equally to prosaic answers put forward by skeptics as solutions to the mystery of the NDE: he notes that none of these explanations have been supported by any research evidence thus far – and most of them are in fact *contradicted* by the evidence currently available. The NDE remains a scientific mystery.

Greyson isn't talking out of school on the matter. In a paper titled "Explanatory Models for Near-Death Experiences", he and co-authors Emily Williams Kelly and Edward Kelly systematically worked through the list of possible 'solutions' that have been offered so far, "paying special attention to how well they can account for the various features of NDEs". These solutions can be separated into two groups – psychological-based theories, and those focusing on physiological factors. In the former category we find offerings such as the 'expectation model' (in which NDEs are seen as products of the imagination, created to protect ourselves when facing threat of death, and which conform to personal or cultural expectations); depersonalization (feelings of detachment and removal from reality when facing threat of death); 'the birth model' (the suggestion that the tunnel, bright light and otherworldly realms of the NDE are memories of our birth experience, reproduced at death); and personality factors (susceptibility to hypnosis and dissociation, fantasy proneness, absorption, dream recall, and so on). Physiologically-based explanations for the NDE include altered blood gas levels (lowered levels of oxygen, known as hypoxia or anoxia, or increased levels of carbon dioxide, known as hypercarbia); neurochemical theories (the release of endogenous endorphins, opioids or psychedelic-like chemicals such as ketamine or dimethyltryptamine (D.M.T.) during times of stress); neuroanatomical models (abnormal activity in parts of the brain, such as the limbic system and temporal lobes, brought on by stress and/or altered gas and chemical levels); and rapid eye movement intrusion (mentation typical of REM sleep intruding into waking consciousness).[15]

But Greyson and his co-authors found that while many of these, in theory, seem like worthwhile candidates, in practice the evidence does not support them. For instance, the birth model is contradicted by the fact that NDE accounts featuring 'travel through a tunnel to another realm' were just as common among those born by Caesarean section as with those born by normal vaginal delivery. Meanwhile, the expectation model is confounded by the NDEs reported by children too young to have formed afterlife expectations, and also that near-death experiences in adults often run sharply counter to the NDEr's specific beliefs about death and the afterlife. Brain stimulation studies have not provided the support for neuroanatomical models that supporters claim, with experiences reported in such situations bearing little resemblance to the NDE. And the altered blood gas levels theory falls flat when we remember that NDEs occur in situations where there are no changes in blood gas levels, such as the afore-mentioned 'fear-death experiences'.[16] Furthermore, as other researchers have pointed out, "any acute alteration in cerebral physiology such as occurring in hypoxia, hypercarbia, metabolic, and drug induced disturbances and seizures leads to disorganised and compromised cerebral function [and] impaired attention," but the near-death experiences reported by those who have suffered cardiac arrest "are clearly not confusional and in fact indicate heightened awareness, attention and consciousness at a time when consciousness and memory formation would not be expected to occur".[17]

The point that Greyson and his fellow researchers make clear is that *in isolation,* individual elements of the near-death experience could possibly be described by one or another of the theories mentioned above, even though there is very little evidence supporting them. But "when several features occur together...and when increasing layers of explanation must be added on to account for them, these hypotheses become increasingly strained". For those who think that the NDE has been satisfactorily explained by science, their advice is sobering: "Theories proposed thus far consist largely of unsupported speculations about what might be happening during an NDE".[18]

Noting this criticism, I ask Bruce Greyson about a recent theory put forward by Dr. Jason Braithwaite of the School of Psychology at the University of Birmingham. Braithwaite has taken elements of a number of the theories outlined above – on their own, lacking as a complete explanation of the NDE – and placed them under the umbrella of one over-arching mechanism known as "neural disinhibition", which he says can be induced or triggered by any one of a number of factors, including anoxia, confusion, trauma, sensory deprivation, illness, pathology, epilepsy, migraine, drug use and brain stimulation. But Greyson is unimpressed. Braithwaite's neural disinhibition explanation, Greyson says, "completely ignores contradictory evidence from NDEs". He debunks Braithwaite's claim that no one so far has measured oxygen levels during NDEs, citing a number of studies that have.[19] And another major problem with Braithwaite's argument, notes Greyson, is that it assumes a material basis for consciousness rather than attempting to prove it – and in doing so, his whole argument becomes an exercise in self-justifying claims. "Braithwaite argues that in order for any experience to be remembered, it must be encoded in the brain, and therefore the existence of NDE memories by definition proves that the brain was functioning during the NDE", Greyson points out. "Of course, if you accept the materialist belief that memories can be created only if the brain is functioning, then that will be your conclusion. But that's exactly the point in question: whether mental functions like perception and memory can occur without the brain. Braithwaite appears not to understand that his argument holds only if one accepts *a priori* the belief that 'the mind is what the brain does'".

This aspect seems to be a major stumbling block for theories suggesting that NDEs are caused by an impaired brain, as experiencer accounts nearly always mention some sort of elevated or enhanced mental activity. "Almost all NDErs report that their thinking processes were 'faster and clearer than they ever have been before', despite their brain being impaired – for example, in cardiac arrest", says Greyson, as if "mind was free of the limitations of the physical brain". He relates the story of a man who had overdosed on medication in a suicide attempt, and began hallucinating small humanoid figures around him. Having second thoughts about leaving this mortal coil, he tried to make it to the telephone to call for help, but his way was being blocked by the figures. At this point the man suddenly had an out-of-body experience, during which his thinking suddenly became clear and the humanoid figures disappeared from view.

> At that point he drew out of his body, and from a position about 10 feet behind his body, his thinking suddenly became crystal clear. And he looked at his body, and his body was looking around confusedly. And from where he was, 10 feet behind, he could not see these humanoid figures. But he remembered being in the body hallucinating. So here we have a brain that's still hallucinating, while the subject, the person, out of the body, is not hallucinating. So how does medical science make sense of that?[20]

Interestingly, Greyson's final word on Jason Braithwaite's neural disinhibition explanation for NDEs includes mention of a few lines of investigation which could offer evidence that mind is indeed a separate thing to the brain.

> The main problem with Braithwaite's position is that he does not consider evidence that contradicts his position...he states that all reported NDE features have been shown to occur 'with pathology, disease, illness, neurological conditions... and direct forms of brain stimulation'. Well, of course, if you limit your consideration of those NDE features that can occur in those conditions, then there will be nothing unique in NDEs that needs to be explained. But he, and many others, completely ignore features like accurate out-of-body perception, encounters with deceased individuals not known to be dead, and so on that do not occur in any pathological condition and defy explanation in terms of brain function.

Wait a second – accurate out-of-body perception? Greyson explains: "There are numerous published examples of experiencers describing accurately unexpected and unpredictable events that occurred when they were unconscious and being resuscitated". These experiences, at face value, should be impossible, especially in cardiac arrest situations where – due to lack of blood flow – there should be no brain activity at all. But could it be possible that the NDE didn't actually happen when experiencers thought it did, and instead were created as 'death memories' in the periods immediately before or after slipping into unconsciousness? Greyson answers that a number of accounts seem to dispute this possibility: "The best evidence for when the NDEs of cardiac arrest patients occur is 'time anchors'," he says – details that patients report "that can be definitively linked to a specific time during their cardiac arrest". And there are a number of cases already recorded which suggest not only that the NDE occurred at a time that it shouldn't have been possible, but also that the experiencer was able to perceive things accurately from a position *external* to their physical body.

Given the significance of these anomalous accounts, if proved true, they comprise their own line of inquiry in the NDE research field, under the term 'veridical perception'. Let's take a closer look at this fascinating subject.

Veridical OBEs

Al Sullivan, a 56-year-old van driver, was at work on a Monday morning in early 1989 when his heartbeat suddenly became irregular. Admitted to Hartford Hospital in Connecticut, Sullivan was undergoing diagnostic testing when one of his arteries became blocked, and he was rushed into the operating room for what became quadruple bypass surgery. During this operation, Sullivan suddenly felt his consciousness separate from his physical body, and after traveling through a "black, billowy smoke-like atmosphere", found himself looking down from above upon his own life-saving surgery:

> I was laying [sic] on a table covered with light blue sheets and I was cut open so as to expose my chest cavity. It was in this cavity that I was able to see my heart on what appeared to be a small glass table. I was able to see my surgeon, who just moments ago had explained to me what he was going to do during my operation. He appeared to be somewhat perplexed. I thought he was flapping his arms as if trying to fly...[21]

At the time of witnessing this strange behaviour from the surgeon, Sullivan also noted that his own chest cavity was being held open by metal clamps, and was equally puzzled by the fact that two other surgeons were working on his leg, rather than his heart. In any case...

> ...It was then that I turned my attention to the lower right-hand side of the place I was at. I saw the most brilliant yellow light coming from, what appeared to be, a very well lit tunnel... The light that came from the tunnel was of a golden yellow hue and although the brightest I had ever looked into, it was of no discomfort to the eyes at all. Then, preceded by warmth, joy and peace and a feeling of being loved, a brown cloaked figure drifted out of the light toward me. As my euphoria rose still more, I, much to my delight, recognized it to be that of my mother. My mother had died at age thirty-seven when I was seven years old. I am now in my fifties and the first thought that came to my mind was how young my mother appeared. She smiled at me and appeared to be shaping words with her mouth and these was [sic] not audible to me. Through thought transfer we were soon able to communicate.[22]

Readers will recognise some of the elements in Sullivan's NDE from other reports discussed above, such as the intense light that doesn't hurt the eyes, and the use of 'thought transfer' for communication.

Sullivan then described how his mother seems to have 'intervened' in the surgery:

> All at once my mother's expression changed to that of concern. At this point she left my side and drifted down toward my surgeon. She placed the surgeon's hand on the left side of my heart and then returned to me. I recall the surgeon making a sweeping motion as if to rid the area of a flying insect. My mother then extended one of her hands to me, but try as I might I could not grasp it. She then smiled and drifted back toward the lit tunnel.[23]

As soon as he regained consciousness and was able to talk, Sullivan told his cardiologist Dr. Anthony LaSala of his amazing experience. Initially skeptical, Dr. LaSala immediately paid more attention when Sullivan described the flapping elbows of the cardiac surgeon, Dr. Hiroyoshi Takata, as this was an idiosyncratic habit of his that Dr. LaSala had witnessed himself – after scrubbing in, Dr. Takata would point at things using his elbows to avoid contamination of his hands, giving the impression that he was impersonating a chicken attempting to fly. However, according to Sullivan, when his extraordinary NDE was reported to Dr. Takata, the surgeon displayed no interest in his account. Later, when Sullivan had a follow-up visit with the doctor and personally brought up his experience, Dr. Takata simply replied "Well, you're here, you're alive, so I must do something right".

Almost a decade later, Dr. Bruce Greyson resolved to investigate this report and spoke to both of the doctors involved in the surgery. Dr. LaSala confirmed that Sullivan had told him about his NDE immediately after regaining consciousness, and also noted the 'flapping' elbows of Dr. Takata – adding that he had never seen any other surgeon do this. Dr. Takata also confirmed that during the operation he stood with hands on chest, pointing at things with his elbows, because after he scrubbed in he didn't want his hands to touch anything until he was ready to do the surgery. Greyson also noted that Sullivan's OBE observations of the open chest cavity and surgeons working on his leg – which he later learned was the stripping of a vein out of his leg to create the bypass graft for his heart – offer a 'time anchor' (as mentioned earlier) which seems to confirm "that Mr. Sullivan's observation of Dr. Takata flapping his arms occurred when he was under general anesthesia and, at least to observers, unconscious".[24] Needless to say, how Al Sullivan 'saw' what he did remains a mystery.

On its own, we might be able to explain this case as an amazing sequence of coincidences, or via some other unexpected explanation. But Al Sullivan's experience is not unique...

The Case of the Missing Teeth

Reports of 'veridical OBEs' during near-death experiences such as Al Sullivan's can be found surprisingly often, such as the following account that graced the pages of the respected medical journal *The Lancet*. In 1979, a 44-year-old man ('Mr. B') was brought into the emergency department at Canisius Hospital in the Netherlands by ambulance, after being discovered comatose, hypothermic and without a pulse in a cold, damp meadow in the middle of the night. Hospital staff, including the senior nurse ('T.G.'), placed Mr. B upon a resuscitation bed, turning him on his side in order to position a heart massage pump (known as a 'Thumper') before turning him onto his back once more. T.G. began to put a ventilation mask on the patient, but noticed that he was wearing dentures, so removed them and placed them on the 'crash cart' before installing the mask. The Thumper was then switched on to restart resuscitation attempts (the patient had undergone resuscitation procedures in the ambulance, but the transfer to the hospital room had taken some minutes, during which only minimal resuscitation was possible). For an hour and a half, hospital staff worked to bring Mr. B back to life, before finally reaching a point where they felt his pulse and blood pressure were stable enough to allow him to be transferred to the intensive care unit, though he remained comatose and ventilated.[25]

It wasn't until more than a week later that T.G. finally saw Mr. B again – he had been transferred from the ICU back to the cardiac ward – while doing his rounds distributing medication. T.G. was astonished when the patient he had brought back to life suddenly exclaimed "Oh, that nurse knows where my dentures are!". Seeing the look of surprise on T.G.'s face, Mr. B explained himself: since coming back to consciousness, Mr. B. had been looking for his dentures. "You were there when I was brought into hospital and you took my dentures out of my mouth and put them onto that cart," he said. "It had all these bottles on it and there was this sliding drawer underneath and there you put my teeth". T.G. was confused by this, as he remembered that he had done this when the patient was unconscious and undergoing CPR to bring him back to life:

> When I asked further, it appeared the man had seen himself lying in bed, that he had perceived from above how nurses and doctors had been busy with CPR. He was also able to describe correctly and in detail the small room in which he had been resuscitated as well as the appearance of those present like myself. At the time that he observed the situation he had been very much afraid that we would stop CPR and that he would die. And it is true that we had been very negative about the patient's prognosis due to his very poor medical condition when admitted. The patient tells me that he desperately and unsuccessfully tried to make it clear to us that he was still alive and that we should

continue CPR. He is deeply impressed by his experience and says he is no longer afraid of death. Four weeks later he left hospital as a healthy man.[26]

The point worth reiterating here is that Mr. B's account took place when he was unconscious, with no blood circulation and thus no brain activity. As T.G. points out, "at arrival in the [CCU] department [the patient had] wide light-stiff pupils, signs of serious oxygen deprivation in the brain, no heart rhythm…there was definitely no blood circulation".[27] By the tenets of orthodox medical science, he could not have observed the removal of his dentures in any normal way, even by some reconstruction through imagination and memory based on touch and sounds, as his brain was shut down at the time of the dentures removal. And yet Mr. B. related that he saw everything from a vantage point near the ceiling in the corner of the room.

But what if, by some chance, Mr. B. *did* hear what was going on and reconstructed the scene from those observations? One skeptic has pointed out how things might have played out: "It was a crash cart with a metal drawer, and one can hear its opening and closing," Gerald Woerlee says, which gave Mr. B. every clue as to where his dentures had been placed. We probably would all make the same assumption, right? The problem with this theory though is that it was not a metal drawer, as most of us might assume: it was a flat wooden shelf (according to T.G., the cart was custom crafted, and unique in this aspect), and it was "already pulled out", as the nurses had used it to prepare bottles and syringes upon hearing a resuscitation patient was on their way – just as described by the patient. And we are still left to explain how Mr. B recognised by sight the nurse who removed his dentures, when he was not conscious during the resuscitation attempts. Furthermore, Mr. B was also able to describe to T.G. the rest of the room, and those working in it: a small niche on the right side of the bed containing a wash basin; where the mirror was; the cart on the left side of the bed with bottles on it, where his dentures were put; a narrow metal storage cabinet; and the appearance of a female nurse in the room as well.

There's Life in the Eye!

Penny Sartori is a British nurse who was awarded a Ph.D. in 2005 for her extensive research into near-death experiences. Amongst her research was one particular case of interest: a 60-year-old man was recovering from emergency surgery for bowel cancer and subsequent complications. In order to begin regaining some muscle tone, his physiotherapist attempted to get the patient sitting upright in a chair, but before long his respiratory rate increased significantly while his oxygen blood saturation levels plummeted. Sartori intervened by manually ventilating the patient with oxygen, but his blood pressure suddenly dropped precipitously and his condition deteriorated further. The nurses moved the patient back into his bed, by which time he was unconscious and not responding to even painful stimuli.

A junior doctor and a consultant anaesthetist performed examinations of the patient and prescribed extra fluids to improve his blood pressure. The doctor checked the patient's eyes for a response by shining a light in each eye, and remarked that they were both reacting, but that the right pupil was larger than the left. Once the doctor returned to his office, the physiotherapist began fretting that she might be responsible for the deterioration in the patient's condition, and stood outside the screen, poking her head around intermittently to check on his status. Meanwhile, a nurse cleaned up some drool that had leaked from the patient's mouth during the episode, firstly with a long suction catheter and then a pink sponge soaked in water. The patient began to return to consciousness some 30 minutes later, though it took a full three hours for him to recover completely.

At this point, the man excitedly tried to communicate something to the medical staff surrounding him. As he was still connected to the ventilator, and thus unable to speak, the physiotherapist provided him with a letter board, through which he spelt out a stunning message for all those in attendance: "I died and I watched it all from above".[28] As Sartori was at that time working on her near-death experience research, she explained her interest in this statement to the patient and asked him to be interviewed about his NDE once he was off the ventilator.

When able, the patient told Sartori what had happened from his point of view:

> They wanted me to get out of bed, with all my tubes in me and sit in the chair. They insisted, especially one sister. I didn't want to because I felt so weak; then eventually I got out. All I can remember is looking up in the air and I was floating in a bright pink room. I couldn't see anything; I was just going up and there was no pain at all. I looked up the second time and I could see my father and my mother-in-law standing alongside a gentleman with long, black hair, which needed to be combed. I saw my father – definitely – and I saw this chap. I don't know who he was, maybe Jesus, but this chap had long, black, scruffy hair that needed combing. The only thing nice about him was his eyes were drawing you to him; the eyes were piercing; it was his eyes. When I went to look at my father, it was drawing with his eyes as well, as if I could see them both [at] the same time. And I had no pain at all. There was talking between me and my father; not words but communicating other ways – don't ask me what, but we were actually talking. I was talking to my father … not through words through my mouth, but through my mind.[29]

As we mentioned earlier, this 'talking using our minds' seems to be a recurring element noted by many near-death experiencers. The patient continued:

> But looking back, I could see other patients as well below me. That's what I couldn't figure out: I could see everybody. I was happy, no pain at all, until I felt somebody going to my eye. I looked back and I could see my bed, my body in the bed. I could see everything that was happening on the floor. I saw doctors when I was up there; I was looking down and could see the doctors and even the sister, what she was actually doing in the ward. It was marvellous; I could see nurses around me and the doctors. I was still going up in the air and I could feel somebody going like this to my eye. [He raised his finger up to his eye.] I eventually looked back and I could see one of the doctors pulling my eye, what for I didn't know. One doctor was saying: "There's life in the eye."

> I could see everybody panicking around me. The blonde lady therapist boss, she was panicking; she looked nervous because she was the one who got me out in the chair. She hid behind the curtains, but kept poking her head around to check on me. I could also see Penny, who was a nurse. She was drawing something out of my mouth, which looked to me like a long, pink lollipop, like a long, pink thing on a stick – I didn't even know what that was. I was still going up, and eventually the gentleman said to my father and my mother-in-law, "He's got to go back; he's not ready yet"... I looked up and Mam [his mother-in-law] said a few words and Dad.

> Eventually, I felt myself coming slowly back into my body. I went in my body on the bed and I was in terrible pain; the pain was worse then than it had ever been before. All

these cables were in me, as they were before I went up. I couldn't speak because I had tubes in my throat and my nose. Then [the physiotherapist] came to speak to me and it was frustration really, because they were all asking me what happened, how I was feeling… The physiotherapist wanted to know what happened. I couldn't speak, so she got a book with words and sayings on it. Eventually she came to a page I recognized and I pointed to that and said, "I was dead".[30]

The patient was bemused as to why his mother-in-law – whom he had never actually met in person, as she died from cancer before he married his wife – appeared along with his father, and wondered why his own mother didn't appear. But Sartori had other things on her mind: as part of her research into NDEs, she had placed cards with images on them out of everyday sight on top of the monitors in patients' rooms, hoping that any near-death experiencers might be able to prove that they were truly out of their body by accurately describing the images as seen from near the ceiling. Sartori asked the patient whether he had noticed anything on top of the monitor…but unfortunately the patient was 'looking' the wrong way: "I didn't twist my head back that way", he apologized. "I was just looking at my side. I could see you and the doctor and two to three others around me".[31]

Nevertheless, Sartori was at a loss to explain how the patient knew the physiotherapist was glancing around the screen nervously, and that she used the suction catheter and sponge to clean up the drool, when at this time the patient was unconscious and had his eyes closed. Despite this, the patient adamantly claimed that he "could see that, as plain as I can see you now". Adding to the mystery, a strange outcome of the experience was that the patient was partially cured of a lifelong problem: due to cerebral palsy, his right hand had always been severely contracted into a fist. But after the NDE, he could now open it.

A Proliferation of Cases

On their own, anecdotes of this kind are certainly perplexing – but in isolation we might be tempted to simply write them off due to their singular nature. However, again and again we find examples in the medical literature of veridical observation during the near-death experience. For example, Canadian neuroscientist Dr. Mario Beauregard reported in the journal *Resuscitation* that a patient he interviewed had a "subjective experience" that raised "a number of perplexing questions". In a retrospective study of patients who had undergone deep hypothermic cardiocirculatory arrest (cooling the patient down to around 18°C/64.5°F in order to allow a complete stop of blood circulation while heart defects are operated on, without causing lasting damage to the body or brain), Beauregard's team found that three patients out of thirty-three "reported conscious mental activity" during their surgery. But the account of one of those three seemed to offer evidence that their mind was outside of their body at this time.

The patient, 'J.S.', was 31 weeks pregnant when, on October 26, 2008, she woke up feeling short of breath and weak. The 31-year-old expectant mother was transported to Hôpital Sacré-Coeur in Montreal by ambulance, where it was found she was suffering from a serious heart condition known as an ascending aortic dissection:

> J.S. first underwent an emergency caesarean section. After having successfully delivered a baby boy, she was then transferred to a surgery room to undergo the replacement of the ascending aorta. She did not see or talk to the members of the surgical team, and it was not possible for her to see the machines behind the head section of the operating table, as she was wheeled into the operating room. J.S. was given general anesthesia and her eyes were taped shut.

At one point during surgery, J.S. claims to have had an out-of-body experience (OBE). From a vantage point outside her physical body, she apparently "saw" a nurse passing surgical instruments to the cardiothoracic surgeon. She also perceived anesthesia and echography machines located behind her head. We were able to verify that the descriptions she provided of the nurse and the machines were accurate (this was confirmed by the cardiothoracic surgeon who operated upon her). Furthermore, in the OBE state J.S. reported feelings of peace and joy, and seeing a bright light.[32]

A similar case from the 1990s, well-known to many, is the seemingly veridical out-of-body experience reported by musician Pam Reynolds during surgery to fix a brain aneurysm. Initially believed to be inoperable, Reynolds was given hope by neurosurgeon Dr. Robert Spetzler, who believed that he could do the surgery by using a radical procedure nicknamed 'Standstill' – like the case of J.S. above, Reynolds' body would be cooled down, and her heart (and thus blood circulation) brought to a halt. The surgeon would drain the blood from her head while in this cooled state, and then repair the aneurysm.

Against all odds, the operation was a success, and Reynolds survived. But her doctors were astounded when Reynolds reported that, while she was apparently unconscious (though before her heart was stopped), she had left her body and watched part of the operation from beside the surgeon's shoulder. Reynolds recounted that she had...

...suddenly been brought to consciousness by the piercing sound of the cranial saw. She said the saw emitted a natural D tone and that it pulled her out of the top of her head. She came to rest at a location near Spetzler's shoulder. She described a sense of awareness far greater than she had ever experienced before, as well as greatly enhanced "vision" with which she saw with clarity and detail the cranial saw, her head, the operating room (OR), and OR personnel. She saw things that she had not expected or that contradicted her expectations, such as the appearance of the cranial saw, the interchangeable saw blades in a socket-wrench-type case, and the way her head was shaved. She also was somewhat dismayed to see someone conducting a procedure in her groin area when this was supposedly brain surgery. From that area, she heard a female voice report that the vessels were too small on the right side, and a male voice directing her to try the other side.[33]

At a later point, Reynolds moved from the operating room to an 'afterlife environment' where she encountered deceased loved ones, including her grandmother and an uncle. Later, this uncle accompanied her back to the surgery to assist her in returning to her physical body. But upon seeing the terrible condition of the body, she recoiled: "I didn't want to get into it... It looked terrible, like a train wreck". Her uncle gave her a sudden push, and she woke suddenly back in the 'real' world. According to Reynolds the re-entry was "like diving into a pool of ice water...it hurt!".[34] On a lighter note, when she awoke the music being played in the operating room was 'Hotel California' by The Eagles, right at the line "You can check out anytime you like, but you can never leave" – Reynolds later joked with her doctors that it was an incredibly insensitive choice of music.[35]

The Pam Reynolds case is of special interest because it is difficult to explain away simply by saying she reconstructed the scene from sounds that she heard, as one aspect of the operation was that it required a loud clicking noise to be played directly into her ears throughout the surgery in order to monitor her brainstem activity. This click was played 11 times per second at a level of 95 decibels (rather loud), through small speakers that had been molded and glued into her ears, and which were then covered over by "mounds" of tape and gauze. The man responsible for inserting these speakers has openly stated that he doesn't believe a person would be able to "hear through the stimuli" that Reynolds was presented with. And according to the neurosurgeon that saved her life, Dr. Robert Spetzler:

> I don't think that the observations she made were based on what she experienced as she went into the operating theater. They were just not available to her. For example, the drill and so on, those things are all covered up. They aren't visible; they were inside their packages. You really don't begin to open until the patient is completely asleep, so that you maintain a sterile environment... At that stage in the operation nobody can observe, hear in that state. And I find it inconceivable that the normal senses, such as hearing, let alone the fact that she had clicking modules in each ear, that there was any way for her to hear through normal auditory pathways. I don't have an explanation for it. I don't know how it's possible for it to happen.[36]

Also of interest in the Reynolds case is that her expectations were confounded: she did not see what her mental representation of the operating room was. Instead, she was surprised by the appearance of the cranial saw and the blades in their case, as well as the way her head had been shaved. We see this in other cases of out-of-body experiences during NDEs; for instance, in some accounts, the NDEr is shocked to see what they actually look like to others, rather than what they themselves thought they looked like: "Boy, I sure didn't realize that I looked like that!' one NDEr reported. "You know, I'm only used to seeing myself in pictures or from the front in a mirror, and both of those look flat. But all of a sudden there I – or my body – was, and I could see it...it took me a few moments to recognise myself".

Reynolds' surgeon Dr. Robert Spetzler isn't the first to be perplexed by veridical reports during a patient's operation. In an interview posted on YouTube, pioneering cardiac surgeon Dr. Lloyd Rudy tells of a certain incident that convinced him personally that there's more to human consciousness than just the electrical activity of the brain.[37] After performing bypass surgery on a patient to correct a valve defect, Rudy was devastated to find that he and his team couldn't get the patient off the bypass machine – each time they tried, the patient's blood pressure would plunge. Eventually, they were forced to give up. They turned off the heart-lung machine, pronounced him dead, and his surgical assistant did a 'temporary close' of the patient's body in preparation for the impending autopsy (required by law in deaths on the surgical table).

The anaesthesiologist went to go grab some food as he hadn't eaten all day, and Rudy and his assistant left the room to take off their surgical gowns while assistants began cleaning up the theatre. The pair returned in their street clothes, and were standing in the doorway with their arms folded, discussing the operation, when they noticed some electrical activity on the echocardiogram (ECG). As this sometimes happens in the wake of death – the heart twitches, but is unable to start pumping blood under pressure – they didn't think too much of it, not least as some 20 minutes had passed since they had pronounced the patient dead. But then the activity began turning into a heartbeat, and slowly the patient's pressure began to rise. Dr. Rudy was astounded, and leapt into action while yelling orders to anyone that could hear him: "Get anaesthesia back in here, get the nurses!"

Eventually they were able to fully resuscitate the patient and stabilise him enough to be transferred to the Intensive Care Unit. And he not only recovered, but showed no signs of any neurological deficits, despite not having any blood-flow to his brain for an extended period. An amazing story, but the best was yet to come.

A few days later, Rudy was talking to the patient about the operation, asking him if he had felt or experienced anything during this strange situation. The patient told Rudy about having seen a bright light at the end of a tunnel – standard fare for an NDE – but it was what he related about the Earthly realm that "astounded" the experienced surgeon: "He described that operating room [and] floating around and saying 'I saw you and the [other doctor] standing in the doorway with your arms folded talking...I didn't know where the anaesthesiologist was but he came running back in. And I saw all of these post-it notes, sitting on this TV screen'." This particular aspect was the most intriguing to Rudy – during a surgery, if he received any phone calls he would get the nurse to answer and then write down the name and number on a post-it note, and stick it to the monitor so that he could call them back once the operation was finished. Dr. Rudy laughs at this point and exclaims animatedly: "HE DESCRIBED THAT!! I mean there's no way he could have described that before the operation because I didn't have any calls...he described the scene, things that there is no way he knew". With a flabbergasted look on his face, Rudy clarifies: "I mean he didn't wake up in the operating room and see all this – he was out, and was out for a day or two while we recovered him in the Intensive Care Unit".

The experience changed Dr. Lloyd Rudy in a profound way. "It always makes me very emotional," he confesses. "It has convinced me that there's something out there".

Almost a century previous, the Scottish surgeon Sir Alexander Ogston also related an anecdote which seemed to confirm that mind can operate beyond the brain – although in this case, it was his own experience near death's door. Ogston was no stranger to skepticism from the establishment – his ground-breaking discovery of the *Staphylococcus* bacteria in the 19th century was met with disbelief and in some cases outright hostility by medical authorities. One can only imagine then what they made of Ogston's near-death experience during his service in the South

African War. Admitted to Blomfontein Hospital suffering from typhoid fever, Ogston reported that as he lay in a stupor, his mind and body seemed to be becoming two separate entities.

> I was conscious of the body as an inert, tumbled mass near a door, it belonged to me but was not I ... In my wanderings there was a strange consciousness that I could see through the walls of the building, though I was aware that they were there and that everything was transparent to my senses. I saw plainly, for instance, a poor Royal Army Medical Corps surgeon, of whose existence I had not known, and who was in quite another part of the hospital, grow very ill and scream and die; I saw them cover his corpse and carry him softly out on shoeless feet, quietly and surreptitiously, lest we should know that he had died, and the next night I saw him taken away to the cemetery. Afterwards when I told these happenings to the sisters, they informed me that all this had happened just as I had fancied...[38]

Joyce Harmon, a surgical intensive care unit (ICU) nurse, related what seemed to be a minor incident that has similar implications for how we view the 'reality' of the near-death experience. She had just returned from a vacation, during which she had purchased a new pair of rather noticeable plaid shoelaces. She was wearing these laces on her first day back at the hospital, when she was involved in successfully resuscitating a female patient. The next day, Harmon met with the patient and was shocked when the woman recognised her: "Oh, you're the one with the plaid shoelaces!" Harmon was astonished, and says she still remembers feeling the hair on her neck rising up as the lady told her exactly how she knew about her laces. "I saw them," the woman continued. "I was watching what was happening yesterday when I died. I was up above".[39]

Could the evidence found in these 'veridical reports' be put down to educated guesses? Cardiologist Michael Sabom surveyed patients who had undergone resuscitation to find how much of the descriptions of operating theatres given by near-death experiencers could be put down to guesswork and inference. Asking patients to describe what their resuscitation 'looked' like from a third-person perspective, he found that the descriptions of 25 cardiac patients who did not report an NDE were significantly less accurate than the accounts of the 32 NDErs he interviewed. Sabom's research showed that 80% of the 'control' patients (those who didn't have an NDE) made at least one major error in describing the scene – but not one of the near-death experiencers did so. Additionally, six of the 32 NDErs went even further in describing unexpected events that occurred during their resuscitation, that they wouldn't have been expected to have any recall of.[40] Sabom concluded that the near-death experiencers appeared to somehow be describing actual observations of the resuscitation, rather than creating them from their imagination.[41]

NDE researcher Janice Miner Holden has looked further into the prevalence of these types of reports, and published her findings in an article titled "Veridical Perception in Near-Death Experiences". She collected as many accounts from the NDE literature as she could find (purposefully excluding some book genres that might be considered 'untrustworthy'), ending with a total of 107 cases, which she then analyzed and categorized based on how correct the accounts were, and how strong they were as evidence of veridical perception. A typical example offered by Holden was the case of an NDEr who reported that while her body was unconscious, "she saw her stepfather, whom she had always known to be a health-food devotee, buy a candy bar from a vending machine with the intention to eat it; when the NDEr regained consciousness, she told her mother what she saw, and her mother confirmed the accuracy of her daughter's perception".[42] A similar story is that of a woman in childbirth who reported having an OBE, and seeing her mother in the waiting room smoking a cigarette – an unexpected sight, as her mother did not smoke.

However the mother "admitted much later that she had 'tried' one or two because she was so nervous!".[43]

Holden found that the strength of evidence in the cases she collected ranged widely from weak to extremely strong, but what impacted on her was the large number of cases that did suggest 'something' was going on. "The sheer volume of anecdotes that a number of authors over the course of the last 150 years have described suggests [veridical NDE perception] is real," she concludes. While acknowledging that each individual instance on its own might not be absolutely conclusive, she points out that "the cumulative weight of these narratives" should be enough to "convince most skeptics that these reports are something more than than mere hallucinations on the patient's part".

It is difficult to overstate the significance of these types of reports. If these near-death experiencers truly did perceive events from a viewpoint outside their bodies, while it lay inert and on the cusp of death, then it totally overturns the reigning scientific view of human consciousness. The mind is no longer tied to the brain, does not require a functioning human body, and can therefore function independently and in the post-death state. We have already seen that some great scientific figures, including Freeman Dyson, Paul Davies and Sir James Jeans, have stated their opinion that consciousness may be a fundamental aspect of the cosmos, and this opinion is supported by reports of veridical perception during NDEs. But though Janice Miner Holden might think skeptics will be convinced by the 'cumulative weight' of reports of this kind, in practice this is not so likely: instead such reports are generally dismissed as 'anecdotes', not data, and thus cannot be trusted as true scientific evidence (regardless of how thoroughly investigated each case is, or how strong the testimony is). So is it possible to move forward from being intrigued by the multitude of reports of veridical perception, to actually proving in the court of science that human consciousness can separate from the body?

Are you AWARE?

Take away the white coat, and you'd still probably be able to guess that Sam Parnia is a doctor. Even when talking about death, in particular the possibility that consciousness could survive the physical death of the body, he remains calm and dispassionate. Like a personal physician, he talks in bursts of information, before stopping and checking that the listener understands what has just been said with a glance their way and a quiet, questioning "okay?". His softly-spoken manner seems to be evidence that, while Parnia is no doubt fascinated by reports of near-death experiences and the possible implications for human consciousness, he is making a conscious attempt to remain as objective and neutral as possible on a topic that is often debated more emotionally than intellectually. For example, when asked by ABC journalist Bob Woodruff – who had an NDE in Iraq in 2006 when the vehicle he was travelling in hit an improvised explosive device – if his experience was a dream, or if he was really looking down on his physical body from above, Parnia's answer was brutally honest. "I don't know", he told Woodruff, before following with a warning about seeking a definitive answer from others: "And if anyone says they know, they're just speculating". Indeed, Parnia's attempts to stay neutral have landed him in that damned location between the extremes of belief and non-belief that some have labeled 'the excluded middle', suffering criticism directed at him by both skeptics of the NDE as well as believers. But this careful attitude may well pay off handsomely in the long term for Sam Parnia, because through it he has managed to institute perhaps the most daring research study into the near-death experience that could be imagined in the modern world of medicine, dominated by ethics committees and research programs based purely on profit margins: the AWARE, or 'AWAreness during REsuscitation' study.

A critical care doctor and expert in the field of resuscitation, Parnia has been fascinated with the question of what happens to consciousness at the moment of death since the time he lost a patient as a student doctor at the age of 22. Working at Mount Sinai hospital in New York as part of his final year of medical studies, Parnia was called to the emergency ward to examine Desmond, a 62-year-old man of West Indian origin who had come to the hospital after coughing up blood. Parnia detected fluid surrounding the man's lungs, but otherwise his vital signs were strong and so he ordered some tests for Desmond and left the emergency room. As he left, the tall, thin West Indian looked him in the eye and saluted good-naturedly.

Thirty minutes later, Parnia's pager went off again, alerting him that there was a cardiac arrest in the emergency ward. Rushing back to the area, Parnia pulled back the curtains to find that the patient being resuscitated was Desmond. But the news was not good – blood had filled his airways and clotted, stopping oxygen from getting into his system. The announcement came as a shock to Parnia: "It's impossible to resuscitate him".

> Just like that, Desmond was dead. One minute he was here, the next he was gone. What had happened to the person I had been talking to a half hour ago about his surprise birthday party? What was left of his memories, thoughts and feelings? It appeared there was just a lifeless body. This interval between life and death had been so quick. Questions buzzed around my head. What had Desmond experienced? Had he been able to see us trying to resuscitate him? What was happening to him now? Could he have retained some form of consciousness, or was that the end? Even with my medical training, I couldn't even begin to answer those questions.[44]

Desmond's death had a profound impact on Parnia's life. It would lead the young doctor to specialize in the field of critical care and resuscitation medicine (he is now Director of Resuscitation

Research at Stonybrook University School of Medicine), and also into studying the enigma of the near-death experience, of which he has become an expert of world renown.

"Contrary to popular perception," he reveals on the AWARE Project's website, "death is not a specific moment".[45] After a cardiac arrest, Parnia notes, there is a period of time, ranging from a few seconds to multiple hours (usually in cases involving extreme cold), in which emergency medical efforts may succeed in restarting the heart and bringing the patient back to 'life'. We may have laughed when Miracle Max said, in *The Princess Bride*, "There's a big difference between mostly dead and all dead. Mostly dead is slightly alive". But the modern field of resuscitation science is built on this very idea.

Studying the experiences that some patients say happened while they were 'mostly dead' provides "a unique window of understanding into what we are all likely to experience during the dying process," says Parnia. He compares these patients to astronauts, in that they may be able to tell us things about a location that prior to just a few decades ago we had no knowledge of: "These are people", says Parnia, "who have been to the Moon and back".

And the issue that has most intrigued him in a number of these episodes – those where patients have reported highly detailed near-death experiences while their heart was stopped – is that memories of events during this time should not be possible, given our current understanding of how the brain works. "The remarkable point about these experiences," he says, "is that while studies of the brain during cardiac arrest have consistently shown that there is no measurable brain activity, these subjects have reported detailed perceptions that indicate the contrary – namely, a high level of consciousness in the absence of detectable brain activity". This is, to put it mildly, a mystery.

But as we have seen, patients don't just report consciousness during NDEs. They sometimes claim to have seen what was happening in the room, and elsewhere, through their mind 'leaving' their physical body and observing the world from outside of it. These are, to be sure, extraordinary – world-changing – claims. And to Parnia these out-of-body experiences offer a way forward for bringing science to bear on the question of whether NDEs offer evidence for the survival of consciousness beyond the body's death. "If we can objectively verify the claims of these patients," Parnia explains on the AWARE website, "the results would bear profound implications not only for the scientific community, but for the way in which we understand and relate to life and death as a society".

Parnia was not the first to realize that veridical out-of-body experiences could be tested scientifically. In the 1960s consciousness researcher Professor Charles T. Tart ran an experiment with a young lady he knew who had regular out-of-body experiences.[46] 'Miss Z', as Tart referred to her, assented to spending a few nights in his sleep research laboratory where he monitored her physical reactions in various ways during these OBEs (EEG, eye movements, heart rate and blood pressure). But he also decided to test whether Miss Z's out-of-body forays were in any sense 'real': Tart copied a five-digit random number onto a small piece of paper with a black marking pen, and then slipped the piece of paper onto a shelf some six feet above the sleeping subject.

Over the four nights in Tart's laboratory, Miss Z had two full OBEs, one of which provided a stunning hit:

> On the fourth night, at 5:57 AM, there was a seven minute period of somewhat ambiguous EEG activity, sometimes looking like stage 1, sometimes like brief wakings. Then Miss Z awakened and called out over the intercom that the target number was 25132, which I wrote on the EEG recording… The number 25132 was indeed the correct target number…. The odds against guessing a 5-digit number by chance alone are 100,000 to 1, so this was a remarkable event!

As already noted, British nurse Penny Sartori also attempted something similar during her Ph.D. research on near-death experiences in 2005: she placed cards with images on them on top of the monitors in patients' rooms, hoping that they might report back accurate descriptions of the images 'seen' while out-of-body during a near-death experience. Unfortunately, however, she did not have the same success as Charles Tart.

Parnia was inspired to try a similar experiment to Tart and Sartori after personally hearing reports of veridical NDEs. One such case involved a three-and-a-half-year-old boy named Andrew who was admitted to hospital for open-heart surgery. Parnia relates the boy's experience in his recent book, *Erasing Death*:

> About two weeks after the surgery, Andrew started asking his parents when he could go back to "the sunny place with all the flowers and animals." His mother told him that they would go to the park when he was feeling better. He said, "No, I don't mean the park. I mean the sunny place I went to with the lady." When she asked him what lady, he replied, "The lady that floats."

> His mother told him that she didn't understand what he meant and apologized that she must have forgotten where this sunny place was. He said: "You didn't take me there. The lady came and got me. She held my hand and we floated up. You were outside when I was having my heart mended. It was okay, the lady looked after me...the lady loves me...it wasn't scary. Everything was bright and colorful [but] I wanted to come back to see you".[47]

When asked where he was when the lady came to him, Andrew replied that he was "up on the ceiling, and when I looked down I was lying in a bed with my arms by my sides and doctors were doing something to my chest". Andrew was able to recognise the bypass machine used during his surgery ("I had that machine...I know I was asleep, but I could see it when I was looking down"), and would later spook his mother by recognising a photo of his deceased grandmother as the "lady that floats".[48]

Sam Parnia's joint fascination with resuscitation and the near-death experience led him to establish the AWARE project, which is now a major collaboration between doctors and researchers in the coronary units of medical centers and hospitals across the globe. Dedicated to exploring and advancing our knowledge of these two inter-related areas, it began with an 18 month pilot study restricted to just a few hospitals in the United Kingdom, before the AWARE project proper launched on September 11, 2008 with the investigation extended to more locations, including some in Europe and the United States. To examine the veridical out-of-body experience component of near-death experiences, Parnia and his team installed approximately one thousand shelves high up on walls within rooms in the emergency, coronary and intensive care wards of participating hospitals, though they were unable to cover all beds due to time and financial constraints – with 25 participating hospitals, the total number of shelves they would have needed to install for full coverage would have been closer to 12,500. On these shelves they placed a hidden 'target', which they hoped patients who had OBEs might report back on after being successfully resuscitated. By targeting these specific wards they were hoping to cover some 80% of cardiac arrest events with their 'shelf test'.

In the first four years of the study, AWARE has received a total of more than four thousand cardiac arrest event reports – some three per day. But while four thousand events may seem a good sample size for in-depth research into veridical NDEs, it must be remembered that these are *cardiac arrests* – not 'heart attacks', with which many people confuse the term, but cases in which the heart has completely stopped beating. As such, in only a third of those cases were medical staff able to resuscitate the patient – and then, only half of those critically-ill survivors remained alive to a point where they could be interviewed by the AWARE team. Further, those medical staff doing interviews on behalf of the AWARE study had to do so around their normal daily duties, and so not all patients were able to be interviewed post-resuscitation (especially so if they came in on the weekend). And, unfortunately, the team's coverage of cardiac arrest events via shelf positioning was lower than hoped – only 50% occurred in a location with a shelf, rather than the hoped-for 80%.

Now, given that near-death experiences were only reported by 5% of survivors in the AWARE study, and that the out-of-body experience only occurs in a low percentage of NDEs, you might begin to see the problem. Out of some 4000 cardiac arrest events, the AWARE team was left with little more than a hundred cases in which a patient with a shelf in their room reported back after their resuscitation, and then only 5 to 10 of those actually had an NDE. In all, after four years, and four thousand recorded cardiac arrest events, the AWARE study has at this stage documented a grand total of just two out-of-body experience reports during cardiac arrest.

Nevertheless, the few NDEs recorded thus far very much conform to the archetypal experience. One of Parnia's AWARE colleagues, Ken Spearpoint, recounted one patient's experience:

> His journey commenced by travelling through a tunnel towards a very strong light, which didn't dazzle him or hurt his eyes. Interestingly, he said that there were other people in the tunnel, whom he did not recognize. When he emerged he described a very beautiful crystal city and I quote "I have seen nothing more beautiful." He said there was a river that ran through. There were many people, without faces, who were washing in the waters. He said that when the people were washing it made their clothes very bright and shiny. He said the people were very beautiful and I asked him if he recalled hearing anything – he said that there was the most beautiful singing, which he described as a choral – as he described this he was very powerfully moved to tears.

His next recollection was looking up at a doctor doing chest compressions!

For the patient this was a profound spiritual experience, and certainly powerful for me too…unfortunately the event was not in a research area [an area with a board].[49]

It wasn't until 2011 that the AWARE study had its first out-of-body experience report. A 57-year-old man had suffered a cardiac arrest in the cardiac catheterization laboratory in Southampton General Hospital (in the United Kingdom), but unfortunately, in the heads-or-tails odds of whether the patient was in a room with a shelf, Parnia called wrong: the out-of-body experience occurred in an area where there was no target for the patient to view. Nevertheless, the patient was keen to recount his story – despite his family having told him it was likely just an effect of the drugs used – saying he believed "it was important" to tell others about it.

The patient, 'Mr. A', had been at work, and started feeling a bit odd. Being a diabetic, he immediately checked his blood sugar level, but it was fine. He continued to feel increasingly unwell, until he finally asked his fellow office-workers for assistance when he started feeling short of air. They immediately phoned an ambulance, and when the paramedics arrived and hooked the patient up to an ECG, the gravity of the situation became apparent:

[T]hey wanted to whisk me off and not talk to me and just do it. Do you know what I mean, doctor? That unnerved me a little bit because I am not used to anything like that, so I said, "Hang on, what are you doing?" They said, "We need to get you to hospital." Anyway, they did.

…I can remember coming into the [hospital bay] … and a nurse came on board. [The paramedics] had told me a nurse called Sarah would come to meet me when I arrived… She came on board the ambulance like they said she would and then she said, "Mr. A, I am the most important person in your life at the moment. I am going to ask you some questions and I want you to answer every one of them." I said yes. I can remember that I wanted to sleep all the time at that stage and all she kept trying to do, it felt like, was to keep me awake and talk with her. Do you understand what I mean? And that's how it was with her.[50]

The medical team brought Mr. A into the catheterization laboratory in the hospital on a trolley, and placed a sterile drape across his upper body so that they could work on him without him seeing what was happening. As such, he didn't notice when the doctor arrived, nor when the team gave him a local anaesthetic so that they could push a wire into the blood vessel in his groin to feed it up to the heart. At this stage, the patient said, he was still talking to the nurse Sarah, when "all of a sudden, I wasn't". Mr. A's heart had stopped beating. But instead of blacking out, as should be the case once blood flow to the brain stops, the patient said he left his body:

> I can remember vividly an automated voice saying, "Shock the patient, shock the patient," and with that, up in that corner of the room [he pointed to the far corner of the room], there was a person beckoning me. I can see her now, and I can remember thinking (but not saying) to myself, "I can't get up there." The next second I was up there and I was looking down at me, the nurse Sarah, and another man who had a bald head... I didn't even know there was another man standing there. I hadn't seen him. Not until I went up in that corner – then I saw them. You understand what I am saying?[51]

It's interesting to note here that Mr. A seems to have had a cross-over between a death-bed vision and a near-death experience. A large number of death-bed vision reports discuss the apparition as being up in the corner of the room. Similarly, Mr. A initially saw a person in the corner of the room from his 'death-bed' perspective, and then in an instant he was 'up there' with them.

Mr A. went on, describing his view of the man with the bald head who was working on his body, whom he hadn't noticed from his bodily view due to the sterile drape.

> I could see all this side of them. [He pointed to the back.] As clear as the day I could see that. [He pointed to an object.] The next thing I remember is waking up on that bed. And these are the words that Sarah said to me: "Oh you nodded off then, Mr. A. You are back with us now." Whether she said those words, whether that automated voice really happened, I don't know – only you would know those things. I don't know how to be able to confirm that those things did happen. I am only telling you what happened with me and what I experienced.

> I couldn't see his face but I could see the back of his body. He was quite a chunky fella, he was. He had blue scrubs on, and he had a blue hat, but I could tell he didn't have any hair, because of where the hat was.[52]

The robotic-sounding voice that Mr. A had heard initially was an automated external defibrillator (AED), an electronic system that can detect when the heart has stopped beating regularly and is fibrillating, and which issues feedback to the user if an electric shock needs to be administered to the heart. Despite being in cardiac arrest, Mr. A. was able to correctly describe the command given by the AED, as well as describe the doctor in attendance, even though he had not previously seen him due to the drape across his chest. Ultimately, however, to skeptics of the NDE this is yet another 'anecdotal report', inadmissible in the court of science. We will have to wait and see if the AWARE study is able to produce something more conclusive in the years ahead.

The Search Continues

Though Parnia might feel disappointed with the lack of out-of-body experiences in his sample so far, he was probably heartened to hear testimony from other medical professionals at a conference on emergency cardiovascular care that he attended in late 2012. After giving an invited talk on the topic of near-death experiences, a number of audience members volunteered their own experiences of patients who had been resuscitated and subsequently related to them events and conversations that had occurred during the time they were apparently 'dead'. For instance, Dr. Tom Aufderheide, a prominent figure in the field of resuscitation science, volunteered his own story that occurred right at the start of his medical career:

> I walked into the room and introduced myself, and the gentleman introduced himself back. Then at that point his eyes suddenly rolled back in his head, and he fell back into his bed. Being a doctor for just five days, I figured there were probably only two options to account for what had just happened – either he had fainted, or he had suffered a cardiac arrest. I knew it was the latter, as I suddenly saw five nurses run into the room with terrified faces! At that moment my own worst fears had been realized. I was all alone. I had no one to collaborate with, and I had never taken care of a cardiac arrest patient before. A thought directed to my seniors who had sent me to the room alone rushed through my head: "How could you do this to me?"
>
> But I got over that really quickly and started CPR. In those days there was no cath lab. There was no therapy for a heart attack. You would just leave the person to finish his heart attack, and if he had a cardiac arrest you would shock him quickly [give an electrical shock using

a defibrillator]. Finally after ten minutes of CPR, many more people came into the room, but he just kept on rearresting [having cardiac arrests]. This process went on for quite some time, and the doctors who were in the room had other things to attend to – so what did they do? They left the intern to stand by and deliver the shock treatment when he needed it again. So I remained at this man's bedside from 5:00 A.M. to 1:00 P.M. in the afternoon, shocking him repeatedly when he went into ventricular fibrillation. He had a prolonged cardiac arrest. At this point the housekeeping staff came into his room to serve his lunch. I was hungry. So I ate his lunch! I certainly couldn't leave his room, and he wasn't going to eat it!

We finally stabilized him after many hours, and he ended up having a long and complicated hospital course. Then some thirty days later, on his last day before discharge, he said to me, "Can you please shut the door and come and sit down?" I thought that was kind of funny, so I went and shut the door and sat down. He said, "I want to tell you something. I have been meaning to tell someone, and you are really my doctor. You have been here the most, and I felt I can share this with you." He then went on to describe a complete near-death experience. He went down a tunnel. He saw the light. He talked to his dead relatives. He talked to a higher being and was ultimately told he needed to come back. This was a really detailed and prolonged near-death experience, but at the end of it he said, "You know, I thought it was awfully funny … here I was dying in front of you, and you were thinking to yourself, 'How could you do this to me?' And then you ate my lunch!"

So that certainly got my attention in the first five days of being a physician! I have been fascinated by the experience ever since, and I often ask my patients about their experiences.[53]

Though four years have elapsed since the AWARE study was set in motion, and the results so far have shown the difficulty in investigating the out-of-body experience component, Sam Parnia is as keen as ever to continue on with the research, and also to improve the procedures. For instance, he notes that in the case of Mr. A., a shelf in the room might not have made any difference, as the patient said he was floating in the opposite corner of the room, well away from where the shelf would have been placed. Perhaps a review of the most reported OBE viewing positions might allow for better targeting in future?

But this tail-chasing has some researchers more skeptical of the chances of the study finding evidence for veridical OBEs. Dr. Bruce Greyson of the Division of Perceptual Studies is associated with the AWARE study, but he holds doubts that it will yield any meaningful results when it comes to veridical OBEs. "If you were to ask travellers the name on the ID badge of the TSA agent who beckoned them through the metal detector on their last flight, it is highly unlikely any could identify that 'target'," Greyson explains to me. "The designated target – the TSA ID badge – was right in front of them to see, but they had no reason to pay attention to it, and no reason to remember it if they had seen it". The problem with the experiment, he says, is in the design, which doesn't include any reason to expect that experiencers would see or remember the designated target. "Patients who report leaving their bodies in the midst of a near-death crisis have no reason to notice a randomly-chosen target planted in a corner of the room that has no particular significance for them," Greyson asserts, "and if they do happen to see it, they have no reason to remember it. So I do not expect meaningful data from the AWARE study, although it is better than not doing any research at all".

Nevertheless, the AWARE study does survey a variety of aspects of the NDE beyond just veridical perception, allowing other possible insights into its mysteries. For instance, from the data so far Parnia has also been able to put forward a possible reason for why so many people that are resuscitated *don't* remember having a near-death experience. Noticing a correlation between the length of cardiac arrest and whether an NDE was reported, Parnia suggests that "if a cardiac arrest event is relatively short, then the post-resuscitation inflammation and disease that normally engulf the brain and cause widespread damage (including damage to the memory circuits) are also relatively mild by comparison to someone with a prolonged cardiac arrest". As such, says Parnia, those who report detailed near-death experiences may do so "simply because they had suffered less damage to their brains and specifically the memory circuits in the days and weeks after the cardiac arrest".[54]

For now though, Parnia and his colleagues are continuing to collate data from the cases on their files since 2008, and once finalized will publish their results in a reputable medical journal. They will then amend any problems with the study that they have noticed in this initial phase: for example, they hope to provide funding for a dedicated member of staff at each medical centre who can attend every single cardiac arrest, possibly with a tablet computer displaying a random target image that they can place in an elevated position in the room, and who would be able to follow up with each patient within days of their resuscitation.

For the rest of us, we'll just have to wait and see if Sam Parnia and his AWARE colleagues can uncover evidence that the minds of those who die really do 'leave' their bodies. If they do, the discovery would perhaps rank among the greatest discoveries in science, up there with the paradigm-shattering ideas of Copernicus and Einstein. Mind would no longer be seen as arising from the brain, and our perception of ourselves and our part in the universe would be forever changed.

I See Dead People...

While Sam Parnia's attempts to find objective evidence supporting veridical NDEs are the gold standard, it's still worth surveying other areas that appear to offer evidence that the mind survives beyond the death of the physical body. One such area is the near-death experience parallel of the 'Peak in Darien' death-bed vision, in which NDErs returning to life report having seen people in the 'afterlife realms' who were thought to be alive, but turned out to have been dead at the time. In recent times, the popular TV show *Grey's Anatomy* brought such an experience into the public consciousness when the main character, Meredith Grey, had an NDE in which she had a vision of her mother, whom she thought was alive but had actually just passed away elsewhere in the hospital. The scene has a number of parallels with real life events.

For instance, in 1968 a female near-death experiencer reported having the classic OBE view of her hospital room from outside her physical body, before finding herself in 'heaven' with an angel and a familiar-looking young man. "Why, Tom, I didn't know you were up here," she said to the close family friend, with Tom replying to her that he had just arrived himself. Not long after returning to her body, and life, her husband received a phone call with the unfortunate news that their friend Tom had died in a car accident.[55]

In another case, a 9-year-old boy in Pittsburgh suffering from meningitis woke up the next morning and said he'd been in heaven and saw his grandparents and uncle, as well as his older sister, saying "she told me I have to come back, but she's going to stay there with grandma and granddad". The boy's father became upset with him, rebuking the lad before assuring him that his sister was alive and healthy at college in Vermont, as he had spoken with her the previous day. Concerned at the father's state, the doctor told him to go home and get some rest, at which time he found that the college had been trying to call him all night long with news that his daughter had been killed in a car accident the night before.[56]

Evidence for this strange element of some NDEs can be found throughout history. In 77CE the Roman historian and philosopher Pliny the Elder recorded a similar Peak in Darien NDE: a nobleman named Corfidius had died, and preparations were underway for his funeral, when he suddenly awoke and announced that he had seen his younger brother while dead, and that the man had requested that his older brother's funeral arrangements be used for his passing instead. Almost simultaneously, the younger brother's servants arrived with the sad news of their master's unexpected (to everyone but his brother) death. Moving forward through time, in his 1680 pamphlet *The Resurrection Proved*, Dr. Henry Atherton describes how his 14-year-old sister, who those in attendance thought had died after a prolonged illness and seven-day coma, returned from the dead and told of seeing an individual who had died since she originally lost consciousness, even though those present had no knowledge that the person had indeed passed away.[57]

In the mid-20th century, Horace Wheatley, while in a coma, felt himself "floating in an atmosphere of peace and serenity" when he was greeted by the figure of a local man that he was acquainted with. His friend acknowledged his presence, saying "Welcome Wheatley!", before apologising for not lingering to chat: "I shall have to see you later," his friend stated, before fading from Horace Wheatley's vision. Upon recovering from his illness, Wheatley discovered that the local man in question had indeed died while he was in his coma.[58] Another NDEr who was in a coma for nearly three weeks came to what seemed to be an iron fence – likely an instance of the 'final barrier' element often found in NDEs – and standing behind the fence was a family friend (referred to as Mr. Van der G. in the account) who told him he couldn't go any further and that he should turn back. Upon waking from his coma, the NDEr described his experience to his parents, who informed him that Mr. Van der G. had passed away while he was in his coma.[59]

Dutch cardiologist Pim van Lommel recounted a different type of Peak in Darien NDE in his recent book *Consciousness Beyond Life*. During a cardiac arrest, a patient had an NDE in which he saw both his dead grandmother and a man who gave him a loving look, but who he was not familiar with:

> Over ten years later my mother confided on her deathbed that I'd been born from an extramarital affair; my biological father was a Jewish man who'd been deported and killed in World War II. My mother showed me a photograph. The unfamiliar man I'd seen more than ten years earlier during my NDE turned out to be my biological father.[60]

Needless to say, such cases are difficult to explain away via any current scientific theories of mind...

NDEs and Mediumistic Communications

After days of struggle against the disease that had struck him down, Dr. Horace Ackley could take no more. All of a sudden, he felt himself gradually rising from his body, with the distinct feeling that he had been divided, though the parts retained a tenuous connection of some sort. As the organs within his physical body ceased functioning, the feeling of being divided came to an abrupt halt, and he found himself whole again. Except he now appeared to be in a position slightly above his lifeless physical body, looking down on it and those who had been in the room with him. Then, without warning...

> ...the scenes of my whole life seemed to move before me like a panorama; every act seemed as though it were drawn

in life size and was really present: it was all there, down to the closing scenes. So rapidly did it pass, that I had little time for reflection. I seemed to be in a whirlpool of excitement; and then, just as suddenly as this panorama had been presented, it was withdrawn, and I was left without a thought of the past or future to contemplate my present condition.[61]

Dr. Ackley realized that he must have died, and was gratified to learn that it seemed a rather pleasant experience. "Death is not so bad a thing after all," he said to himself, "and I should like to see what that country is that I am going to, if I am a spirit." His only regret, looking down on the whirl of activity in the room, was that he was unable to inform his friends that he lived on, to set their minds and hearts at ease. At this point, two 'guardian spirits' appeared before Dr. Ackley, greeting him by name before leading him from the room into an area where a number of 'spirits' whom he was familiar with had assembled.

By this point in the book, you may well be saying to yourself "ho-hum, another stock-standard near-death experience". You might guess that Dr. Ackley then woke up in his resuscitated body and told an NDE researcher about his experience. But if you did, you would be wrong. Dr. Horace Ackley truly did die that day, never to return to this life. The report that you read above was an account of his death, allegedly given by him through a spirit medium – one Samuel Paist of Philadelphia. And what makes it truly remarkable is that it was written down by Paist in his book *A Narrative of the Experience of Horace Abraham Ackley, M.D.*, and published in 1861 – more than a century before the near-death experience had come to the attention of researchers and the general public. And yet Paist/Ackley tells of an OBE shortly after death, a "panoramic" life review (again, the exact word is used, just as in Admiral Beaufort's NDE and others), and being greeted by spirits who subsequently guided him to an afterlife realm!

The after-death narrative of Dr. Horace Ackley is not an isolated instance. More than a decade before the publication of Raymond Moody's *Life After Life* – the book that started the modern fascination with near-death experiences – another scientist had already investigated and written at length on the topic. In a pair of relatively obscure books – *The Supreme Adventure* (1961) and *Intimations of Immortality* (1965) – Dr. Robert Crookall cited numerous examples of what he called "pseudo-death," noting the archetypal elements that Moody would later bring to the public's attention as the near-death experience. What's more however, Crookall also compared these tales of 'pseudo-death' with accounts of the dying process as told by 'communicators' through mediums – and found a number of these same recurring elements, well before they became public knowledge through Moody's *Life After Life*.

For example, Crookall showed that, according to ostensibly dead 'communicators' talking through mediums, the newly-deceased are usually met by other deceased loved ones: "Usually friends or relatives take the newly-dead man in charge". This of course may not be considered a surprising thing for a medium to say – it's probably what most people would expectantly hope for upon entering the spirit realm. But the common elements continue, and include some of the more idiosyncratic features of the NDE. For instance, Crookall noted that, as with the case of Dr. Ackley above, communicators often declare through mediums that "in the early stages of transition, they experienced *a panoramic review* of their past lives". In one case the communicator recounted that shortly after death "the scenes of the past life" are revealed; another said that upon 'waking' his "entire life unreeled itself". A dead communicator by the name of Scott told medium Jane Sherwood that his thoughts "raced over the record of a whole long lifetime", while another communicator said that he saw "clearer and clearer the events of my past life pass, in a long procession, before me." Crookall even discovered a reference in ancient texts to the experience of dying which agreed with the above accounts: the great Greek philosopher Pythagoras (circa 500 BCE) taught that at the time of death, the soul "sees, over and over again, its earthly existence, the scenes succeeding one another with startling clearness".

Considering how we have already seen that the life review is sometimes considered a personal 'judgement day', with feelings of right and wrong accompanying each scene, it is fascinating to note the recurring motif that accompanies this aspect, as told to mediums by 'dead' communicators. "I saw my life unfold before me in a procession of images. *One is faced with the effects emotionally of all one's actions*", said a communicator quoted in a 1929 book. "Each incident brings with it the feelings not only of oneself alone but *of all those others who were affected by the events*," according to another communicator. And again, this account given by a medium, from 1928: "Like everyone who passes over, he had been through the whole of his past life, re-living his past actions in every detail. *All the pain he had given to people he experienced himself,* and all the pleasure he had given he received back again". Given the similarities to some of the NDE accounts mentioned earlier, we must remind ourselves here that this is the apparent testimony from deceased communicators, speaking through mediums, not accounts of near-death experiencers – and well before the elements of the archetypal NDE were well known. And yet the parallels are extraordinary.

Beyond the meeting with the familiar dead, and the past life review, Crookall's research also found that mediumistic communicators regularly make note of the out-of-body experience component. For example, one communicator noted that he "seemed to rise up out of my body". According to another, "I was not lying in the bed, but floating in the air, a little above it. I saw the body, stretched out straight". Furthermore, they also describe the familiar element of traveling through a tunnel! "I saw in front of me a dark tunnel," said one communicator, before travelling through it and then stepping "out of the tunnel into a new world". Another communicator noted that they remembered "a curious opening, as if one had passed through subterranean passages and found oneself near the mouth of a cave... The light was much stronger outside". And once through the 'tunnel', the environment is once again familiar to anyone who has perused a catalogue of NDEs: "I was with 'B' [her son, killed in the War]: he took me to a world so brilliant that I can't describe it".

The common elements are compelling. For anyone familiar with the NDE literature, these reports through mediums are startlingly similar to the accounts of near-death experiencers – and yet Crookall collected them years before the archetype of the NDE became common knowledge. And not only do they seem to offer support for the validity of the near-death experience, they also hint that there may well be more to the much-maligned subject of mediumship. Do 'spirit mediums' really have contact with the dead? Let's dim the lights, join hands and find out...

THREE

Voices From Beyond?

Of course it's happening inside your head, Harry, but why on earth should that mean that it is not real?

Professor Dumbledore, in *Harry Potter and the Deathly Hallows*

Katharine Sutton held the hands of the entranced medium, quite unable to believe what she was hearing. Despite being introduced anonymously, under an assumed name – 'Mrs. Smith' – it seemed that the medium knew her family intimately. In a small voice, reminiscent of a child, the medium continued: "I want you to call Dodo... Tell Dodo I am happy". The flow of words offered reassurance: "Cry for me no more". 'Dodo' was Katharine Sutton's son George; it was the pet name given to him by his sister, who had died recently. "Her name is Katherine", the medium announced. "She calls herself Kakie".

Mrs. Leonora Piper had done this many times before. Taking her place at a small table, 'sitters' were brought in by scientific investigators, usually under assumed names and with strict instructions not to give away any personal details. Then this ostensibly normal Bostonian housewife would slip into a trance, and her personality would be replaced by that of a certain 'Jean Phinuit

Scliville', more usually known simply as 'Phinuit' (pronounced Fin-wee). Phinuit claimed to be a doctor of French extraction who had died a few decades previously, and who was now Mrs. Piper's 'control' – a separate personality who acted as the mediator between the sitters present and whichever spirits might choose to come through during the séance. In Katharine Sutton's case the spirit was, it seemed, that of her recently deceased daughter.

The low masculine tones of Phinuit's French accent gave way again to the voice of the young child, addressing her father directly. "Papa, want to go to wide horsey." Kakie had often requested to do this during her terminal illness. She had also asked regularly to see her younger sister. "Eleanor…I want Eleanor," came the words from Mrs. Piper's mouth. Then 'Kakie' had one more request: to sing her favourite bedtime song with her parents once more.

> Lightly row, lightly row,
> O'er the merry waves we go,
> Smoothly glide, smoothly glide
> With the ebbing tide.

Then Phinuit hushed the parents, allowing the soft voice of their lost child to finish the verses alone.

> Let the winds and waters be
> Mingled with our melody,
> Sing and float, sing and float,
> In our little boat.

More specific names came during the séance. Kakie asked for 'Dinah' – an old black rag doll she used to play with – and 'Bagie', her pet name for younger sister Eleanor. She asked to see the "mooley-cow", the idiosyncratic pronunciation she used while alive for the family's heifer. And she named correctly her deceased "Uncle Alonzo" and "Grandma Sutton".

The day before the séance, Katharine Sutton had been troubled by her desire to talk to the dead, asking herself if it was right to 'bring them back' for her own gratification. During the sitting, out of the blue the spirit of 'Uncle Alonzo' reassured her: "Do not think it wrong to bring us back – we love to come".

Kakie's parting words for her mother also brought comfort. "I will come to you every day, and I will put my hand on you, when you go to sleep. Do not cry for me – that makes me sad".[1]

Not Dead, But With You Still...

Leonora Piper's sitting with the Sutton family occurred in 1893. By this time, she had undergone more than seven years of rigorous investigation at the hands of the Society for Psychical Research (S.P.R.), an organisation made up of some of the world's leading thinkers – from future Nobel Prize winners to British Prime Ministers – who had devoted themselves to examining paranormal and psychic claims. Already she had built a formidable reputation. She regularly achieved astonishing results during her séances, despite the S.P.R.'s scientists taking every precaution to keep the identities of sitters secret, and to ensure that Mrs. Piper had no other way of accessing the information that came through during her sittings. The S.P.R. had even gone so far as to have Mrs. Piper and her husband shadowed by detectives, but had failed to uncover any damning revelations. Not once in all those years had she been detected using, or attempting to use, the regular fraudulent techniques of fake mediums.

Born Leonora Evelina Simonds on 27 June 1859, Mrs. Piper's alleged abilities are said to have first manifested as a child. When eight years old, she was playing in the garden when "suddenly she felt a sharp blow on her right ear, accompanied by a prolonged sibilant sound", according to her daughter Alta Piper.[2] This sound gradually resolved itself into the letter 'S', and was followed by the words "Aunt Sara, not dead, but with you still". The hysterical child ran to her mother, who struggled to make sense of what young Leonora was saying. But the incident made quite an impact on Hannah Simonds; she duly made note of what had happened in her diary that night. According to Alta Piper, several days later the news came through confirming that young Leonora's Aunt Sara had died at the very hour she 'heard' this message.

Within a few weeks she experienced more strangeness, calling out to her mother during the night that she could not sleep because of "the bright light in the room and all the faces in it", and complaining that her bed wouldn't stop rocking.[3] But there seems to have been little else of note in the early life of Leonora Piper that would point towards her later 'talent'.

In 1881 Leonora married William Piper of Boston, with whom she settled in the suburbs and began a family. However, the newly-wed Mrs. Piper was often ill, as a result of an accidental blow suffered in a collision with a sled in her teenage years. The accident had damaged her knee, giving her a slight limp, but more seriously had also caused some abdominal bleeding which resulted in a persistent dull pain in her midsection. After the birth of the couple's first daughter, Alta, in 1884, the ache intensified. Her husband's parents, who were keenly interested in Spiritualism, urged their daughter-in-law to visit a psychic healer. To please them, Leonora went for a consultation with Dr. J.R. Cocke, a blind professional clairvoyant who was attracting positive reviews on account of his 'psychic' medical diagnoses and cures.

At one of her visits Dr. Cocke put his hands on Leonora's head; she felt at once that she was losing consciousness. "His face seemed to become smaller and smaller," Leonora later related.[4] She saw a flood of light, as well as unrecognised human faces, and a hand which fluttered before her own face. Though afterwards she did not remember what had happened, others present soon told her: in a trance she had risen from her chair, walked to a table in the centre of the room and picked up a pencil and paper. A few minutes of rapid writing ensued, and then Mrs. Piper had handed the note to another person present, a highly-regarded judge from Cambridge, Massachusetts by the name of Frost. The communicator was said to be his dead son, and the message "the most remarkable he ever received" in his thirty years of investigating Spiritualism.[5] Whatever the psychic influence of Dr. Cocke though, it would seem his healing wasn't up to scratch in Leonora's case, as her injury continued to bother her for the next decade.

The report of Judge Frost's experience with Mrs. Piper made waves in the Spiritualist community, but Leonora was expecting a second child (another girl, Minerva, born October 1885); she was nicely settled into middle-class life, and the attention her accidental mediumship had generated was unwanted. Nevertheless, she did feel – perhaps at the urging of her husband's parents – that her 'gift' should not be wasted, and so despite refusing requests from strangers, she assented to giving private sittings for those closest to her family. One of those lucky enough to be be granted a sitting was Anne Manning Robbins, a young stenographer who had recently moved to the Boston area, and who was becoming interested in Spiritualism. In the winter of 1884-5 she was invited to a family gathering of about a dozen people at the Piper's house. During the course of the evening Mrs. Piper...

> ...retired with one or two of her friends to a small room adjoining and opening into the large room in which the company was assembled, and, as I understood, "went under control," whatever that might mean. It was something new and strange to me. I think she had not then begun to give sittings outside of the immediate circle of her own family, but was in the process of developing her powers. Her husband explained to me that she was a little bashful about going into trance under the eyes of other people, and for that reason had retired to the smaller room.[6]

It was no wonder that Mrs. Piper was "a little bashful" about being seen going into the trance. At this time the onset of the condition was accompanied by groaning, grinding of teeth, and significant convulsions of the body and face. In fact one sitter, Professor Barrett Wendell, described the onset of Mrs. Piper's trance as the most shocking sight he had ever witnessed.[7] Another sitter suggested the trance must have been genuine, simply because he did not think someone "could go through the teeth-grinding she did without shuddering".[8]

Leonora Piper's own description of what she experienced during this time is interesting. To start it was "as if something were passing over my brain making it numb; a sensation similar to that I experienced when I was etherized, only the unpleasant odor of ether is absent". The sitters present would begin to shrink; the room chilled. Then all would go black.[9]

Once entranced, the 'controls' would take over the medium's body. Whether these controls were genuine individuals who had died and returned is debatable; it is perhaps more likely that they were fictitious creations of Mrs. Piper's subconscious mind. Fantastic deceased personages including J. Sebastian Bach, an Indian girl going by the unlikely name of "Chlorine", and the recently dead American entrepreneur Cornelius 'Commodore' Vanderbilt apparently jostled for a chance to use the psychic telephone that was the body of Leonora Piper. Similarly, during Anne Manning Robbins' visit, even the spirit of poet William Longfellow – who had died just two years previous – claimed to have taken a turn as control. But the most prominent personality to take control of Mrs. Piper that night was 'Phinuit'.

Speaking in a loud masculine voice with a French accent, Phinuit seemed the complete opposite of the demure American housewife whom 'he' had taken over from. Most sitters found him to be opinionated and mischievous, even deceptive. One researcher referred to him as a "grotesque and somewhat saucy personage";[10] Phinuit was given to vulgar expressions and on occasion even threatened sitters who challenged him. But the trance personality was also capable of stunning sitters with his apparent knowledge of the most intimate secrets of their friends and family.

A Fateful Meeting

William James, educated and employed at Harvard University, was rather unimpressed with the fast-developing 'church of science' which dismissed all reports of mystical and supernatural experience. "Although in its essence science only stands for a method and for no fixed belief," he wrote, "it is identified with a certain fixed belief, the belief that the hidden order of nature is mechanical exclusively, and that non-mechanical categories are irrational ways of conceiving and explaining even such things as human life". James was uniquely suited to contemplating these ideas: as a child, his father had immersed him in the teachings of the mystic scientist Emmanuel Swedenborg. Though academically brilliant, the young William James initially had his heart set on taking an apprenticeship as a painter in the art studio of William Morris Hunt, before moving into the study of physiology. He graduated from Harvard with an M.D., but then moved into the study and teaching of philosophy and psychology, as the mind was where his real interest lay. He would become one of the most highly-regarded thinkers of the 19th century; his texts *Principles of Psychology* and *The Varieties of Religious Experience* are classics in their respective fields.

Investigation of mystical experiences and supernatural occurrences was a constant throughout James's life. He experimented with the consciousness-bending chemical nitrous oxide (better known as 'laughing gas') in 1882, and fourteen years later even tried ingesting peyote, the cactus used by shamans in the New World – some seven decades before the psychedelic revolution of the 1960s. But he also took an interest

– if a rather skeptical one – in the claims made by Spiritualists of communication with the dead.

It therefore seems as if it was the hand of fate that brought Leonora Piper and William James together. In the summer of 1885, James's mother-in-law Eliza Gibbens had heard about the budding medium through word-of-mouth (through a friend, who had in turn heard about Mrs. Piper through their maid), even though the talents of Mrs. Piper were not public knowledge at that time.[11] Despite not having any previous experience with mediums, curiosity got the better of Mrs. Gibbens, and she requested a sitting. Lucky enough to be granted time with Mrs. Piper, what transpired during the sitting astonished her; Mrs. Gibbens later related that during the séance Mrs. Piper had given her a long string of names of members of her family (usually Christian names), along with intimate details regarding the persons mentioned and their relationships.

Perhaps Mrs. Piper had researched Eliza Gibbens before the sitting, found out her family details and committed it all to memory? Her interest piqued, Mrs. Gibbens's daughter Margaret booked a sitting with Leonora, and brought with her a more searching test of the medium's abilities: a private letter from a person "known to but two persons in this country", and written in Italian. The entranced Mrs. Piper held the letter to her forehead, and went on to describe the writer in a way which identified him unmistakably.[12] (Two years later, Mrs. Piper would suddenly reveal the name of the person during a trance).

William James was much amused by the excitement of his in-laws regarding Mrs. Piper – no doubt, he thought, a wily trickster who had researched his family beforehand. Nevertheless, being the open-minded scientist that he was, James felt the case worthy of further investigation:

> I remember playing the *esprit fort* on that occasion before
> my feminine relatives, and seeking to explain, by simple

considerations the marvellous character of the facts which they brought back. This did not, however, prevent me from going myself a few days later, in company with my wife [Alice], to get a direct personal impression. The names of none of us up to this meeting had been announced to Mrs. Piper, and Mrs. James and I were, of course, careful to make no reference to our relatives who had preceded. The medium, however, when entranced, repeated most of the names of "spirits" whom she had announced on the two former occasions and added others.

James was especially intrigued by the manner in which the medium announced the names. It was as if the control had cotton wool stuffed in 'his' ears, and was being fed information by a third party whom they couldn't hear properly. His father-in-law's name (Gibbens) was first announced as Niblin, then afterward as Giblin. But the name that really caught William and Alice James's attention was the one first spelt out as Herrin.

'The Flower of Our Little Flock'

In January of 1884, the James family was thriving. Alice James had just given birth to the couple's third son, Herman, and William was at home in high spirits with the intention of editing his late father's works for publication. The new addition to the family brought joy to William and Alice James; a pudgy and placid boy whom William described as "the flower of our little flock".[13] But dark clouds were gathering on the horizon.

At the beginning of March 1885, Alice contracted scarlet fever, which began a long period of isolation for her; while fighting the disease her children were removed to their grandmother's house, and William could only talk to her through the bedroom door. After six weeks, Alice had finally recovered enough to be able to see her children again. But another month later, at the start of June, Herman came down with a bad case of whooping cough. In mid-June, Alice contracted the disease as well. But the focus was all on Herman: the James's darling child, not yet 18 months old, had developed complications of bronchial pneumonia and, by early July his condition had worsened. Suffering high fevers, his tiny body was wracked by almost daily convulsions.

Despite being severely unwell herself, Alice took Herman to her bed and nursed him around the clock, sleeping less than three hours each night. William James would later write of being awestruck by Alice's determination to care for Herman at this time, saying "the passionate devotion of a mother – ill herself, perhaps – to a sick or dying child is perhaps the most simply beautiful moral spectacle that human life affords. Contemning every danger, triumphing over every difficulty, outlasting all fatigue, woman's love is here invincibly superior to anything that man can show".[14]

William's little "flower" fought on with a strength which surprised the doctors tending him; almost each day the boy suffered a severe convulsion which they suspected would be his last. But finally, on July 9, young Herman's reserves were spent. Gasping for breath until the bitter end, Herman James died that night on his mother's bed.[15]

The impact on any family that suffers this nightmarish scenario can barely be fathomed. Alice's grief was intense, while William felt numb, his emotions "abstract". He described Herman's life and death as "one more taste of the intolerable mysteriousness of this thing called existence". But he would also later appreciate the blessing of those 18 months of life: "the mere fact that matter could have taken for a time that precious form, ought to make matter sacred forever after".[16] Alice would never forget her lost child, nor his fate in this world. "Had I tried to tell him, he would have shrunk back in terror and begged to stay safely in his mother's womb," she wrote.[17]

In her book *Genuine Reality: A Life of William James,* Linda Simon describes the melancholy beauty of Herman's funeral:

> The next day, in a haze of grief, William and Alice planned their son's funeral. They chose a small wicker basket as a coffin and lined it with soft flannel. They engaged the venerable Unitarian minister Andrew Preston Peabody to conduct the service. At six o'clock on Saturday morning, July 11, they took a buggy the few miles from Cambridge to Belmont where, in the woods, they gathered birch branches and pine boughs, ferns, grasses, and wild flowers to cover the wicker coffin. Laying their dead child gently in the basket, they arranged sprays of leaves at his head, grasses at his feet, flowers on his chest. "I have always looked down on these dressings," James wrote to [his] Aunt Kate, "but there is usually a human need embodied in any old human custom, and we both felt this most gracefully."

Herman's death left William James in desperate hope of the reality of an afterlife existence. "It *must* be...that he is reserved for some still better chance than that, and that we shall in some way come into his presence again," he would write.[18] It is hardly surprising then that – just months after their son's death – the James's found great solace in the messages coming through Leonora Piper.

When the name Herrin came through, in Mrs. Piper's usual piecemeal fashion, Alice and William knew who was meant. The medium went on to give further personal details and circumstances which confirmed the identity to them: Alice later recalled that Mrs. Piper described Herman "with his hands full of daisies", despite not knowing the special meaningful burial they had designed. Alice also told of how Mrs. Piper related "other sweet nothings (from the point of view of science) which meant everything to me".[19]

William James was, naturally, more suspicious. But though he thought it likely that a fake medium could put together a fair amount of information about his own famous family (in addition to his own high profile, his brother Henry James is regarded as one of the great novelists of the modern era), he was surprised to find so much information coming through Mrs. Piper about his wife's family. The facts given regarding "the persons named made it in many instances impossible not to recognise the particular individuals who were talked about", James reported. He was careful to note: "We took particular pains on this occasion to give the Phinuit control no help over his difficulties and to ask no leading questions".

Additionally, James could not work out how the medium would have 'worked up' the intimate details of his own household: Mrs. Piper described in disturbing detail the death throes of a cat that William had recently put down with ether; she mentioned that he had just lost his waistcoat, and she gave correct information about Herman's now-unused – and seemingly haunted – room. "She was strong on the events in our nursery," William James would recount, "and gave striking advice during our first visit to her about the way to deal with certain 'tantrums' of our second child, 'little Billy-boy', as she called him, reproducing his nursery name. She told how the crib creaked at night, how a certain rocking-chair creaked mysteriously, how my wife heard footsteps on the stairs".[20]

Information produced at other séances organized by James was also striking. His mother-in-law had, on her return from Europe, lost her bank-book. At a sitting held soon afterwards Phinuit was asked if he could help her to find it – he told her correctly where it was.[21] A man by the name of Minot Savage sat anonymously with Mrs. Piper, telling her only that he'd heard of her trances and wished to observe one. At his first sitting, Mrs. Piper referenced his dead father. "He calls you Judson," she said, correctly noting Savage's middle name – the name which only his father and another family member (also deceased) had ever called him.[22]

Beyond the evidential conversations with the medium however, William James was perhaps most impressed with her manner. He had investigated other mediums before Mrs. Piper; often they were self-promoting and devious, their apparent paranormal abilities disappearing like a ghost themselves under sustained investigation. But Leonora was different: she was shy and unassuming. Unlike other mediums, she didn't advertise herself in the Spiritualist journals – instead, she seemed reluctant to give sittings and for others to know about her talent. Mrs. Piper didn't even claim to have psychic abilities – all she knew about it was from what others had told her, as she had no memory of what went on during the trance. It appeared to baffle her as much as it did others.

It may be also that William and Alice found a certain kinship in Mrs. Piper through her daughter Alta, who was almost the same age as Herman at the time of his death – not to mention that the medium was also heavily pregnant at their first meeting. But regardless of that possibility, William James was first and foremost astounded by the information that came through Leonora Piper in their first encounter:

> My impression after this first visit, was, that [Mrs. Piper] was either possessed of supernormal powers, or knew the members of my wife's family by sight and had by some lucky coincidence become acquainted with such a multitude of their domestic circumstances as to produce the startling impression which she did.

James's skepticism is evident in the statement above; he was always considering other possible explanations for the seemingly miraculous information offered by Mrs. Piper. However, further investigation led him "absolutely to reject the latter explanation, and to believe that she has supernormal powers":

I am persuaded of the medium's honesty, and of the genuineness of her trance; and although at first disposed to think that the 'hits' she made were either lucky coincidences, or the result of knowledge on her part of who the sitter was and of his or her family affairs, I now believe her to be in possession of a power as yet unexplained.[23]

William James knew that he had found a medium worthy of extensive investigation. At his suggestion, the Society for Psychical Research made Leonora Piper their primary research focus, paying her a modest annual salary to be exclusively available to them for testing and not hold private sittings with anyone else without their permission. Their investigation of her mediumship would last more than two decades, and was spearheaded by one of the toughest judges they could find.

The Miraculous Mrs. Piper

Richard Hodgson arrived in Boston in 1887, ready to dismantle the growing legend of Leonora Piper. He had already made his name via a high-profile debunking of the 'magical powers' of the leader of the controversial Theosophical movement, Helena Blavatsky, as well as highly critical papers pointing out the poor observational ability – and some might say gullibility – of sitters at séances. "Nearly all the professional mediums," he scowled in a report, "are a gang of vulgar tricksters who are more or less in league with one another". Originally from Australia, Hodgson arrived at his first meeting with Mrs. Piper anonymously, sent by the S.P.R. with the initial assumption that she was fraudulent. Wise to the techniques of deception used by fake mediums, and with the benefit of his remote geographical origin, he was committed to not giving her any information about his life from which she could 'construct' the impression of a successful sitting.

"Mother living, father dead, little brother dead", said the entranced Mrs. Piper, through the voice of Phinuit. "Four of you living besides mother". In response, Hodgson simply noted "True". A surprising direct hit, but perhaps Mrs. Piper had somehow got wind of his arrival, and gone in search of records about his family. But what came next was more difficult to explain.

> Phinuit mentioned the name "Fred". I said that it might be my cousin. "He says you went to school together. He goes on jumping-frogs, and laughs. He says he used to get the better of you. He had convulsive movements before his death, struggles. He went off in a sort of spasm. You were not there.

Hodgson was intrigued. "My cousin Fred far excelled any other person that I have seen in the games of leap-frog, fly the garter etc.," he reveals in his notes to this sitting. "He took very long flying jumps, and whenever he played, the game was lined by crowds of school-mates to watch him. He injured his spine in a gymnasium in Melbourne, Australia, in 1871, and was carried to the hospital, where he lingered for a fortnight, with occasional spasmodic convulsions, in one of which he died".

At a follow-up sitting, Mrs. Piper continued discussing Fred, noting correctly that he had died as the result of a fall from a trapeze. Fred also wanted to remind Hodgson of "Harris", from the school they attended, who they both thought was a "very able man". Hodgson noted Fred's statements through Mrs. Piper were "all true".

But perhaps more persuasive was the personal information about a girl he formerly knew – a lost love from Australia by the name of Jessie Tyler Dunn (discreetly referred to in Hodgson's reports under the simple pseudonym of 'Q'), who had died in Melbourne some 8 years previous, in 1879. Phinuit described a lady with dark hair, dark eyes and a slim figure, who was "much closer" to Hodgson "than any other person". He then correctly stated that "the second part of her first name is –sie". Hodgson noted other statements about 'Q', both correct and incorrect, though he wasn't always able to share the details due to their extremely personal nature:

(a) That I had given her a book, Dr. Phinuit thinks, of poems, and I had written her name in it, in connection with her birthday. [Correct]

(b) . . . . . . [Correct. This includes a reference to circumstances under which I had a very special conversation with 'Q'. I think it impossible that 'Q' could have spoken of this to any other person. It occurred in Australia in 1875.]

(c) That she "left the body" in England, and that I was across the country. [This is incorrect. 'Q' died in Australia. I was in England.]

This intermingling of highly specific, correct information with occasional incorrect statements was no doubt infuriating to Hodgson. He notes that Phinuit seems to have been party to the details of a "very special conversation" between just himself and Jessie, half a world away and many years before. But surely, if it was truly the deceased person talking through the medium, they wouldn't make such elementary mistakes as not knowing the country that they died in? At another point, Phinuit noted that 'Q' was showing him her beautiful teeth, but Hodgson was quick to point out that this was beyond wrong; "on the contrary, a year or two before her death, the state of her teeth compelled the drawing of a large number of them." But, just as quickly, Hodgson was jolted by a description that seemed to defy any rational explanation:

Phinuit then proceeded to give a general description of 'Q', right so far as it went, and described the eyes as "dark". She then began to rub the right eye on the under side, saying, "There's a spot here. This eye (left) is brown, the other eye has a spot in it of a light colour, in the iris. This spot is straggly, of a bluish cast. It is a birth-mark. It looks as if it had been thrown on."

...I asked her to draw it, the result being the figure, a reproduction of which is attempted below:—

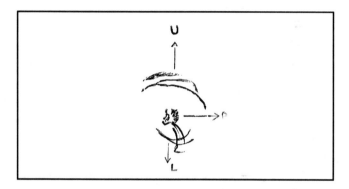

This was drawn with the block-book held away from Mrs. P., where she could not see what she was drawing, her eyes being behind and close to the block-book. "This (U) is the top part of the iris. This (L) is the bottom. This (P) is the pupil. The light part is here" [making the other lines in the figure].

'Q' had a splash of what I should call *grey* (rather than blue) in the right eye, occupying the position and having very nearly the shape assigned by Phinuit. I should have drawn it as I remember it, thus:—

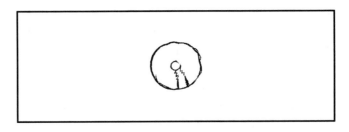

It was very peculiar; a little jagged in the edges, and sharply and distinctly marked off from the rest of the *brown* iris. I asked Phinuit how he obtained the information about the eyes. He said that 'Q' was standing close to him and showing him her right eye so that he could see it clearly, and saying that was what I wanted. *This peculiarity in the eye was what I had in mind when I asked Phinuit for a detailed description of 'Q's face.* [my emphasis]

This is an astounding 'hit'. Hodgson was seeking proof of Jessie's identity via a unique mark in her eye, and *somehow* Phinuit/Mrs. Piper was able to provide it. It is difficult to explain how this was achieved without resorting to some paranormal explanation – a facile "lucky guess" just doesn't seem to do it justice.

To test whether Mrs. Piper was truly in a trance, Hodgson pinched her suddenly ("sometimes rather severely"), held a lit match to her forearm, and made her take several deep inhalations of ammonia (another researcher poked her with needles without warning). The entranced Mrs. Piper showed absolutely no reaction to these tests – though, as Hodgson rather coldly noted, she "suffered somewhat after the trance was over".

Then Along Came G.P.

Four years into Hodgson's investigation of Mrs. Piper, the loquacious Dr. Phinuit gained some competition for the mouthpiece of the medium, when other 'spirits' began apparently taking control of her hand in order to communicate via writing. For the next couple of years, sittings would be a mix of both written and spoken communication – sometimes at the same time! Hodgson noted that at one sitting Phinuit kept up an especially "rapid and vigorous" hour-long conversation with two female sitters, while another spirit simultaneously 'discussed' other matters with a separate sitter via writing. The skeptical investigator was so intrigued by this development that he wondered if the left hand could join in as well; "that it might be possible to get both hands writing and Phinuit speaking all at the same time on different subjects with different persons". And this in fact did happen at a sitting in 1895!

But one of the first – and most convincing – written communications came in 1892, from a spirit claiming to be a recently deceased friend of Hodgson's named George Pellew (referred to in Hodgson's reports simply as 'G.P.', and sometimes under the pseudonym of 'George Pelham'). Pellew had died from an accidental fall in February 1892, aged just 32. Just over a month later, one of his intimate friends had a sitting with Mrs. Piper (as usual, anonymously, this time under the pseudonym "Mr. Hart"), and during a conversation with Phinuit regarding the sitter's deceased Uncle George, the recently dead Pellew appears to have begun his post-mortem communication. Phinuit announced suddenly "there is another George who wants to speak to you". He went on to give G.P.'s full name correctly, as well as the names of several of his close friends, including the supposedly anonymous sitter. G.P., through the intermediary of Phinuit, also mentioned a number of incidents relating to friends which the sitter was not aware of, but which were confirmed after the sitting. For example, G.P. had a message for one Katharine Howard:

"Tell her, she'll know. I will solve the problems, Katharine."
Mr. Hart notes: "This had no special significance for me at the time, though I was aware that Katharine, the daughter

of Jim Howard, was known to George, who used to live with the Howards. On the day following the sitting I gave Mr. Howard a detailed account of the sitting. These words, 'I will solve the problems, Katharine,' impressed him more than anything else, and at the close of my account he related that George, when he had last stayed with them, had talked frequently with Katharine (a girl of fifteen years of age at the time) upon such subjects as Time, Space, God, Eternity, and pointed out to her how unsatisfactory the commonly accepted solutions were. He added that some time he would solve the problems, and let her know, using almost the very words of the communication made at the sitting.

Beyond the evidential statements made, 'John Hart' was just as impressed by the *vraisemblance* – what we might call the impersonation – of the alleged communicator to his deceased friend, notably through the use of the idiosyncratic words of greeting and occasional remarks that the living G.P. had employed.

G.P. gradually superceded Phinuit as Mrs. Piper's chief control personality, and as he did the majority of communication slowly changed from spoken words to written. During one of the early sittings with G.P. speaking, the young Katharine Howard mentioned above came in person. She was greeted by name, and G.P. asked about her violin, saying it was horrible to hear her playing it (the living George Pellew had often been annoyed by Katharine's violin practice sessions as a child and would let her know it). At a subsequent sitting, Katharine's younger sister Evelyn was present – G.P. apologised for the great deal of teasing that the living George had indeed tormented the young girl with, and then asked if she remembered the little book that he had given her which he had written her name in. Evelyn noted that she had pulled the book out just a few days before to look at it. And when the girls' father James Howard asked for specific evidence to prove his identity, G.P. offered some extremely private information that moved Mr. Howard to remark that he had been "perfectly satisfied" as to the continued existence of his friend. All in all, Hodgson noted, there were at least 150 people who had sittings with Mrs. Piper after the first appearance of the G.P. personality, and of those 30 were connected with the living George Pellew. G.P. recognised all 30, though one was only a partial recognition – and interestingly, this individual was a lady who was only a girl when the living George Pellew last saw her, some nine years previous to the sitting. Of the other 120+ sitters not connected to Pellew, there was not one case of false recognition by G.P. Additionally, though the reports on the G.P. sittings contain a mass of hard-to-explain 'proofs' of his identity, Hodgson was at pains to point out that "the most important evidence tending to show that the real G.P. was in some way 'communicating' cannot be published". We have to remember the era in which the Piper sittings took place: a time when discretion in private affairs was the mark of a proper gentleman or lady. This "most important evidence" that Hodgson refers to concerned "the confidential remembrances of friends, dealing...with incidents of a private nature relating to other persons living" (at the time of Hodgson's report).

Richard Hodgson continued to investigate Mrs. Piper's mediumship until his own death in 1905 – almost two decades of constant research in which the initially skeptical investigator never once found serious reason to believe she was a fraud. He collected thousands of pages of testimony and analysis, and reams of evidence suggesting that Mrs. Piper had access to information beyond her normal senses. Hodgson's official conclusion was paradigm-shattering. He was, he said, convinced "that the chief 'communicators'...have survived the change we call death, and... have directly communicated with us...through Mrs Piper's entranced organism".

Hodgson was not alone in his summation. Another researcher who devoted a number of years to studying Mrs. Piper, Professor

James Hyslop, concluded that her mediumship provided solid evidence "that there is a future life and persistence of personal identity". Frederic Myers, one of the founding members of the S.P.R., said of his own sittings that they "left little doubt – no doubt – that we were in the presence of an authentic utterance from a soul beyond the tomb".[24]

You read that right. Some of the most learned individuals of the late 19th century investigated a medium for more than two decades, applying skepticism at every point, and came to the conclusion that they were talking to dead people. I'll bet you weren't taught that in school...

The Medium and the Message

Mediumship is often described as a phenomenon that appeared in the mid-19th century with the birth of the 'religion' of Spiritualism, and is even sometimes specifically dated to 1848, when three young sisters – Leah, Margaret and Kate Fox – caused a sensation by claiming to be in contact with a spirit via rapping or knocking sounds in their family home in New York. The identification with this period is so strong that if you mention the word 'medium' to someone these days, they will likely perceive a darkened séance room from Victorian times (or more recently, someone like John Edward interacting with his audience on TV). But the phenomenon of mediumship goes back well before Western culture of the last 150 years. Indeed, it is as old as human history itself – the archaeological record and historical literature are full of references to apparent communication with the spirit world.[25]

Perhaps the most well-known 'ancient' reference to mediumship is the Biblical case of the 'Witch of Endor', mentioned in the First Book of Samuel. King Saul, in trying to determine the best course of action against the forces of the Philistines, requests that his servants find him "a woman that divineth by a ghost, that I may go to her, and inquire of her". Told that such a woman could be found at Endor, Saul sets out (in disguise) to seek her counsel. The 'witch' raises the spirit of the recently deceased prophet Samuel, who tells Saul in no uncertain terms that the Lord is a bit miffed with him, and as such that both Israel and Saul himself will be delivered into the hands of the Philistines. If that wasn't bad news enough, Samuel then informs Saul that "tomorrow shalt thou and thy sons be with me" – that is, dead. According to the Biblical narrative, the following day Saul's army was indeed defeated at the Battle of Gilboa, with three of his sons dying, while Saul committed suicide.

In China, spirit-mediums are known as *wu,* or *ji-tong,* and their historical origin can be traced back to at least two thousand years before the time of Christ.[26] In Japan, the *itako* were blind, usually female, shamans from northern Japan who were said to have the ability to communicate with the dead. And the original word shaman, which most of us know today, is taken from the Evenki people of northern Siberia, and denotes a person who, among others duties, could act as a vehicle for making contact with deceased ancestors. The Spiritualism of the last two centuries is just one more example of this apparent human ability, though it is perhaps more familiar to most of us due to its proximity in time, not to mention the cultural similarities.

The terms 'medium' and 'psychic' are often used interchangeably, but they actually do have specific, and quite separate, meanings. To be 'psychic' simply means that a person gains access to information via some source beyond our normal senses (e.g. possibly using telepathy, or clairvoyance), while the word 'medium' itself points clearly to its own definition: a person who acts as the medium, or conduit, for communication from the spirit world to our world (and vice versa). So, a medium can always be labeled psychic – and thus to call someone a 'psychic medium' is stating the obvious – but a psychic might not always be a medium.

Mediums also come in different flavours. *Physical mediumship* is where the communicating spirit allegedly interacts with the physical world: objects are moved (sometimes even teleported), lights are seen and winds are felt, and sometimes the dead even seem to appear in physical form and walk around the room. While it may be the most spectacular form of mediumship, it is also the most closely associated with fraud – with séances often held in the dark (light apparently interferes with the manifestation of spirits; and also, conveniently enough, interferes with manifestations of fraudulent techniques of deception), it is very difficult to come to a certain conclusion as to whether the 'spirit' that appeared was a genuine paranormal occurrence. While accounts of physical mediumship certainly make for good Hallowe'en tales – and some cases remain a mystery due to the inexplicable happenings during séances – they are a topic that we will not cover in detail.

As opposed to physical mediumship, *mental mediumship* is concerned with spirit communication through the mind of the medium, rather than physical manifestations. And mental mediumship is often divided into two particular types: *trance* and *non-trance*. Leonora Piper was an example of a trance medium – she would slip into unconsciousness, her normal personality would be 'put aside', and an intruding intelligence, apparently that of a deceased person, would take over the medium's mind. The trance personality would then communicate with sitters by controlling the medium's body – sometimes holding conversations through the voice of the medium, sometimes via writing (as already mentioned, Mrs. Piper did both – and at times simultaneously), and through general use of the body (wagging fingers, crossing arms etc.) Often in the case of trance mediumship, a certain spirit comes to be the main 'control' of the medium – the designated driver, so to speak – and acts as the intermediary in the spirit world between sitters and those queueing up to talk to them on 'the other side', retaining direct control of the medium's body during séances over the course of many years. In the Piper case, the first main control was "Dr. Phinuit", who was succeeded by the "G.P." control many years later, among others.

Non-trance mental mediumship includes the sub-group most are familiar with today – the John Edward-style medium who remains conscious, but gets feelings, hints and visions from the dead communicator. They might get the letter of a name, or be shown an object that is a metaphor for some important facet of the sitter's relationship with the spirit; in many ways, communication through this type of medium seems to be symbolic, delivered through impressions rather than direct contact. But this is not the only type of non-trance mental mediumship. Another claimed way of conversing with the dead is through the use of 'motor automatisms', where conscious control of parts of the body is relinquished, allowing (supposed) outside intelligences to take control. Most readers would be familiar with one such method that has become a stock standard of the supernatural and horror genres: the Ouija Board. A person (or group) puts their hand on the pointer ('planchette'), and without consciously willing it to move, allows it to spell out words and messages, or answer questions, via the markings on the board. Another method is what is known as automatic writing, where the medium relinquishes conscious control of their writing arm, and through either trance, or usually at least entering a slightly dissociative state, allows the arm to 'be controlled' and write messages.

The Enigmatic Mrs. Leonard

When the Society for Psychical Research set out to investigate the possibility of there being an afterlife, they investigated all types of mediums. But over the following few decades, the real 'stars' who seemed to offer evidence of the survival of human personality after death were mental mediums, and of those, most often trance mediums. As we have seen, Leonora Piper was of this type. Another trance medium who impressed the S.P.R. was Mrs. Gladys Osborne Leonard. Like Mrs. Piper and many other mediums (and shamans, it might be noted), Mrs. Leonard's ability manifested at an early age – she often saw visions, but the expression of her talent was frowned upon and discouraged by her conservative parents.[27] As an adult though, her mediumship manifested again when, at a 'fun' table-tipping séance with friends, she suddenly fell into trance, and was told afterwards that the spirit of her mother, and a young girl of Indian descent called 'Feda', had apparently spoken through her. Feda went on to become Mrs. Leonard's control during her occasional trances, and as the First World War approached, warned of an impending catastrophe that would require Mrs. Leonard to devote all her time to acting as a medium to help people connect with the other world.

Like Mrs. Piper, Mrs. Leonard allowed herself to be studied by the S.P.R. for a large portion of her life, from the beginnings of her career with the First World War until after World War II had come to an end. And as with Mrs. Piper, the S.P.R. applied a skeptical attitude to their investigation, to the point of having detectives shadow Mrs. Leonard to determine if she was researching sitters' details. Today Mrs. Piper and Mrs. Leonard are considered the two foremost mediums to have undergone scientific testing. We have already seen some of Mrs. Piper's work, so let's take a quick look at some of Mrs. Leonard's sittings.

In one case, the Reverend Charles Drayton Thomas was asked by a well-known critic of survival research to attempt to contact a deceased individual, one Frederic William Macaulay, on behalf of his daughter, Mrs. Lewis. The following passage gives Feda's communication, with Mrs. Lewis's later feedback:

> FEDA: There is a John and Harry, both with him. And Race...Rice...Riss...it might be Reece but sounds like Riss, and Francis. These are all names of people who are connected with him or linked up with him in the past,

connected with happy times. I get the feeling of an active and busy home in which he was rather happy.

[MRS LEWIS: This is a very curious passage… Probably the happiest time of my father's life was in the four or five years before the war, when we, his five children, were all at school, and the home was packed with our friends during the holidays. John, Harry and Francis could be three of these… But the most interesting passage is 'It might be Reece but it sounds like 'Riss'… My elder brother was at school at Shrewsbury and there conceived a kind of hero-worship for one of the 'Tweaks' (sixth form boys) whose name was Rees. He wrote home about him several times and always drew attention to the fact that the name was spelt 'Rees' and not 'Reece'. In the holidays my sister and I used to tease him by singing 'Not Reece but Riss' until my father stopped us…]

FEDA: I get a funny word now…could he be interested in…baths of some kind? Ah, he says I have got the right word, baths, He spells it, BATHS. His daughter will understand, he says. It is not something quite ordinary, but feels something special.

[MRS LEWIS: This is, to me, the most interesting thing that has yet emerged. Baths were always a matter of joke in our family – my father being very emphatic that water must not be wasted by our having too big baths… It is difficult to explain how intimate a detail this seems.][28]

The final point from Mrs. Lewis above is worth emphasizing. When we discuss the topic of afterlife evidence, it's very easy to get into "explain it away" mode – in the above case, we could all fit the word 'bath' into our upbringing and relationship with our father somehow. What's the big deal? But Mrs. Lewis makes the point that this really was more than just a general statement – the word 'bath', in relationship to her father, held such personal meaning for her that she struggled to put into words exactly "how intimate" this communication was.

But even if we discard this extremely meaningful and successful hit, we still have the idiosyncratic "Not Reece but Riss" comment to explain away. And, beyond that, Feda kept piling on the extra evidence:

> FEDA: Godfrey; will you ask the daughter if she remembers someone called Godfrey. That name is a great link with old times.

> [MRS LEWIS: My father's most trusted clerk, one who specially helped in [his] hydraulic research, was called William Godfrey. He was with my father for years and I remember him from almost my earliest childhood.]

> FEDA: What is that? Peggy…Peggy…Puggy… He is giving me a little name like Puggy or Peggy. Sounds like a special name, a little special nickname, and I think it is something his daughter would know.

> [MRS LEWIS: My father sometimes call me 'pug-nose' or 'Puggy'.]

When we see a number of intimate details such as in the above sitting – culminating in the medium accurately offering the father's special name for his daughter – it's hard to dismiss the feeling that perhaps, just perhaps, something interesting might be going on. And after the sittings on behalf of Mrs. Lewis, the skeptic who instigated the contact – classical scholar E.R. Dodds – was moved to much the same conclusion. In contemplating the summary of the sittings – of 124 pieces of information given, 95 were classified under 'right/good/fair', and only 29 as 'poor/doubtful/wrong' – he noted that "the hypotheses of fraud, rational influence from disclosed facts, telepathy from the sitter, and coincidence cannot either singly or in combination account for the results obtained". The experiment, he said, seemed to present investigators with a choice between two paradigm-shattering conclusions: either Mrs. Leonard was reading the minds of living people and presenting the information so obtained, or she was passing on the thoughts of minds "other than that of a living person". Dodds concluded that he could see no plausible means of departing from this "staggering dilemma".[29]

As with Mrs. Piper, books could be (and have been) filled with the fascinating evidence provided by Mrs. Leonard, but we'll have to settle here for just one more case. Mary White was a distraught wife who wrote to the researchers of the S.P.R. when her husband Gwyther died from stomach cancer, aged just 38. The couple had shared a deep love, and Mary had taken the loss so hard that her friends feared for her life.[30] In a fit of desperation, she reached out to the investigators of the S.P.R. to help her find reassurance that Gwyther lived on in some fashion.

An investigator by the name of Nea Walker responded to Mary, offering to sit with mediums on behalf of the bereaved widow in an effort to contact Gwyther. She managed to collect a substantial amount of evidence from a number of mediums, one of whom was Mrs. Leonard. For example, just as in the case of Mrs. Lewis mentioned above, the medium was able to offer the pet names that Mary and Gwyther had for each other. Mrs. Leonard asked: "What am I getting B for?", despite not knowing that Mary's pet name for her husband was 'Bee'. Mrs. Leonard's control personality, the child-like 'Feda', then referred to a piano: "Mrs. Nea, you know the piano, you tap on his teeth, the one with the big white teeth?" When Mary read the transcript of this sitting, she was amazed. "Gwyther often called my piano 'the animal with the big white teeth'," she noted.

Nea Walker then organized for Mary White to have a sitting with Mrs. Leonard, but as an anonymous guest so that the medium was unaware of her identity. In the very first sitting, Mrs. Leonard spelled out Gwyther's pet name for his wife: 'Biddy'. Mary noted that this particular name was very special, as it was only Gwyther that used it. He also mentioned "the house of sweet scents", which was a specific phrase that he had invented to describe potpourri.

But again, as with Mrs. Piper, perhaps the strongest evidence was unable to be shared due to the private nature of the communication. "Do you know what he means about the Shrine?", Mrs. Leonard said. "It is connected with that chair… He likes to go in there at night. That is our Holy of Holies – where I meet you, so specially, so spiritually. I speak of my love to you. And there – and there, you make me feel I am going to have you again". Mary White was unequivocal in her reading of this particular communication, though reticent to share the details. "I do not wish to annotate this", she stated, but was at pains to confirm that it was "full of meaning. Gwyther can give me no greater evidence of his nearness or of his intimate association with my inmost self".

And, as with Mrs. Piper's 'impersonations', beyond the provocative evidence that comes down to us today in written form, there was even more to the sittings for those present in the way the medium transmitted the personality – dare we even say the 'soul' – of the deceased individual, in a way that was immediately recognizable.

Explaining It Away

Before we go too far down the rabbit-hole though, perhaps we should stop for a second and stand in front of a fire hose of ice-cold water. Mediumship is an area that has had, throughout its history, more than its fair share of charlatans, con-men and, frankly, rather unhinged people. There's a reason for that: people die all the time, and always leave behind other devastated, vulnerable people, who in some cases will give anything to feel connected to their lost family members and friends one more time. It is therefore not surprising that con artists have at times profited handsomely by exploiting this misfortune and desperation. After all, what price would you put on being able to talk once more to your lost child or spouse, whom you thought you had lost forever?

So, could it be that the extraordinary examples of 'afterlife contact' that we've seen in the preceding chapters were produced by all-too-worldly means? Throughout history, various techniques of fake mediums have come to light. Perhaps the most well-known, at least in recent years, is what is known as 'cold reading', or 'fishing': the medium starts with vague, educated guesses and then focuses on only the positive responses from the sitter, becoming more specific as the sitter continues to 'bite' on the successes and offer useful feedback. By the end of the sitting, it seems as if the medium has absolutely nailed the identity of the 'communicator', though in reality the sitter has provided nearly all the information. For instance, a fake medium sitting with a middle-aged British person in the last couple of decades might offer something like: "I'm getting a father or grandfather figure, connected with a J name". Given the plethora of 'J' names (John, Jim, Jack etc), and the weasel word of "connected" (perhaps his wife Jane, his friend Jerry?), the medium is likely to get some sort of positive feedback from the sitter as to the identity of the loved one, which they would then focus on further. They might throw in something like "there's a connection with the army, or a war", knowing full well that both parents and grandparents of middle-aged British people lived through the era of the two World Wars. If they got a hit on that, then they could begin focusing on that aspect. And so on.

Fake mediums also use what is termed the 'Forer Effect' to their advantage. This is the tendency for people to ascribe a personal connection to vague, very general statements about human personality that apply to most people (also known as 'Barnum statements', in reference to a quote by the famous entertainment businessman P.T. Barnum: "we've got something for everyone"). The Forer Effect gets its name from psychologist Bertram R. Forer, who in 1948 gave a "unique personality test" to each of his students, which he asked them to rate – on a scale of 0 (very poor) to 5 (excellent) – according to how well it matched their own personality:

> You have a great need for other people to like and admire you. You have a tendency to be critical of yourself. You have a great deal of unused capacity which you have not turned to your advantage. While you have some personality weaknesses, you are generally able to compensate for them. Your sexual adjustment has presented problems for you. Disciplined and self-controlled outside, you tend to be worrisome and insecure inside. At times you have serious doubts as to whether you have made the right decision or done the right thing. You prefer a certain amount of change and variety and become dissatisfied when hemmed in by restrictions and limitations. You pride yourself as an independent thinker and do not accept others' statements without satisfactory proof. You have found it unwise to be too frank in revealing yourself to others. At times you are extroverted, affable, sociable, while at other times you are introverted, wary, reserved. Some of your aspirations tend to be pretty unrealistic. Security is one of your major goals in life.

The average rating from students was 4.26 out of 5, right at the upper end of the scale, despite every student getting exactly the same personality test. It is quite obvious how similar statements could be used by psychics and mediums in order to forge a connection with their sitters, who would come out afterwards with the feeling that the medium somehow 'knew' their innermost thoughts.

Cold reading and the Forer Effect can even be found in cases where the medium actually believes their own abilities are genuine – they simply pick up the information they need during the sitting through intuitive hunches and unintentional fishing, and sprinkle their reading with Barnum statements. By the end, both medium and sitter are pleasantly surprised by how many items they got right!

But the same does not apply to 'hot reading', which is the generally wilful act of collecting information prior to the sitting taking place. For instance, at the time of the S.P.R.'s investigations, it was well-known that some fake mediums would search through newspaper obituaries, town records, and graveyards for information that they would 'miraculously' pull out of thin air at the later sitting. Such mediums could also form a 'gang' of sorts, sharing information between themselves, ranging from their original research through to specific (often emotionally charged) facts and relationships that came to light, directly from the sitter, during subsequent sittings. In his 1976 exposé *The Psychic Mafia*, fake medium M. Lamar Keene told of eavesdropping on sitters' conversations before meeting them in person using an "electronic sound collector"; visitors to a 'psychic centre' in the United Kingdom were told to leave their belongings in the cloakroom, which were then rifled through for personal information.[31] We can only imagine how important Facebook has become as an information-gathering tool for modern-day fake mediums...

Beyond those techniques, some fake mediums also employed the techniques of stage magic in order to achieve amazing effects. Many of these were limited to the 'tricks' of physical mediumship, but some methods were still successfully employed to create the illusion of mental mediumship. Perhaps the most jaw-dropping of these, at least in its effect, is what is known as 'muscle reading'.

Muscle reading takes advantage of the ideomotor effect, where very slight involuntary reactions to questions, and even your innermost thoughts, can be ascertained through physical contact, often by holding a person's hand or wrist. For example, some magicians have a stock trick of getting an audience member to hide something in the performance hall, which they then go about locating simply by holding the wrist of the person who hid the item, in order to detect their unconscious muscle movements that betray the correct location. Some magicians have even been successful in city-wide versions of this find-and-seek game. By holding the hand or wrist during a sitting, a medium could ascertain the answers to questions that they pose, amazing those present.

There are even more techniques than I have mentioned here, but this short education on the techniques of deception used by fake mediums should at least, I hope, make it absolutely clear that we need to be especially careful not to blindly accept claims of mediumship. But conversely we should also be careful not to extend the existence of fake mediums, and the numerous ways that we can be fooled, to a broad conclusion that there are no genuine mediums. We should always examine cases on their merits, by looking at the evidence, and applying what we know about deception (including self-deception), in order to come to some sort of a conclusion, even if we just mark it as 'provisional'. I bring this point up because in recent times there seems to be a tendency to quote skeptical opinions as the final word on this topic, even though sometimes they might contain as much dubious information as a fake medium's séance. As an example, let's look at the case of Mrs. Piper.

The Skeptical Gardner

There have been few professional skeptics of the standing of Martin Gardner. A brilliant academic who was also well-versed in magic techniques, Gardner – who passed away aged 95 in May 2010 – published more than seventy books on such diverse topics as mathematics, science, philosophy, literature and skepticism. Douglas Hofstadter, no slouch on the intellectual front himself, described Gardner as "one of the great intellects produced in this country in this century." He was also one of the pioneers of the modern 'organised skepticism' movement, writing a deconstruction of pseudoscience in the 1950s titled *In the Name of Science* that would inspire many to become champions of critical thinking. In the summation of one authority, Gardner was "the single most powerful critic of the paranormal in the second half of the 20th century".

Gardner famously wrote a critical piece on the mediumship of Mrs. Piper, with the title "How Mrs. Piper Bamboozled William James", which is regularly quoted by skeptics in response to any discussion of her mediumship (it is also cited in her entry on Wikipedia). In Gardner's summation, the legend of Mrs. Piper grew out of the poor investigative skills of William James: "Had James been better informed about techniques of deception, practiced by magicians and mediums, he would not have been so impressed by Mrs. Piper's carefully contrived persona", said Gardner. "Moreover, James had only a weak comprehension of how to conduct controlled tests of mediums".

He pointed out that "Mrs. Piper usually held a client's hand throughout a sitting", implying that she used muscle reading to ascertain some of her information about sitters. He also suggested that she used hot reading to 'get up' information about her clients before they arrived. But his main accusation was that she used cold-reading extensively: according to Gardner, records of Mrs. Piper's séances "show plainly that her controls did an enormous amount of what was called 'fishing', and today is called 'cold reading'."

All this seems like a fairly comprehensive debunking of Mrs. Piper's apparent talents. Martin Gardner, the intellect and magician, saw right through her deception, and has pointed out to the rest of us exactly how she did it. Perhaps a casual reader would think so, but the case of Mrs. Piper has been a special interest of mine for a number of years, and with the benefit of reading all the original research I have to say that Gardner is leading readers astray. For instance, to arrive at his conclusion that "cunning cold reading may account for most of Mrs. Piper's hits", Gardner appears to have completely ignored the testimony of the original researchers. One of the primary investigators of the case, Professor James Hyslop, said he "applied fishing, guessing, shrewd inference, and suggestion" as explanations for her hits "and found them wanting". Professor William Newbold noted that both he and Richard Hodgson "have seen much of professional mediums, and are thoroughly familiar with the methods of 'fishing' upon which they generally rely. Hence we always had such possibilities in mind, and it would have been impossible for any large amount of detailed information to have been extracted from us in this way without our knowledge". Even Frank Podmore – the resident curmudgeon of the S.P.R., always willing to put forward a skeptical view on mediums – explicitly noted that the hypothesis of cold reading was "clearly inadequate to explain even a small fraction" of Mrs. Piper's sittings.

On the charge of muscle reading, Gardner appears to have ignored the testimony of Sir Oliver Lodge, who explained that he was "familiar with muscle-reading and other simulated 'thought-transference' methods", and avoided any sort of contact that could offer the chance of this taking place. Lodge also offered clarity on Gardner's statement that Mrs. Piper usually held people's hands: "Although Mrs. Piper always held somebody's hand while preparing to go into the trance, she did not always continue to hold it when speaking as Phinuit". Gardner also failed to note that, for the majority of her mediumship – from 1892 onwards – Mrs. Piper communicated via writing and didn't hold people's hands at all.

And in terms of hot reading, we can only ask how Mrs. Piper got up information on sitters when they were usually booked anonymously, many had never been to a medium before, and the S.P.R. had Mrs. Piper and her husband shadowed by detectives. As Frank Podmore noted regarding the possibility that Mrs. Piper could have acquired information on sitters before they arrived:

> [Mrs. Piper] ...did not even know their names... The sittings were fixed sometimes a fortnight, sometimes only two or three days beforehand; the dates were sometimes changed... in one or other of these instances the precautions taken may have been insufficient... But it would be very difficult to suppose that that loophole was always left open, that malign chance favored Mrs. Piper for nine years so punctually that the sittings which have to be written down as failures now number barely 10 percent.
>
> That Mrs. Piper should have worked up the dossiers of all the sitters some time before was practically impossible.

And Richard Hodgson, the primary investigator in the Piper case, who arrived full of skepticism and with a comprehensive knowledge of techniques of deception, made clear that all of Gardner's possibilities were in his own mind before he set out on his investigation. He was, he said...

> ...compelled to assume, in the first instance, that Mrs. Piper was fraudulent and obtained her information previously by ordinary means, such as inquiries by confederates, etc... further information given in various ways by the sitter, consciously or unconsciously, by speech, gesture, and other muscular action.

Who should we trust more? The original investigators, who covered all of these areas in their investigation, or Martin Gardner, writing a century later, who appears to have disregarded all of the original research and testimony? Regardless of anyone's final conclusion on the topic, superficial debunkings such as Gardner's are detrimental to our understanding of the phenomenon of mediumship – the case of Mrs. Piper (and other impressive mediums) *demands* detailed and fair discussion and debate, purely on the evidence collected and the ramifications of a positive conclusion. To give the S.P.R.'s skeptical voice, Frank Podmore, the final say on the Piper case and the evidence that needs to be produced to level a charge of fraud:

> [T]he abundance of the material, the fullness of the records, the watchful supervision exercised over the medium herself for some years past, and the extraordinary and almost uniformly high level of success, make these records much more noteworthy than any previous accounts of the kind... In all these years – now thirteen or more – during which Mrs. Piper has been under the close observation, first of Professor William James, and afterwards of Dr. Hodgson and other competent persons – though she has been shadowed by detectives, though her personal luggage, as Professor Lodge has told us, has been searched, her correspondence read, her goings-out and comings-in closely watched – during all these years not the smallest circumstance has come to light reflecting in any way upon her honesty. Certainly no other medium has been exposed to so stringent an ordeal... Dr. Hodgson himself...[has] succeeded in bringing home the charge of dishonesty to very many professional mediums, that this medium should have passed through the most searching and prolonged inquiries without even a rumour of an exposure, or the discovery of any suspicious circumstances, is a fact entitled to some weight.

In a word, if Mrs. Piper's trance utterances are entirely founded on knowledge acquired by normal means, Mrs.

Piper must be admitted to have inaugurated a new departure in fraud. Nothing to approach this has ever been done before. On the assumption that all so-called clairvoyance is fraudulent, we have seen the utmost which fraud has been able to accomplish in the past, and at its best it falls immeasurably short of Mrs. Piper's achievements. Now, that in itself requires explanation... On the assumption of fraud the tremendous gulf between her and them is an almost insuperable obstacle.

Martin Gardner's oft-cited debunking of Mrs. Piper's mediumship shows a tendency in many scientists and skeptics to quickly (and far too eagerly) write off anything that seems outside the boundaries of orthodox science, without giving the evidence due respect. This isn't exactly a new phenomenon – William James wrote more than a century ago of the rather ironic tendency to resort to unscientific thinking in order to try and protect the edifice of science from 'outside invaders' such as afterlife research. In response to a critic who had taken him to task for his thoughts on the evidence for survival after death, James eloquently bemoaned the difficulties involved in getting a fair hearing for this heretical subject:

> ...The scientific mind is by the pressure of professional opinion painfully drilled to fairness and logic in discussing orthodox phenomena. But in such mere matters of superstition as a medium's trances it feels so confident of impunity and indulgence whatever it may say, provided it be only contemptuous enough, that it fairly revels in the untrained barbarians' arsenal of logical weapons, including all the various sophisms enumerated in the books.

In dismissing the history of research into mediumship, modern skeptics often seem all too willing to ignore the calibre of the researchers involved, and the techniques they brought to bear in ruling out deception. For example, the 'proxy sitting' – in which an individual with little knowledge of the sitter and their relationship with the communicator takes their place in talking to the medium – arose as a new technique to try and remove the possibility of cold reading. In the case of Mary and Gwyther White, Nea Walker served as a proxy sitter with Mrs. Leonard, and with no real knowledge of the Whites was unable in any capacity – consciously or unconsciously – to give feedback and clues to the medium's probing statements. As author Michael Grosso notes, the object in this case "was to get as much evidence as possible of the personality and identity of Mr. White through mediums who had never seen or heard of either Mr. or Mrs. White, working with sitters who had also seen neither and who practically knew nothing of them and their life together".[32]

Super-Psi: Leaps Every Mystery in a Single Bound

The proxy sitting technique was also devised to address another possible explanation for mediumistic communications, though it's one that you definitely won't hear too often from skeptics: the possibility that the information being given was gained via telepathy from the minds of the living (or via other 'paranormal' means, such as clairvoyance, or precognition). This theory, known as the 'super-psi' explanation, says that if such powers exist – as is suggested by a number of (much-debated) recent scientific reports – then we have no need to entertain the added idea that people are communicating from the afterlife. While this is logically true, in many ways the super-psi explanation feels like a bit of a cop-out – in this scenario, the medium becomes 'all-seeing', and any anomalous information can be explained away by her alleged super-powers. So much so that we start wondering whether such a scenario is any more likely than the afterlife explanation.

For an example of the disruptive force of the super-psi explanation, consider this fairly convincing case from the investigation of Mrs. Leonard. One of the S.P.R.'s members, one Lionel G. Aitken, had lost his son in an accident, and information about the deceased young man began appearing at sittings between Charles Drayton Thomas and Mrs. Leonard. Much of the information given was regarded as highly evidential by Mr. Aitken, but he was baffled by a few items. For instance, at a sitting in January 1939, 'Feda' noted that "there was somebody else he was very interested in, that perhaps you don't know…a name that starts with the letter B, and I think there is an R in it…it might be a Mr. Brick". A couple of weeks later, Feda once again brought up "a name starting with BR", and asked "if there is anything to do with him like a little ship…or a little model of a ship". According to Feda this young man had also passed over, "rather early in his earth life".

Mr. Aitken could not make any sense of this 'Br' individual, connected with a ship. It wasn't until his other, still living son read the details of the sitting that the mystery was solved – it was information that he had 'requested' that his dead brother send him to prove that he lived on:

> He and his deceased brother had been friends at an RAF Station with a young officer called BRIDGEN – whom we had not heard of – and who had been killed about a year after my son.

> This young man, before joining the RAF, had worked for a firm which made *scale models of ships* for shipping companies, and he had shown my son a photograph of one of these models which he had made himself and which he said his people still had at home. *My son had felt sure that this matter of the model ship would be given as a sign* if they were unable to get the name through correctly.[33] [my emphasis]

In a corroborating letter, the son himself noted that he was the only member of the family still alive that knew of Bridgen, and that prior to the sittings he had specifically asked his dead brother to communicate the identity of this common friend through the medium, in order to prove it was really him 'talking from the other side'. To the living son, "the reply was unmistakable".[34]

So how do we explain this case? First, this was a proxy sitting, with Thomas standing in for Mr. Aitken. Beyond that, information came through that wasn't even known by the elder Mr. Aitken, but was only known to the two sons, one living and one dead. What's more, the living son *had directly requested his deceased brother send the information that appears to have come through the medium.* The afterlife explanation seems to fit perfectly. Skeptical theories seem unable to account for the case. But the super-psi explanation says there is no need for the afterlife hypothesis: instead, the medium simply fished this request, and the required answer, out of the living son's head. We cannot disprove this notion, so it largely comes down to a question of which seems more plausible to us. For those who are, for whatever reason, against the notion of an afterlife, the super-psi explanation would seem to be a 'less complicated' solution – removing the whole question of a location of post-death existence, and concentrating simply on as-yet unexplained powers of the mind. But if we look closer at cases like the above, we start to wonder whether it really is simpler. Why would the medium 'fish' the request from the mind of the young Mr. Aitken? Did his desire link his mind somehow to hers? How do minds 'read' each other? And, extending that, if minds can do these amazing things, then perhaps mind is made of a thing beyond the physical, and is not restricted to life in a physical body? That is, once we begin exploring the idea of super-psi, we often end up standing in the same neighbourhood that we do with the afterlife hypothesis.

Once again, we are left with a judgement call on evidence that seems to suggest an afterlife, but which could also be 'explained' by other convoluted processes. Why do we struggle to take that leap to the answer that seems the simplest explanation?

The Cross-Correspondences

To try and beat the super-psi explanation, a further technique was developed: the *cross-correspondence*. Meant to ascertain whether the communication through mediums was truly from 'the dead', this may be perhaps the most ironic invention ever, because it was, apparently, devised by a dead person and communicated through a medium!

At the turn of the 20th century the S.P.R. had suffered two mortal wounds, with the deaths of co-founders Henry Sidgwick and Frederic Myers, in 1900 and 1901 respectively. Until that point the two men had been driving forces of the society for two decades, pouring all their efforts into trying to answer the question of whether there was an afterlife. But when another member of the S.P.R. began receiving messages via automatic writing that were signed off with the name "Myers", it seemed that they intended to continue their efforts from beyond the grave. And they did so via the cross-correspondences.

The basic premise of what became known as the cross-correspondences was outlined very simply by one of the communicators: "Record the bits and when fitted they will make the whole". The plan, it seems, was for a communicator on 'the other side' to begin with a coherent idea, which would then be divided into pieces – like a jigsaw puzzle – and distributed to a number of mediums scattered around the world. The pieces on their own would not make sense to each medium, or those sitting with them, but once they had been recognised as pieces of the puzzle and reassembled, the overall picture would become apparent. Also, as further proof this revealed 'picture' would be seen to relate to the personality of the deceased communicator in some way. To make an analogy, we might compare it to a game where we telephone (or email) various friends around the world, giving them a piece of information related to ourselves, and then get them all to reassemble the pieces to reveal a coherent, idiosyncratic idea that identifies us as the communicator.

The main communicators in the cross correspondences claimed to be the afterlife incarnations of Myers, Sidgwick, and another important S.P.R. member, Edmund Gurney, who had died in 1888. However, the cross-correspondence method was used for a long period (some 31 years, between 1901 and 1932), and as such there were numerous others involved at various times. Interestingly, the mediums who were given the puzzle pieces were nearly all 'amateurs' – S.P.R. members who had developed the skill of automatic writing out of their own personal interest (one major exception being the leading light of the S.P.R.'s research effort, Mrs. Piper), and so had no financial stake in success. A number of these amateur mediums were referred to under pseudonyms in reports on the case in order to protect their reputations. They included Mrs. Margaret Verrall and her daughter Helen, 'Mrs. Willett' (Mrs. Winifred Coombe-Tennant, a prominent British suffragette, politician, and philanthropist who would become the first British woman elected to the League of Nations), and 'Mrs. Holland' (Mrs. Fleming, the sister of Rudyard Kipling).

Given the academic experience of the alleged communicators, the cross-correspondence puzzles often involved literary themes related to their interests (many from the Classics). As such, they often seemed obscure until the key was given. However, along with the complex reconstruction of the overall picture, there were often little hints that pieces were related, and sometimes these on their own were suggestive that an individual intelligence was transmitting through multiple mediums. As an example, let's look at one of the more well-known cross-correspondences, known as the "Hope, Star and Browning" case.

In a sitting with Mrs. Piper in January 1907, one of the S.P.R.'s investigators, Mr. J.G. Piddington, suggested to the 'Myers' personality who was communicating through the medium that he should make things a little easier for researchers by indicating when a cross-correspondence was being attempted, by perhaps drawing a symbol beside the text. Piddington suggested 'Myers' use a circle with a triangle inside it.

A week later, Mrs. Verrall provided a message from 'Myers' (via her automatic writing) suggesting to Piddington that "an anagram would be better" – anagrams being a personal interest of the living Myers. "Tell him that – rats, star, tars and so on". Five days later, writing through the same medium, 'Myers' played with some anagrams, writing 'Aster' and 'Teras' (Greek words for star and wonder, respectively), before seemingly free associating on those themes via a string of quotations from the poetry of Robert Browning. Following this outpouring of ideas, 'Myers' signed off with drawings of a triangle inside a circle, a clear reference to Piddington's original request through Mrs. Piper the week previous.

Then, at the start of February, Mrs. Verrall's daughter Helen also received a message from 'Myers': "A monogram, the crescent moon, remember that, and the star." And through Mrs. Piper, the 'Myers' personality seemed to offer another proof that he was transmitting through multiple mediums, by asking if Mrs. Verrall had received his message, with specific reference to the information he had provided: "I referred also to Browning again. I referred to Hope ["Evelyn Hope", the title of a Browning poem on the rather relevant theme of death] and Browning... I also said star... look out for Hope, Star and Browning." And in another message through Helen Verrall shortly after, he drew a star, played with the same anagrams, and referenced Browning again (via his poem about the Pied Piper of Hamelin). Pointing to the drawn star, 'Myers' noted "That was the sign she will understand when she sees it... No *arts* avail... and a *star* above it all *rats* everywhere in Hamelin town." [my emphasis]

Finally, in March, 'Myers' explained the thinking behind the various scripts. Communicating through Mrs. Piper, he noted that he had drawn the circle and triangle through Mrs. Verrall as requested by Piddington, but that in doing so the idea of anagrams came to him, and these in turn "suggested a poem to my mind" – that is, the work of Robert Browning. And, to top it all off, he subsequently noted that he had also drawn a crescent moon...which brings to mind the script received by Helen Verrall which explicitly said "the crescent moon, remember that".

This case alone appears to offer substantial evidence that a single intelligence was speaking through multiple mediums. But one has to understand the various literary allusions, and keep track of which mediums were providing information confirming previous sittings with other mediums, to get a sense of its strength. And yet, believe it or not, this is one of the simpler cases – many of the cross correspondences extended over a number of years and contained extremely obscure literary references. This raises a problem with the cross-correspondences as proof – while in theory they seem like a great method of negating skeptical explanations, in practice their complexity and personal nature make them very difficult to explain to the casual observer. In total, over 50 papers were written analysing the cross correspondences, many of those book-length, with complex analyses of how the literary puzzle pieces fit together. It's therefore almost impossible for a lay-person to grasp the subtleties of any one case in detail. The best we can do is, as I have here, grab one of the 'simpler' examples to show how information appears to have been shared between mediums.

But while we moan about the difficulties re-assembling the pieces on our side, perhaps we should also consider the obstacles faced by those attempting the communication. 'Myers' himself, speaking through Mrs. Willett in 1910, noted that his use of "different scribes" – from the classically trained Mrs. Verrall, through to an American housewife like Mrs. Piper – meant that he needed to show "different aspects of thought, underlying which unity is to be found".[35] This idea, that the communicator is using the medium like an instrument – and is therefore somewhat restricted by the capabilities of each one – may perhaps offer one reason why we get the mix of both highly specific and completely wrong information through mediums, and also why some mediums are better than others. It's very difficult to play "Flight of the Bumblebee" on a double-bass, but if you can find a piano you might stand a better chance (though even after much practice, you're likely to still flub more than a few notes).

Once we consider the idea that communicators might also be facing their own difficulties – something like living in a location with only a few phone lines available, all of varying quality (and in this case, attempting a *seriously* long-distance call) – then some of these errors also perhaps become more understandable. For instance, when Phinuit was incorrectly telling Hodgson that his lost love Jessie had perfect teeth, could the 'Jessie' communicator have simply been trying to indicate that her teeth were a particularly recognisable feature, but in translation it became her showing off her teeth? Pure speculation, of course, but these issues are certainly something we need to keep in mind when we evaluate communication through mediums. As the deceased 'Myers' once grumpily noted, conveying his thoughts through a medium was like "dictating feebly to a reluctant and somewhat obtuse secretary [while] standing behind a sheet of frosted glass which blurs sight and deadens sounds".[36]

But similarly, we should also note that – even if we accept that mediumistic communications are truly originating from the consciousness of the dead – we need to be careful in trusting any information that comes through a medium. Just because you go to a medium and get a highly evidential piece of information about Aunt Sally, doesn't mean you should then follow the next piece of advice given through the medium to quit your job and try to make a living via professional water-skiing. Even if you are not dealing with a fraud, a very good medium might still impose their own subconscious thoughts on the sitting, or mistranslate a message from the dearly departed.

Because let's face it – we really don't know what we're dealing with here. To many of us, even if the evidence seems convincing, we still simply imagine our loved ones in their everyday clothes, standing beside the medium and whispering in their ear, à la Whoopi Goldberg's Oda Mae in the movie *Ghost*. But if there *is* an afterlife existence, could we really understand exactly what that is from our own limited perspective? We'll discuss some of these possibilities in a later chapter, but for now the simple message is that we need to be careful in our assumptions and expectations of communications through mediums. Richard Hodgson made the analogy that it seemed that communicators were within an imperfect transmitting machine filled with a gas "which produces a partial loss of consciousness", the effects of which accumulated the longer the communicator stayed within the 'machine' (the medium). The veteran investigator offered words of advice for future researchers, stating that "unless the presence of such conditions is constantly recognised" by those investigating, then "further research in this field will be futile".

But what of this "further research". A century ago, the eminent investigators of the S.P.R. came largely to the conclusion that they had collected enough evidence to prove that consciousness survived the physical death of the body. Their conclusions seem to have slipped into obscurity, with very few people today knowing anything about the Society's comprehensive research into the topic. Are there any investigators today who are continuing to research the question of whether mediums offer a line of communication with the dead?

Modern Investigation

In the past decade, public interest in mediumship has surged, with fictional television series such as *Medium* and *Ghost Whisperer* rating highly, while a number of professional (self-proclaimed) mediums – including John Edward, Allison DuBois, and James Van Praagh – have become near household names, appearing on popular television shows and publishing bestselling books.

On the flipside, the scientific view of mediumship has plummeted since the time of the S.P.R.'s investigations of the likes of Mrs. Piper and Mrs. Leonard, an era when some of the most respected scientists and members of society believed they had found evidence for life after death. Today, most scientists and skeptics view mediums as frauds, and the excited public as gullible fools or victims. To pursue research in the field and attempt to publish scientific papers on mediumship experiments seems often to be taking the short route to professional suicide for scientists.

But some modern researchers are still willing to risk their reputation and investigate the question of whether mediums have access to information from beyond the grave, and in doing so they have been bringing modern scientific procedures to the field. Psychologist Dr. Richard Wiseman (well-known for his media appearances as a skeptic, which perhaps gives him more freedom in pursuing research on this topic) co-authored a paper in 2005 with Dr. Ciarán O'Keeffe of Liverpool Hope University, titled "Testing alleged mediumship: Methods and results", in which the two researchers attempted to develop a standard method of testing mediums which would eliminate the potential for the various "psychological strategems" which non-genuine mediums might use (e.g. cold reading). They focused on three potential problems that might arise during tests of mediums, which dictated the structure of their experimental set-up:

(a) the need to control for potential sensory leakage,

(b) the need to accurately assess the generality of the mediums' statements, and...

(c) the need for 'blind' judging.

The need to control sensory leakage covers much ground, from potential 'hot-reading' prior to a sitting (i.e. by researching the sitter in advance, or listening in to conversations immediately before the sitting begins), through to 'cold-reading' during the sitting (from remarks and gestures made by the sitter, through to their appearance and mode of dress). To achieve this, the medium needs to be isolated from any normal means of gaining information about the sitter – including information learned through third parties, such as those running the experiment.

The second problem noted, regarding the generality of statements made by the medium, is meant to address the Forer/Barnum effect that we have mentioned previously. If we simply ask the sitter how the medium performed, they may feel that the information given was impressive, and count the sitting as a success, despite the fact that general statements were used to give that false impression, as with Forer's personality test. So researchers now aim to get sitters to mark not only their own sitting, but also those of the other sitters, without being aware which is theirs. If the medium's statements were truly accurate, then the correct sittings should have a higher score than the 'decoy' sittings.

And lastly, the the need for 'blind' judging addresses the subjectivity involved in rating the sittings. If the sitter knows which reading is theirs, and which are the decoys, then they may unwittingly attribute more weight to some of the statements made in their sittings, seeking a successful hit (subtle biases would be amplified when there is a need to believe a member of the family 'lives on'). And alternatively, if the sitter is an avowed skeptic or atheist, who desired to see the experiment fail, then they might rank their sitting lower to sabotage any chance of success. To remove these possibilities, experimenters get sitters to rate the accuracy of the medium's statements 'blind' – that is, without informing them whether they are from the 'target' or 'decoy' sittings.

O'Keeffe and Wiseman assembled a group of five mediums and a group of five sitters, with each researcher dealing solely with their respective group to eliminate the chance of leakage of information between sitters and mediums. Each sitter – all males, between the age of 25 and 30 – was placed in an acoustically isolated room, with the medium taken to another. The medium was then asked to attempt contact with any spirits associated with the sitter, and to report on the information given for the next 60 minutes. The sitting was recorded on videotape, and after all had been completed the mediums' comments were transcribed and broken down into a series of statements. Sitters then blindly rated each statement with a score between 1 (not applicable) and 7 (very applicable), and an overall score for each sitting was created by summing up the ratings given to the entire series of statements.

However, contrary to all the convincing evidence for mediumship we have seen so far in this book, the experiment was a bust. The analysis showed no significant findings, with the highest rating only matching up with the correct sitting on one occasion. So what went wrong? Were the mediums used of a poor quality? O'Keeffe and Wiseman made sure that they picked from a pool of some reputation (as far as mediums go at least): they recruited them from a list of certified mediums provided by the Spiritualists' National Union (SNU) in the United Kingdom. Perhaps the mediums were having an off day, or weren't used to the conditions of isolation? Or perhaps, as the two researchers noted, it is possible that genuine mediumistic ability simply does not exist, and that "the apparent accuracy of mediums' readings are entirely due to the type of psychological stratagems" that the experimenters attempted to eliminate via sensory isolation, scoring with decoy sittings, and blind judging.

However, there is one other element to the study that may be important. As we've already seen, mediums nearly always get at least a few things wrong in sittings. Sometimes, the sitting is a complete write-off, except for one highly specific piece of information that stands out from the background, almost causing whiplash in the sitter. Researchers label these small but convincing personal details given through mediums as "dazzle shots". To use an example from popular culture, it's when Demi Moore in *Ghost* is stopped in her tracks by the mention of one familiar word from Whoopi Goldberg's Oda Mae: "He says 'Ditto'". It might be only one piece of information out of ten that is correct or specific enough to get the attention of the sitter, but it is *so correct* that it stands out above everything else. When the self-admitted "skeptical by nature" science author Mary Roach was researching her book *Spook*, it was Allison DuBois' off-the-cuff, post-sitting statement "I'm showing a metal hourglass... does your brother have one?" that impressed her, after a less-than-impressive one-on-one with the famous medium. Roach's brother collects hourglasses.

These "dazzle shots" seem to be the key to further research with mediums, and the study by O'Keeffe and Wiseman, though for the most part highly laudable, blunted this important aspect of mediumship by scoring a sitting by adding the ratings *for each individual statement*. In this way, any quality 'signals' (that is, the dazzle shots) are bound to get lost in the quantity of noise (the vague and incorrect statements also made during a sitting). As Mary Roach mentioned in her book: though the one, very specific and obscure call by DuBois was mighty impressive, it was equally hard for Roach to dismiss all the incorrect statements that the medium made during the actual sitting. If she scored her sitting as per O'Keeffe and Wiseman's experimental set-up, it would no doubt have gone down as a low-scoring failure. But if she were asked to pick the correct sitting based on *an overall feeling,* from a number of decoys, she might well pick that sitting out of the rest based on that one, head-turning dazzle shot.

And So Faintly You Came Tapping, Tapping

In July 2002, life was going along rather nicely for Trevor Hamilton
and his wife Anne. They had both retired and moved to a lovely,
quiet English village. And now, their plane had just landed at Bristol
after a week holidaying in Paris in the summertime. But as the
plane taxied to its arrival gate, a message came over the intercom:
"If a Mr. and Mrs. Hamilton are on board, would they please
remain seated until the other passengers have left". Aware that such
a message never precedes good news, Trevor and Anne anxiously
waited as other travellers fussed over their bags and slowly made
their departure, oblivious to the couple's growing dread. As they
disembarked, a policewoman met them at the bottom of the steps,
and asked if their son Ralph drove a car with a certain numberplate,
before going on to ask them to identify some personal items:

> Yes, that was his watch given to him by the girl who had
> nearly broken his heart. Yes, yes, yes (hurriedly to get it over
> with) to all the other effects. Everything was just plain unreal,
> as if we were being forced to take part in a film and speak
> lines that referred to the tragedies of other people. I wanted
> to stop the kind police woman and say, OK, I realise you are
> just doing your job, but you've got the wrong parents.

Then she told us the details.[37]

The Hamilton's son Ralph had died the previous day at 12.45 p.m.
in a car accident, after colliding with a bus. Strangely enough, at
this very time the previous day in Paris, Trevor and Anne had
been lazing about in the Jardin du Luxembourg when Anne had
experienced a sudden feeling of desolation. But, however odd,
that was a fleeting sensation, whereas now the desolation was
permanent. "We spent the next three days in bed," says Trevor,
"cold and stunned with grief and clinging to each other."

...We identified Ralph's body at a local hospital. We could only look at him through a window. Insanely, I felt that if we refused to look we could somehow turn the clock back and not be forced to take part in a play we hadn't written and would never have wanted to write. We would not be grieving parents. Ralph would not be dead. But we had to look.

It was him and wasn't him and there was a bruise on his face.[38]

How does a parent cope with such a loss? How does one motivate themselves to get out of bed in the morning once their child has died? I can't imagine being able to cope with the pain, and I hope I never find out. For Trevor though, his coping mechanism was to address the question of whether Ralph's consciousness 'lived on' in some way beyond the threshold of physical death. Throughout his life, Trevor and his family had experienced minor 'paranormal' events (he had personally experienced poltergeist-like activity, while his brother had twice encountered an apparition of their deceased father on the landing of their house). And in the weeks after Ralph's death, both Trevor and Anne had noticed appliances doing strange things (the TV turned itself on, the stereo changed volume spontaneously, and the light outside Ralph's room seemed to have a mind of its own), and both of them had felt his 'presence' about the house. So Trevor wasn't opposed to the idea that there was something beyond death, but he was also wary of being 'a believer' without any evidence, simply as a consequence of his grief. So he decided that he would go in search of evidence himself... though he wasn't sure at all where to start:

[H]ow was I to find him? Where was I to look? Who could I turn to for advice? How could I be sure that grief and loss hadn't weakened my judgement? And what did finding him actually mean?

...I was worried that I might be led astray by a mixture of over-imagination and wishful thinking if I started my quest – however that might shape up – without guidance and structure. So, in what might seem rather a cold-blooded way, I developed a strategy which would give me structure and guidance and prevent me from deluding myself. I would join the Society for Psychical Research (the oldest and most prestigious organisation working in this field in the UK), I would read all I could on the history of the subject and, informed by this reading, I would visit a number of mediums to see if there was anything in it at all.[39]

The results of Trevor Hamilton's 'experiment' are laid out in his fascinating and moving book *Tell My Mother I'm Not Dead: A Case Study in Mediumship Research*. In visiting ten mediums, he noted down all statements made and then marked them as 'True', 'False', 'Other' and 'Predictive'. In total, he found that three of the sittings were between 85 and 90% accurate, four were between 68 and 79%, while the other three scored from 38% to 61%. He noted that the number of false statements across all mediums was very low, and two of them made no errors at all!

Trevor also realized, however, that though a number of statements were factual and true, they were also very general in scope, and perhaps would have applied to most sitters: the Forer Effect in action. And he was cautious in giving too much credence to answers that he felt may have been generated through fishing, or other techniques mentioned earlier. But then, there were also a number of rather specific statements that he found difficult to explain away:

The colour of Ralph's bedroom wallpaper (an unusual lilac which we remarked on when we moved in); the name Mrs. Bennett who, with my grandmother, babysat him and Daniel and spoilt them rotten with sweet treats; the car park replacing the gardens at the back of their houses; the fact that I had six siblings; the 24 chapters in my [book] draft (which I have never counted); the angel lamp which we had taken from our first house and which fascinated Ralph as a child; my love of Chopin and my music teacher Elizabeth (Richards not Roberts – I considered this a reasonable enough approximation to score as true) of whom I had been particularly fond because of the earnest conversations we used to have at the keyboard; and the importance of the dates 22nd November and the 6th July.[40]

And in the sitting with 'Medium 3', which both Trevor and Anne were 'partially disappointed' by overall, there was one, stand-out statement. The medium was given a mental picture of Trevor "agitated at a table, tapping on it with a penny, in the registry" – a seemingly random and obscure statement that was in fact spookily correct. "I had to sort out the legal matters to do with Ralph's death," Trevor notes. "I remember going to the registrar to prove probate and get the death certificate, and sitting outside her office staring at the little table in front of me, tapping aimlessly with a couple of pennies on the table top, confronted by the utter meaninglessness of it all".

I ask Trevor how he interprets this sitting, given that apart from this one outstanding hit, he had overall considered it disappointing. For him, that one 'signal burst' seems enough to overwhelm the 'noise' of the rest of the sitting, given the manner in which it conformed so closely with his memory of that day. "I remember the actual event, winding up his personal affairs according to the law, vividly", he tells me. The precision of the hit has led Trevor to consider it as "a useful piece of evidence possibly indicating Ralph's continued awareness of what is happening to his family". He does however retain the healthy questioning attitude that is a hallmark of his research, wondering aloud to me whether the penny-tapping incident could possibly be "the kind of well-rehearsed miniature scene" that a fake medium might have as a standard line, hoping for a lucky hit. He is quick to qualify, however, that he does not believe this particular medium was a fake. In fact, Trevor believes that, despite the largely incorrect sitting, this particular medium may well be genuinely talented, but needs further development: "He seemed always to be on the brink of making good contact but misinterpreting the images he was receiving".

It strikes me that the penny incident is yet another prime example of how a 'dazzle shot' can triumph over a sitting's worth of incorrect or vague information, so I ask Trevor his thoughts on how science can best approach the topic. "The question of how to score and judge the sittings of mediums is a complex and under-researched area", he admits. "I kept my system as simple as possible because I was writing for a general but thoughtful audience and not for specialists". But he notes that this approach, as with the one taken by Wiseman and O'Keeffe in their study, was certainly not ideal. "The danger of the individual hit approach is that it does not discriminate between levels and qualities of hit", he warns. Trevor also takes issue with researchers formatting or editing the medium's statements to create a list of discrete, measurable items in order to easily tally the hits and misses in a sitting, noting that "some of the most suggestive and interesting statements can be in the language and the turn of phrase and the total cumulative effect". To filter this element out, Trevor says, "is not fair".

Trevor has continued to study and write about mediumship, though he has performed no further research attempting to make contact with Ralph. Nevertheless, he purposefully maintains a very low profile online, avoiding social media and email communication where possible, in case he ever desires to restart his experiments with mediums. "I may do so in the future provided I can be reasonably confident in the arrangements", he says, informing me that he was wary that fake mediums might look up information about him on the web (one major complication that he is aware of though is the public nature of the information in his book). Trevor does mention to me though one "remarkable event" that didn't make it into his book, as it occurred during the proofing stage. A medium in Australia, whom Trevor knows and respects for their integrity and intelligence, used a copy of Ralph's photo in an exercise with twelve trainee mediums. After concealing the photo in an envelope, the medium asked the trainees to write their impressions on a sheet of paper. The results, Trevor tells me, "were remarkable":

> They all picked up highly relevant material about his life/ personality/appearance; that he had died in an accident; and that he was a young male (only one didn't specifically state this but you could argue that it was implied). 69 statements were made and they were all accurate, some just by one trainee, but many of them picked up by a substantial number of the other trainees.

Trevor continues to welcome all voices in the debate over the validity of mediumship, from scientific evidence for survival to fair criticism from skeptics. "If there is anything ultimately in the survival hypothesis", he tells me, "it will be all the stronger for really understanding, appreciating and dealing with the criticisms of scientists of a strongly materialistic ideology and skilled magicians". Like them, he says he has zero tolerance for fraudulent mediums – "they should be exposed and put out of business" – and acknowledges that there are some valid reasons why mediumship in general is often held in such low esteem, telling me that "there is a great need for quality control and greater professionalism in mediumship, and a lessening of the show business element".

But in the end, he says, arguments over the survival hypothesis may just be "an endless debate". For a critical thinker like himself, he admits, there is a perpetual fear of "false hopes and being deceived, which will never go away". Conversely though, Trevor explains that even if he had found no evidence for survival, he still would have "doubted the null hypothesis (that there is no survival) given the wide range of testimony from credible sources to the contrary".

Black Licorice and a Chicken Killer

Recently, two other researchers have taken on the yoke of investigating mediumship within a scientific framework. Dr. Emily Kelly of the University of Virginia and former hospice chaplain Dianne Arcangel undertook a study of the information given by mediums to recently-bereaved persons, the results of which were published in early 2011 in the *Journal of Nervous and Mental Disorders*. As opposed to the results from the research done by Richard Wiseman and Ciaran O'Keeffe however, some of Kelly and Arcangel's findings *do* appear to offer support for the validity of mediumship.

In one experiment, Kelly and Arcangel employed nine mediums to offer readings for 40 individual sitters – two of the mediums doing six each, while the other seven mediums did four readings each (each sitter had just one reading done). Similarly to Wiseman and O'Keeffe's protocol, the sittings were done without the actual sitter present (the researchers acted as a 'proxy' to keep a blind protocol), and audio recordings of the mediums' statements were later transcribed. And addressing the need for blind judging, each sitter was then sent six readings – the correct reading, and five 'decoy' readings drawn from those given for others in the group – but were then asked to rate each *overall reading* on how applicable they thought it was to them, and comment on why they chose the highest rated reading. Thirty-eight of the forty participants returned their ratings – and, amazingly, 14 of the 38 readings were correctly chosen (while at first sight 'less than half correct' may seem a rather poor success rate, given there were six readings to choose from, this is actually a number significantly above what would be expected by chance). Additionally, seven other readings were ranked second, and altogether 30 of the 38 readings were ranked in the top half of the ratings. What's more, one medium in particular stood out above the others: all six of this person's readings were correctly ranked first by each sitter!

Of the people who correctly chose their own reading, it's interesting to note that many didn't just 'lean' toward that reading – they made comments such as "I don't see how it could be anything other than (X reading)"; "one reading stood out from the rest"; and "I feel certain this is the correct choice and would bet my life on it". What convinced them? The dazzle shots.

For instance, the person who made the "I would bet my life on it" statement in choosing the correct reading...

> ...cited the medium's statement that "there's something funny about black licorice... Like there's a big joke about it, like, ooh, you like that?" According to the sitter, his deceased son and his wife had joked about licorice frequently. Also, the medium had said "I also have sharp pain in the rear back of the left side of my head in the back, in the occipital. So perhaps there was an injury back there, or he hit something or something hit him." The deceased person had died of such an injury incurred in a car crash.[41]

Another of the sitters also noted how specific details had convinced them as to which reading was theirs. The medium, looking at a photo of the subject, said "I feel like the hair I see here in the photo is gone, so I have to go with cancer or something that would take the hair away...her hair – at some point she's kind of teasing it, she tried many colors. I think she experimented with color a lot before her passing." The deceased girl's mother confirmed that she had died of cancer, and had dyed her hair "hot pink" before her cancer surgery (the girl's hair was normal-looking in the photo, so there was no clue for the medium there). She later shaved her head when her hair began falling out. The medium also described a feeling of being "up in Northampton, Massachusetts... Northampton does have that kind of college town beatnik kind of feel to it." This was another source of confirmation for the sitter, as although the girl lived in Texas, Northampton was apparently where she wanted to go to college.

Again and again in the experiment we see that it is certain, specific and seemingly personal details given by the medium that stand out to sitters:

> In another example, among many other details the sitter commented especially on the statement "he said I don't know why they keep that clock if they are not going to make it work. So somebody connected directly to him has a clock that either is not wound up, or they let it run down, or it's standing there just quiet. And he said what's the point in having a clock that isn't running? So, somebody should know about that and it should give them quite laughter." The sitter did laugh (and cry) over this, because a grandfather clock that her husband had kept wound had not been wound since his death. The medium had also commented that "he can be on a soap box, hammering it"; his children when young had frequently complained about "Dad being on his soap box."

> ...the sitter...noted the medium's comment that "I think she collected some small things...either little china or glass things. Like little knicknacks. But I keep seeing an elephant with the trunk up, so this might be a special object or something that people would understand." The sitter subsequently sent E.W.K. [researcher Emily Williams Kelly] a photograph of a small ceramic elephant with its trunk up, part of his deceased wife's larger collection and an item sitting on a table in their front hall.

...the medium referred to "a lady that is very much, was influential in his [the deceased person's] formative years. So, whether that is mother or whether that is grandmother... She can strangle a chicken." The sitter commented that her grandmother (the deceased person's mother) "killed chickens. It freaked me out the first time I saw her do this. I cried so hard that my parents had to take me home. So the chicken strangling is a big deal...In fact I often referred to my sweet grandmother as the chicken killer".[42]

The weak link in these experiments, no doubt, was that in Kelly and Arcangel's study the mediums were given photographs of the recently deceased individuals they were meant to be contacting, which breaches the 'no sensory leakage' rule set by O'Keeffe and Wiseman. However, it must be said that Kelly and Arcangel were aware of this weakness, and tried to control for it as much as possible. For example, the most obvious things that can be read, or leaked, from a photograph – age and gender – were eliminated as factors by sending sitter's decoy readings which were from the same age and gender group. The researchers also pointed out that many of those who chose the correct reading did so on specific details that really could not be "read" from a photograph – for example, how many people could tell that someone's Granny was a 'chicken killer' from a photo of her deceased son, or that a family had an in-joke about black licorice?

But why did Kelly and Arcangel allow this 'weakness' in their experiment? The answer is that they felt the minimal amount of information given in more stringent experiments (only the name and birthday) might be "insufficient to focus the medium on the deceased person" – that is, in an attempt to make experiments fool-proof, perhaps mediums were being short-changed in terms of the conditions under which they were being expected to operate successfully.

A Scientist Among the Mediums

Dr. Julie Beischel, who has been investigating mediums for more than a decade now, agrees that there have to be some concessions when testing them. An important facet of any study, Beischel says, is having "an environment that mimics how the phenomenon exists in nature". In the case of mediumship, she says, there is a need to provide the medium with some sort of 'jumping-off' point: "a nugget of information that she can use to focus or connect". In their 'natural habitat', says Beischel, mediums might be given the name of a deceased person and a photograph, or at the very least have a sitter present who has a strong connection to the deceased. And so, in her peer-reviewed research studies, Beischel provides the medium with "a necessary trigger" in the absence of the usual sitter.

"Creating an experimental environment too far removed from the natural mediumship process would be like placing an acorn in your palm, waiting a few minutes, and then calling it a fraud when it didn't turn into an oak tree," Beischel counsels. "Like the acorn, mediums need the equivalent of soil, water, and sunlight to effectively do what they do".[43] As such, she tells me, her experimental designs are not always those desired or recommended by skeptics, as her primary aim is to provide the right setting for the phenomenon to occur: "We don't do this research to please skeptics; we do it to gain new knowledge". Nevertheless, Beischel remains on guard against producing flawed results, and keeps effective controls in place as much as possible. For instance, she ensures that the first names given to the mediums as 'triggers' do not provide enough information for the mediums to be able to intentionally or subconsciously 'read' information from them.

Julie Beischel is well-placed to discuss issues to do with research into mediumship, given her many years of full-time study of the phenomenon. It's a career choice that would have surprised Beischel herself if told about it in early 2003 though. After graduating from North Arizona University with a Bachelor of Science degree in Environmental Sciences (with an emphasis in Microbiology), she went on to complete a Ph.D. in Pharmacology and Toxicology at the University of Arizona in Tucson.

Her time at university had not been a smooth road: at age 19, she woke up one morning with only peripheral vision in one eye, unable to see anything in the center of her field of vision; a battery of tests resulted in a diagnosis of multiple sclerosis. But even that paled into insignificance beside the other personal issue she had been forced to deal with during this time: her mother's suicide.

"My relationship with my mother had been strained. Thus, her death was sadly a relief", Beischel confesses in her semi-autobiographical book *Among Mediums: A Scientist's Quest for Answers*. With her mother diagnosed as suffering from the disorder alexithymia, which is characterised by the inability to identify and describe emotions, Beischel's upbringing had been so turbulent that in the wake of her mother's suicide, she felt that "I had to get past her life more than get over her death". Her mother's passing would provide a new beginning though: in the years subsequent to the tragedy, Beischel became interested in the apparent mediumistic abilities displayed by John Edward (his show *Crossing Over* was at its peak at that time). She was surprised to learn that Edward had been scientifically tested by a psychologist at her own university, Dr. Gary Schwartz, as part of a pioneering study examining the efficacy of mediumship. Through a mutual acquaintance, she received a recommendation from Schwartz for another medium that he considered of similar ability to Edward. Beischel decided to have a sitting with her.

She was more than aware, however, that her emotions might well overwhelm any rational judgement of the sitting. As such, Beischel was determined to approach it as a scientist – so much so that she kicked herself for giving away information about herself when telling the medium over the phone that she would "drive *up* to Phoenix", as well as when she discussed her choice of clothing upon meeting in person.

Beischel was surprised when the sitting began with a number of pieces of very specific information – though in a negative way, as none were correct. But the medium seemed to warm to the task, going on to offer some interesting hints at communication from Beischel's grandmother, before hitting stride with phrases describing her mother including the suggestion that she "feels removed", had a "chemical imbalance", "can't express emotions" and "ingested pills". The medium then said that there was a Dalmation with her mother. "Does that makes sense?" she asked, only to be rebuked by Beischel's perhaps over-the-top skeptical attitude. "Well, sort of", Beischel responded. "Our dog was half-Dalmation and half-black Lab".

The medium followed up by piling on hit after hit. "In the course of those two hours, I was more or less convinced that my mother was still around and that she and my grandmother had spoken to me that day", Beischel remembers. "I systematically scored the reading and found that the percent accuracy was 93% for the items related to my mom". And she might not have even picked up on all the pertinent information: when Beischel later asked her aunts to provide a separate perspective on the 'presence' of her mother by judging the reading themselves, they scored items as accurate that hadn't made any sense to Beischel.

Intrigued by these 'impossible' results, Beischel met with Dr. Gary Schwartz to discuss her experience and find out more about his research. It resulted in a job offer: a post-doctoral fellowship in Schwartz's laboratory, studying mediums professionally. Beischel would go on to serve as co-director of the research program, experimenting with the mediums there for some four and a half years. And when the funding for that role expired she had become so fascinated by the topic that she co-founded her own organization in order to continue studying the topic: The Windbridge Institute for Applied Research in Human Potential.

If there truly is anything to mediumship, Beischel figured that at Windbridge she needed to optimize her chances of uncovering concrete evidence by testing only the best mediums that could be found. "If we wanted to study the phenomenon of high jumping, we would find some good high jumpers", she notes. "We wouldn't invite some people off the street into the lab and tell them, 'go jump over that bar'. When those people couldn't do it, we wouldn't have learned anything at all about high jumping. In mediumship research, we would select participants with a track (and field) record of reporting accurate information about the deceased".[44]

As such, Beischel and her research team have employed an extensive screening, training, and certification procedure that consists of eight steps, during which prospective mediums are firstly interviewed, and then tested to see if they can achieve a certain level of accuracy with their readings. Approximately 25% of applicants have been cut during this stage, though Beischel is unwilling to suggest that those mediums have no ability. "It only means that the readings they performed on those days…did not achieve the level of accuracy we require", she clarifies. Those that pass the testing stage are then put through a training schedule in which they learn about regulations governing research with human subjects, the history of modern research into mediumship, and grief. Once they have completed all the necessary steps – which, Beischel tells me, takes each medium several months to complete – the medium is then inducted as a 'Windbridge Certified Research Medium' (WCRM). At this time, Beischel has around 20 WCRMs available for research, a number that is perhaps limited by the fact that the entire cost for the screening, testing and training process can reach $10,000 per medium.

It should be noted, however, that the expenses incurred are in no way contributed to by fees charged by the mediums, as they all donate their time freely. "No money changes hands as part of the WCRM-Windbridge Institute relationship", Beischel affirms. "We do not pay them for participating in research and they do not pay us to screen and certify them". Instead – contrary to the much-propagated perception of mediums as money-hungry fraudsters – each Windbridge-certified medium donates at least four hours per month of their own time, submitting themselves to the spotlight of scientific testing, as well as agreeing to a code of ethics "which includes confidentiality regarding the content of readings and not performing readings outside of those specifically requested". Beischel makes clear that these mediums are willing, for the purposes of science, "to attempt experimental protocols that go well beyond their comfort zones" – for instance, in an upcoming psychophysiological study, part of the experiment will involve the drawing of blood for testing. "The WCRMs are scientifically-minded", she notes. "They have a genuine and personal interest in our research questions and are willing to volunteer their time to assist in answering them".

This close working relationship between mediums and researchers, however, does not mean that the testing process is relaxed. Beischel is clear that, in order to properly investigate the phenomenon, it is imperative that proper experimental controls are instituted where possible:

> We need to eliminate all the normal explanations for how the information the medium reports could be accurate. To rule out fraud, we have to make sure the medium can't look up information about the sitter or the deceased person online or in any other way. We also need to account for cold reading… To prevent that from happening, the medium will be what's called masked or blinded to the sitter. The medium won't be able to see, hear, smell, etc., the sitter during the reading: but, as stated above, the sitter should be involved somehow in order to optimize the environment, so we'll just make sure his intention is that his discarnate communicates with the medium. Now if I as the experimenter know things about the sitter or the discarnate during a reading, I could also cue the medium… So in our design, let's also blind me to the information about the

sitter and the discarnate… That just leaves the sitter. When a person reflects on the accuracy of a mediumship reading that he knows was intended for him his personality and psychology affect how he rates the statements. A person who is more laid-back and forgiving may score more of the items as accurate whereas someone more cynical and strict may only score a few as right. That phenomenon is called rater bias… To maintain blinding, the sitter won't be able to tell which reading is which… So, to account for fraud, cold reading, experimenter cueing, general statements, and rater bias, we…design an experiment in which the setting is similar to a normal mediumship reading but where the medium, the sitter, and the experimenter are all blinded.

Beischel and her team score sittings by both of the methods we've mentioned, item-by-item and also on the whole sitting. "I think the difference is one between statistical evidence and evidence that is meaningful to a sitter", she tells me. "A p-value won't convince a sitter of communication and a dazzle shot doesn't provide objective evidence that can be statistically analyzed. [So] in addition to item-by-item and whole reading scores, we also have raters choose which blinded readings they believe were intended for them so if one reading contains true dazzle shots but not a lot of other correct information, that may be reflected in the raters' choices".

So after going to all this trouble, what has Beischel learned about mediums? "When I applied the scientific method to the phenomenon of mediumship using optimal environments, maximum controls, and skilled participants", she states, "I was able to definitively conclude that certain mediums are able to report accurate and specific information about discarnates without using any normal means to acquire that information". The data from her experiments, she believes, effectively refute both the idea that mediums use normal, sensory means to find out information about the deceased, as well as the more controversial super-psi theory. "This leaves only communication with the deceased as a plausible explanation for the source of their information," Beischel claims – though she makes clear that she is open to revising her assertion as more data becomes available.

Her conclusion is, you can imagine, as controversial as it is worldview-shaking. But it is based directly on the data from her research: in a 2012 research brief on Windbridge's ongoing experiments with mediums,[45] 21 blind readings had been evaluated, with 16 of those 21 being correctly chosen by the sitters (76%), as well as scoring significantly on an item-by-item basis. Beischel is currently writing a paper reporting the positive results of her proof-based mediumship research, and is hoping that other labs begin the process of replicating her results in order to help solidify the case for mediumistic communication.

In fact, the evidence seems so strong to Beischel and her team at the Windbridge Institute that they have now moved beyond just seeking proof that mediumship works, and are looking into other aspects of the phenomenon. Their research is split into three strands, code-named 'Information', 'Operation' and 'Application': respectively, "proof-focused research" (finding evidence for survival of consciousness through mediums, the experiments we've just discussed), "process-focused research" (how mediumship works: the physiological, psychological and phenomenological aspects) and "social application research" (the impact mediumship has on people).

The latter area in particular is a current focus for Windbridge. Regardless of how mediumship works, Beischel notes, if it makes people feel better then it's worth investigating further. She cites the testimony of a sitter named Bill who had suffered the devastating loss of two sons. "This work has proven to me that we survive the death of our bodies", he told Beischel, "and has made my life not only bearable but worthwhile again". Another sitter testified that "the medium helped me manage the grief that has been with me for more than 20 years". And in a survey that asked

83 people to rate their levels of grief before and after sitting with a medium, the average score moved from slightly above "I felt a somewhat high level of grief" to slightly below "I felt a somewhat low, manageable level of grief".

But Julie Beischel recognizes anecdotes are not enough. "Although we have collected data from sitters who reported recalling dramatic reductions in their grief after past readings with mediums, this is far from conclusive", she points out to me. "We have begun a systematic investigation of whether mediumship readings are helpful in grief recovery". The Bereavement and Mediumship (BAM) Study is a trial at the Windbridge Institute that will examine the potential clinical benefits of personal mediumship readings. "Only with controlled research such as the BAM Study can we effectively determine if receiving mediumship readings is helpful, harmful, or neither for the bereaved", notes Beischel. She and her team have created a website for those looking to assist with the study,[46] and believe that if the results are positive, we may one day see credentialed mediums working together with licensed mental health professionals to help the bereaved manage their grief.

Given his familiarity with both mediumship and the grieving process, I ask Trevor Hamilton for his thoughts on the possibility that it might one day be used as a clinical tool to treat bereavement: "The relationship between a good sitting with a medium and the easing of grief is a complex one," he cautions, "and there is no way one can predict the result. [Our] first sitting which was so powerful and fluent (no fishing, no hesitation) made quite an impact on us. But the grief still has to be worked through regardless of the apparent evidence indicative of some form of survival". He does have great respect for Julie Beischel and her work, and what she has achieved on a modicum of funding. But, he says, "the relationship of mediumship to counselling is formally a minefield, even if informally some very useful and helpful relationships can be built up. How many counsellors and medical and psychiatric staff are prepared, for example, to acknowledge a level 5 Windbridge accredited medium and give the level 5 equal status with their own professional qualification?"

Nevertheless, the research being done at the Windbridge Institute seems a worthwhile effort in trying to better understand this neglected and often ridiculed field. And it continues to turn up interesting information. For example, around 90% of the mediums with Windbridge are female, a ratio that Beischel thinks accurately reflects the proportion of females to males in the ranks of practicing mediums in America. Furthermore, when researchers queried the current WCRMs about any health issues they had, it became clear that chronic medical problems were a serious concern for those with mediumistic talents. They had seven times the incidence of autoimmune disorders compared to the general US population; cases of diabetes were nearly twice the national prevalence; and the incidence of migraines in female WCRMs was almost two and a half times that of the average woman in the United States.

Also, as mentioned earlier, the Windbridge Institute's research has touched on the 'super-psi' problem. Some of their mediums reported that there were two entirely different 'feels' to performing mediumship readings versus performing psychic readings for the living. In response, Windbridge researchers set up a study in which mediums were provided with the first name of a target person at the start of a reading, some of whom were living while the others were deceased, though the medium and the experimenter were blinded to this knowledge. The medium then went on to answer questions about the target personality, and also completed a standardized questionnaire about his/her experiences during the reading. When these were analyzed, Julie Beischel informs me, "a statistically significant difference was found for blinded readings for living targets versus blinded readings for deceased targets". This gives credence to some mediums' opinion that they are not using telepathy or other 'psi' talents to acquire information about the deceased target. In short, Beischel says, "they know what psi feels like and mediumship feels different even under blinded conditions".

Beyond those discoveries however, the overall ramifications of positive results from research into mediumship by groups such as the Windbridge Institute – as well as other areas suggesting survival of consciousness – would be profound. Our entire approach to death would be forever changed: how we treat the dying (medically and socially), our grief at losing loved ones, and our own desire for physical immortality (and anxiety about our inevitable date with death).

But instead, this area of research has largely been ignored (and mediums themselves often ridiculed or attacked) even though there definitely seems to be something worth exploring further with smart, scientific research. "Mediumistic experiences are common and normal", Julie Beischel notes in her book *Among Mediums*. And yet "people who believe in phenomena like mediumship are labeled ignorant, gullible, or delusional, and the unfortunate individuals who experience mediumistic communication are called frauds, con-artists, schizophrenics, evil, or worse". Given the antipathy of skeptics and orthodox scientists toward the topic of mediumship, there is a sad irony to Beischel's final plea, asking for a more rational response to the possibility that consciousness survives the physical death of our body: "What if we calmed down, put aside our assumptions about how the world works, and actually applied the scientific method to the phenomenon of mediumship?"

Or as Emily Kelly and Dianne Arcangel so eloquently put it in the conclusion to their research paper:

> We hope that this study might suggest to readers that mediums are neither the infallible oracles that many people in the general public seem to believe they are, nor the frauds or imposters that many scientists assume they invariably are. The history of research on mediumship shows that the phenomenon should be taken seriously, and we hope that

the results of our study might encourage other scientists to do so.[47]

We can only hope that these types of study are the start of a new chapter in exploring the possibility of post-mortem communication through mediums.

FOUR

Broadening Our Horizons

Up to the Twentieth Century, reality was everything humans could touch, smell, see, and hear. Since the initial publication of the chart of the electromagnetic spectrum, humans have learned that what they can touch, smell, see, and hear is less than one-millionth of reality.

Buckminster Fuller

On September 13th, 1848, a stocky railroad construction foreman by the name of Phineas Gage was using a tamping iron to pack explosive powder in preparation for a blast, when the powder suddenly detonated. The force of the explosion thrust the 43-inch-long tamping iron violently upwards, where it encountered the flesh and bone of 25-year-old Gage's head. With its 1 inch diameter tapering to a point over the last 12 inches of its length, the 13 pound shaft speared into Gage's left cheek, pierced the top of his mouth, and continued on through the left side of his brain before exiting in its entirety through the top of his head and continuing on its way skyward.

Gage was knocked to the ground and was blinded in his left eye, but apart from that he miraculously survived this massive trauma to his brain – in fact, it is believed that he did not even lose consciousness. And as if that didn't earn him enough toughness points, it is said that when the physician arrived to treat his injuries, Gage greeted him, lucidly and calmly, with the words "Doctor, here is business enough for you".

While his survival alone might have been enough to guarantee him lasting fame, the reason Gage's name is remembered today is that the accident did have other effects, the most noticeable of which was a change in his personality. Despite previously being one of his employer's most trusted and capable foremen, his friends and family said he was now "no longer Gage", and the doctor treating him noted that Phineas would now utter gross profanities, could not follow through on plans, was impatient, obstinate, and showed "little deference" for others. After the railroad-construction company refused to take him back, Gage took a number of other jobs before dying in May 1860 after a series of seizures. He was just 36 years old.[1]

The influential story of Phineas Gage contributed to the development of the hypothesis that trauma to certain areas of the brain could cause changes in personality, and that certain areas of the brain therefore appear to perform individual roles (known as 'functional specialization') – after all, Gage's motor skills seemed to survive intact, so the inference was that his destroyed left frontal lobe was responsible for his personality, but not for moving his body around. As such, the case of Phineas Gage has often been embraced as a fine example of how the mind is produced by the brain, as Gage's 'mind' was severely disrupted by damage to the instrument that apparently 'produced' it. Change the brain, and you modify the mind. This is not a new idea: the ancient Roman philosopher Lucretius Carus argued against survival of consciousness after death some 2000 years ago by pointing out how diseases and blows to the head affect the mind.[2] I am myself all too familiar with the example of those suffering from Alzheimer's Disease, with the winking out of abilities as the illness progresses and gradually shuts down the individual functions of the brain. The straightforward conclusion taken by orthodox science from such examples is that the mind is entirely created by the brain.

Some doubt has recently been cast as to what degree Gage's personality actually changed, and for how long (some say he returned to a functional personality), but regardless of this there is a more important reason to challenge the 'production' theory of mind when based on cases such as that of Phineas Gage and illnesses including Alzheimer's Disease: it's bad logic. Such changes could also be accounted for just as easily by considering a 'transmission' model of mind. A modern analogy would be to consider the brain as a television. The signal is produced elsewhere, and a television on a certain channel will pick up that signal and display it on the screen. Throw a tamping iron through the television though, and its functioning will no doubt be compromised in some manner – but the original signal continues to exist. And, to extend the analogy to post-death, if you pull out the power cord of the television, never to power it up again, the signal again still remains.

The influential psychologist William James, who we met earlier when discussing the medium Leonora Piper, offered a different analogy as far back as 1898. "Everyone knows," James admitted, "that arrests of brain development occasion imbecility, that blows on the head abolish memory or consciousness, and that brain-stimulants and poisons change the quality of our ideas." But using the analogy of a pipe organ, James pointed out that its keys "have only a transmissive function" – they don't produce the air, just modify it into a certain form:

> They open successively the various pipes and let the wind in the air-chest escape in various ways. The voices of the various pipes are constituted by the columns of air trembling as they emerge. But the air is not engendered in the organ. The organ proper, as distinguished from its air-

chest, is only an apparatus for letting portions of it loose
upon the world in these peculiarly limited shapes.

James's thesis was that when we investigate the idea that thought
is simply a function of the brain, we should not only consider
productive function; "we are entitled also to consider permissive
or transmissive function". Embracing this alternative idea would
certainly provide an explanation for some of the strange phenomena
near the time of death that we have covered throughout this book.
Terminal lucidity, for example, could be accounted for by a mind
that disengages sufficiently from the diseased or injured parts of the
brain to exhibit normal function for a period of time.[3]

Similarly, a transmission theory of mind could possibly account
for the strange outcome of operations such as hemispherectomy,
in which one half of the brain is entirely removed. The incredible
result of this drastic surgery is often only specific impairment of
motor skills and vision, while the personality and memory of the
patient apparently remains intact and unaffected.[4] The same applies
to the anomalous brain scans of hydrocephalic patients undertaken
by Professor John Lorber in the 1970s and 1980s. He found that,
despite missing 95% or more of their brain tissue, around 30
individuals had a global IQ above 100. One was even a university
student with an above-average IQ of 126, who had completed a
degree in maths, despite having "virtually no brain". These findings
prompted Lorber to provoke fellow physicians with the question,
"Is your brain really necessary?"[5]

The question may have been asked (or is at least often taken)
facetiously. But could Lorber, in some sense, be correct?

Beyond the Umwelt

Transmission theories of mind are certainly a different way of
looking at the mystery of consciousness, but surely if consciousness

is floating about like electromagnetic waves, waiting for a brain to pick up the signal like a cerebral aerial, such 'waves' would have been detected and measured by now? Hubris in science is always a dangerous thing, and is perhaps best addressed by a famous Shakesperean quote. "There are more things in heaven and earth, Horatio, than are dreamt of in your philosophy", the Bard wrote so many centuries ago, and the sentiment still resonates in the modern age – especially when it comes to the question of consciousness, given how some scientists have suggested it may be a fundamental aspect of the universe.

For example, it has been pointed out by a number of thinkers that up until recent centuries, 'reality' was restricted to things that humans could experience via the five senses, but in recent years scientific knowledge of what exists beyond our senses has expanded tremendously. Neuroscientist David Eagleman is clear on the matter, noting that humans really "don't have a strong grasp of what reality 'out there' even is, because we detect such an unbearably small slice of it". Eagleman uses the German word *umwelt* – meaning "environment" or "surroundings" – to describe that tiny slice of reality that we are aware of, and that we often mistakenly assume is the entirety of existence:

> Each organism presumably assumes its *umwelt* to be the entirety of objective reality. Until a child learns that honeybees enjoy ultraviolet signals and rattlesnakes see infrared, it is not obvious that plenty of information is riding on channels to which we have no natural access. In fact, the part of the electromagnetic spectrum visible to us is less than a ten-trillionth of it. Our sensorium is enough to get by in our ecosystem, but no better.[6]

The expansion of our *umwelt* in the past couple of centuries has been dramatic, based on numerous jumps forward in our knowledge of the cosmos, from the atomic to galactic scales. Do we have the hubris to think that we have now discovered all there is to find? Or could a new level of scientific knowledge, one which incorporates consciousness as a fundamental part of the cosmos, be around the corner? As we saw in the introduction, there are a number of world-class scientists who believe that may be the case. Professor Paul Davies thinks it unlikely that mind was just "a lucky fluke of biological evolution", given the way it is linked to the inner workings of the cosmos, suggesting "that there is something truly fundamental and literally cosmic in the emergence of sentience".

Another theoretical physicist, Professor Andrei Linde, has wondered whether we could investigate the possibility "that consciousness may exist by itself, even in the absence of matter, just like gravitational waves, excitations of space, may exist in the absence of protons and electrons?"[7] He points out that we should perhaps keep the previous history of scientific discoveries in mind when considering consciousness. "Prior to the invention of the general theory of relativity," he notes, "space, time, and matter seemed to be three fundamentally different entities...[Einstein's] general theory of relativity brought with it a decisive change in this point of view. Spacetime and matter were found to be interdependent, and there was no longer any question which one of the two is more fundamental".[8]

If we consider the current orthodox assumptions about consciousness in the same way, it may be that we will one day find that *they* were flawed. "The standard assumption is that consciousness, just like spacetime before the invention of general relativity, plays a secondary, subservient role, being just a function of matter and a tool for the description of the truly existing material world," Linde notes. "[But] could it be that consciousness is an equally important part of the consistent picture of our world?"[9] But through what sort of mechanism would the stuff of mind interact with the world of matter? It is at this point that we cannot help but explore the mysteries of the quantum world.

Quantum Weirdness

As noted in the introduction of this book, at the level of quantum physics consciousness suddenly appears to be of fundamental importance in the 'creation' of reality: it is not until the process of observation that the particles upon which the physical world is constructed solidify ('collapse') from a probabilistic cloud of possibilities ('quantum superposition') into concrete existence – an attribute which appears to "deny the existence of a physically real world independent of our observation of it", according to some physicists.[10] Now, I feel compelled here to add a cautionary note: many modern writers, especially in the New Age genre, have seized – despite having minimal knowledge of the field – on the strange elements of quantum theory and its links to consciousness to produce all manner of nonsensical 'quantum woo', as skeptics have derisively named it. Indeed, in the words of one scientist, "presenting this material to nonscientists is the intellectual equivalent of allowing children to play with loaded guns".[11] There is no doubt good reason to criticize much of this sort of nonsense, and I'm extremely wary of committing the same sin myself. But we should also be careful not to throw the baby out with the proverbial bathwater, because there *are* a number of experts on the topic who see more of a mystery here than many orthodox-leaning scientists and skeptics would have us believe. Indeed, physicists Bruce Rosenblum and Fred Kuttner describe the requirement of consciousness in quantum mechanics as physics' "embarrassing skeleton in the closet".[12] According to acclaimed physicist Anton Zeilinger the notion of a reality independent of us is "obviously wrong".[13] More plainly, one of the founders of quantum theory, Werner Heisenberg, cautioned that "some physicists would prefer to come back to the idea of an objective real world whose smallest parts exist objectively in the same sense as stones or trees exist independently of whether we observe them. This however is impossible".[14] And another of the original pioneers of the quantum, Max Planck, stated clearly the conclusion that the new physics had led him to:

> I regard consciousness as fundamental. I regard matter as derivative from consciousness. We cannot get behind consciousness. Everything that we talk about, everything that we regard as existing, postulates consciousness.[15]

Furthermore, if we look around, it quickly becomes evident that there are a number of outstanding scientists and thinkers who have put forward interesting ideas about how the quantum world offers a way for mind to manifest in the physical brain. It would, therefore, be foolish for us not to at least discuss them as possibilities (a quick note: doing so will require *some* technical/scientific terminology; if that's not your cup of tea, please don't fret or put down the book, as it is only a brief exploration).

One of those scientists is the distinguished physicist Professor Henry Stapp. He too has noted that the determinism of Newtonian physics still exerts a dominant influence over many fields of science – including consciousness studies and philosophical questions regarding free will – despite that model of physics having been superseded a century ago. "Most quantum physicists", Stapp notes, "have been reluctant even to try to construct an ontology compatible with the validity of the massively validated pragmatic quantum rules involving our causally efficacious conscious thoughts." As such, influential intellectuals often pretend to speak for science, Stapp says, on the basis of the "grotesquely inadequate old scientific theory" of Newtonian physics.[16]

> [T]he scientific ideas that prevailed from the time of Isaac Newton to the beginning of the twentieth century proclaimed your physical actions to be completely determined by processes that are describable in physical terms alone. Any notion that your conscious choices make a difference in how

you behave was branded an illusion: you were asserted to be causally equivalent to a mindless automaton.

The conflating of Nature herself with the impoverished mechanical conception of it invented by scientists during the seventeenth century has derailed the philosophies of science and of mind for more than three centuries, by effectively eliminating the causal link between the psychological and physical aspects of nature that contemporary physics restores.

But the now-falsified classical conception of the world still exerts a blinding effect. For example, Daniel Dennett says that his own thinking rests on the idea that "a brain was always going to do what it was caused to do by current, local, mechanical circumstances". But by making that judgment he tied his thinking to the physical half of Cartesian dualism, or its child, classical physics, and thus was forced in his book *Consciousness Explained* to leave consciousness out, as he himself admits, and tries to justify, at the end of the book.[17]

As a consequence of this incorrect belief pervading academia, Stapp laments, modern society is built upon a "fundamentally false", deterministic conception of reality in which consciousness is seen as an incidental byproduct of brain processes, and humans are thus seen as the flesh and blood equivalent of mechanical automata. This out-dated model of reality lies "like the plague on Western culture, robbing its citizens of any rational basis for self-esteem or self-respect, or esteem or respect for others", while on the other hand the modern science of quantum physics "brings our human minds squarely into the dynamical workings of nature...the responsibility that accompanies the power to decide things on the basis of one's own thoughts, ideas, and judgments is laid upon us [leading] naturally and correctly to a concomitant elevation in the dignity of our persons and the meaningfulness of our lives".[18]

But of particular interest to our discussion of the brain as a possible receptor of consciousness is Stapp's theory of 'quantum consciousness', in which mind, as a fundamental element of the cosmos, interacts with the matter of the physical world at the quantum level within our brains – specifically, at the level of calcium ions, which have been found to trigger the release of neurotransmitters between synapses in the brain – via conscious intent.[19] By making the conscious decision to do something, we collapse the smear of possibilities of the calcium ions into a particular manifestation, and by other quantum effects can then maintain that brain state until our conscious intent has been achieved. Thus, rather than humans being subject to the random 'bouncing of billiard balls' in a clockwork universe, our conscious intent becomes the driving force behind changes in our reality.

Additionally, despite personally being a skeptic of the idea of an afterlife, Stapp believes there *is* enough accumulated evidence for 'something' going on (reports of NDEs, death-bed visions and so on) for the topic to be worthy of open scientific debate. He draws a parallel with the change of paradigm brought on by Copernicus's heliocentric theory, noting that – despite his personal views – he doesn't wish to be seen as one of the "doubters who refused to look through Galileo's telescope". So as a thought experiment, he decided to see if – assuming the collected evidence for survival of consciousness does point at something beyond the current paradigm – the idea of an afterlife could be reconciled with contemporary science. Taking into consideration the laws of quantum physics and the philosophy of mind, Stapp came to the stunning conclusion that "aspects of a personality might be able to survive bodily death and persist for a while as an enduring mental entity...capable on rare occasions of reconnecting with the physical world".[20] Contrary to the opinion of materialist-leaning scientists and atheist pundits, he found that survival of consciousness after the death of the physical body was within the bounds of science as we currently understand it. "I do not see any compelling theoretical reason why this idea could not be reconciled with the precepts of quantum mechanics," Stapp states.[21] In a paper titled "Compatibility of Contemporary Physical Theory with Personality Survival", he sums up the take-away message in these words:

> [S]trong doubts about personality survival based *solely* on the belief that postmortem survival is incompatible with the laws of physics are unfounded. Rational science-based opinion on this question must be based on the content and quality of the empirical data, not on a presumed incompatibility of such phenomena with our contemporary understanding of the workings of nature.[22]

According to Stapp, his interpretation of quantum mechanics would both "allow our conscious efforts to influence our own bodily actions, and also allow certain purported phenomena such as 'possession', 'mediumship', and 'reincarnation' to be reconciled with the basic precepts of contemporary physics".[23]

Another scientist who has voiced a similar opinion is anaesthesiologist Dr. Stuart Hameroff, who along with renowned scientist Sir Roger Penrose has proposed another theory of 'quantum consciousness' (though it should be noted that the Penrose/Hameroff theory of quantum consciousness is at odds on various points with Stapp's theory). Penrose and Hameroff hypothesize that consciousness arises at the quantum level within structures inside brain neurons known as microtubules.

With his clean-shaven head, goatee and easy-going mannerisms, Hameroff might at first glance seem more likely to be a biker or a construction worker. However, once he begins talking, jumping effortlessly between complex concepts ranging from neurobiology to quantum physics – often leaving a layman like myself in his wake – you begin to believe that he may have come up with a way to integrate multiple scientific threads into a solid theory of consciousness (a conversation with Hameroff includes lines like "megahertz coherence, quantum conductance, and topological qubits in microtubules at room temperature…very exciting work!").

Hameroff, like Stapp, agrees that it makes sense to look for quantum theories of consciousness. "Quantum mechanics has a crisis in that the measurement problem is unresolved," he tells me. "Why don't we see superpositions in our perceived world? None of the usual explanations make any sense". He notes that Henry Stapp favours the explanation that consciousness *causes* collapse of the wave function, but Hameroff feels that by doing so the acclaimed physicist "puts consciousness outside science", whereas his and Penrose's theory "puts consciousness in science, precisely at the instant of (self-) collapse". Nevertheless, Hameroff's ideas still certainly challenge the mainstream scientific view of how consciousness emerges:

> The prevalent paradigm is that brain neurons (nerve cells) and synapses (connections between nerve cells) act like bits and switches in computers, that consciousness is essentially computation, essentially no different (except in degree of complexity) from what is happening in your laptop.
>
> Microtubules are the structural components inside neurons, part of the cell cytoskeleton. But in addition to being bony girders, they seem to also process information – the nervous system within each cell. The Penrose-Hameroff quantum consciousness hypothesis proposes that quantum computations in microtubules inside the brain's neurons convert pre/subconscious possibilities (manifest as dream-like quantum information) to particular information (choices, perceptions) by a type of quantum state reduction, or collapse of the wave

function. The reduction itself – an instantaneous event connected to the fundamental level of reality, as suggested by Penrose – is a conscious moment. A sequence of such moments gives our stream of consciousness.

The Penrose-Hameroff theory of quantum consciousness began its life under heavy attack from skeptics, most often based on the presumption that delicate quantum effects could not occur in warm, wet biological tissue. But in the intervening decade or so, there have been a number of discoveries in the field of 'quantum biology' that appear to have diminished the gravity of that criticism. For example, recent studies have identified quantum effects being used by plants during the light-harvesting stage of photosynthesis. And Hameroff is excited by developments related to these discoveries which seem to offer significant support for his own theory, such as recently conducted experiments which found quantum effects in microtubules that are almost identical to the mechanism for quantum coherence in photosynthesis proteins. Additionally, a group of researchers in Japan found quantum resonances in microtubules,[24] while another group has shown that general anaesthetics selectively erase consciousness by acting on microtubules.[25] Meanwhile, says Hameroff, "conventional approaches [to consciousness] continue to flounder". He and Penrose continue to modify the details of their theory as new discoveries are made, though the central core has not only remained intact, but now seems more likely than ever. "The future's so bright we gotta wear shades", he jokes to me.

When I first spoke to Hameroff about this topic almost a decade ago, I asked him the rather controversial question of whether his 'quantum consciousness' hypothesis might provide a model for explaining anomalous phenomena such as the near-death experience. His answer at that time surprised me, given his qualifications and standing in the medical and scientific community. "I would say possibly yes," Hameroff replied without blinking. Expanding on his initial short answer, he explained further in more technical terms: "Under normal circumstances consciousness occurs in the fundamental level of spacetime geometry confined in the brain. But when the metabolism driving quantum coherence (in microtubules) is lost, the quantum information leaks out to the spacetime geometry in the universe at large. Being holographic and entangled it doesn't dissipate. Hence consciousness (or dream-like subconsciousness) can persist". Perhaps more surprising to me though is that in the intervening ten or so years since he first told me this, Hameroff's opinion has not changed: he still thinks the mind may well be able to 'break free' of the physical brain.

Now, if you're like me, between the neurobiology and the quantum physics that are involved, a lot of these concepts are a bit hard to grasp. But my point in presenting these cutting edge ideas about consciousness, and the possibility that it might survive the physical death of our body, is simply to make clear that – beyond the orthodox view of the mind-brain relationship – there are well-respected scientists out there who have alternative hypotheses, and see them as possible solutions to the impasse that has been reached in our (lack of) understanding of the 'hard problem' of consciousness. When I ask Stuart Hameroff why many 'orthodox' scientists not only dismiss any possibility of consciousness being an important element of the cosmos, but will often actively make fun of the idea and those investigating it, he is blunt in his assessment. "They are trying to protect their turf as the high priests of knowledge," he says. "There have not been any developments minimizing the role of consciousness that I'm aware of. Just the opposite".

When You Assume, You Make An...

Just as we should be wary of assuming that our *umwelt* encompasses the entirety of 'reality', so too should we be careful not to just embrace a few models of consciousness that seem likely based on our current scientific knowledge, simply in an attempt to satiate our appetite for theories. Similarly, we should be careful of falling into the trap of thinking about an afterlife existence based on the religious or cultural models we have been brought up with. Most people who were exposed to some sort of religion in their upbringing are imprinted with the fairly simplistic idea that surviving death means a transparent, ethereal version of you floats 'up' to a heaven of fluffy clouds, and lives there for eternity in happiness. Who knows, perhaps elements of this are correct – some of the experiences that we've mentioned in this book actually do correlate in some respects with these ideas. But perhaps also these experiences are filtered through an overlay of our own expectations and cultural beliefs, and the 'true' experience could be fundamentally different. It's fun to consider some of these possibilities.

For example, the standard belief is that it is 'us' that moves on to the afterlife realm. But perhaps the true self is the mind or consciousness that originates from that other realm, and who we are in the material realm is a transient, modified version, constricted by the requirements of existence in the physical world. This is a more specific aspect of the transmission theory of consciousness, often referred to as 'filter' or 'permission' theory. Whereas 'transmission' suggests "faithful conveyance from one place to another", these alternative terms represent the possible "selection, narrowing, and loss" that might occur when mind is filtered through the physical brain.[26] As the celebrated writer Aldous Huxley remarked in his classic *The Doors of Perception*...

...each one of us is potentially Mind at Large. But in so far as we are animals, our business is at all costs to survive. To make biological survival possible, Mind at Large has to be funneled through the reducing valve of the brain and nervous system. What comes out at the other end is a measly trickle of the kind of consciousness which will help us to stay alive on the surface of this particular planet.

Another possibility could be, as the philosopher C.D. Broad suggested, that mind and matter combine to form a third substance with its own intrinsic properties, like the formation of salt from the atoms sodium and chlorine. The compound can at some point be dissolved into its constituent elements again, but while engaged with each other the elements act as one unit with its own unique properties.[27] Alternatively, author Alan Gauld has put forward the analogy of consciousness as possibly being similar to a parasite, attached to a host (the physical brain/body), which suffers when the host gets ill and eventually disengages when it can no longer support it. We think of our identity in terms of our physical body, but is it just something that we – as only a consciousness – simply use as a vehicle? These are interesting ideas, at the very least as thought experiments to help us understand there are more possibilities than we sometimes realize.

The way our view of an external realm 'beyond reality' can change is illustrated well by the science fiction blockbuster *The Matrix*, with Neo taking the red pill and 'waking up' into the 'real' world, despite having thought until that point that the computer-generated Matrix was the real world. Before the age of computers the idea that we might be inside some sort of virtual reality, with the 'real us' residing in another realm, was barely known. Certainly, versions of this idea existed before the computer age, notably in discussions of the strange world of dreams. For example, the ancient Chinese philosopher Zhuangzi once remarked on the difficulty of distinguishing where 'reality' lies with the following words: "Once upon a time, I dreamt I was a butterfly, fluttering hither and thither, to all intents and purposes a butterfly. I was conscious only of my happiness as a butterfly, unaware that I was Chou. Soon I awaked, and there I was, veritably myself again. Now I do not know whether I was then a man dreaming I was a butterfly, or whether I am now a butterfly, dreaming I am a man".

The influential 17th century philosopher René Descartes also wondered how we could actually *know* what reality is, given that our senses can be so unreliable, and yet it is only through these senses (and then subsequent interpretation by the brain) that we comprehend the world 'out there'. Descartes deduced that all we can be sure of about 'reality' is just one thing – that if we think, then we must in some way exist, at the very least as just a mind. He summarized this view with his well-known maxim *'cogito ergo sum'* ('I think, therefore I am'). Beyond that, for all we know, we could just be a 'brain in a vat' – a piece of meat hooked up to sensors that trick our mind into thinking it is undergoing experiences in a virtual world. The fact that all of our sensorial experience of 'reality' must necessarily be filtered subjectively through the brain – and thus isn't 'reality' at all (for example, we apprehend the world very differently to an infrared-sensing rattlesnake) – was enunciated in Hindu culture via the term *maya* (illusion): the idea that we can never identify or comprehend the actual truth or reality of the world, only (at best) a fragment of it.

But in the 21st century, the 'simulation argument' – the suggestion that all of what we think of as 'reality' is actually a simulation, and that until now we have been unaware of the fact – has gone mainstream. Not only through the popularity of *The Matrix,* but through first-hand experience: many computer gamers now spend several hours a day immersed in the virtual worlds of first-person shooters. Given the speed of technological development, it no longer seems impossible that one day a computer might be able to be hooked up directly to our brain, and be able to 'trick' us into thinking we are in another world. In fact Nick Bostrom, Professor of Philosophy at Oxford University, has said that he feels there is about "a 20 percent chance we're living in a computer simulation".[28] Meanwhile, physicist Frank Tipler believes that, through extrapolation of the laws of physics, it is inevitable that the sentient beings of the far distant future will be virtually omnipotent, given the likely scale of information processing at that time. This 'Omega Point', as Tipler terms it, will be a time in which such beings will be able to 'see' the future, as well as all of history up until that point, which will allow them to 'resurrect', within a virtual universe, every being that has lived.[29] Certainly a different type of 'heaven' than we normally contemplate...

The small selection of ideas outlined above range all the way from 'plausible' to 'what the hell were they smoking?'. My point in mentioning them, however, is to show that our everyday assumptions about the world – as per the current orthodox scientific *and* religious views – may be only part of the picture, or perhaps even largely wrong. At any point in history until now, our assumptions about both ourselves, and the cosmos, have often been incorrect. For example, for thousands of years up until the 16th century, most people believed our Sun, the planets and the heavenly sphere rotated around the Earth – and though it now seems silly, it was actually common-sense based on their observations and the knowledge they had available to them at that time; from the human frame of reference, we do indeed appear to remain still, while the heavenly bodies rotate around us across the sky. We should therefore be careful in assuming that any of our current views are correct – from a belief in a God that will resurrect us once dead, through to thinking that we're simply meat puppets of little to no significance to the cosmos.

What cannot be denied, however, is the power of science in leading us to better ideas. Science should not be discarded just because we don't like what it is telling us. In the last few centuries we have discovered an enormous amount through the use of rational thinking and the scientific method (although as the eminent American physicist John Archibald Wheeler once remarked, "As our island of knowledge grows, so does the shore of our ignorance"). But we should also be careful of the dangerous assumption that what we know now is the limit of knowledge, or at least that we have most things correct and only need to finesse the details from here. Such assumptions have resulted in some genuine scientists becoming outcasts simply due to the 'fringe' topics that they research, even though they believe in the efficacy of science and that it is the correct tool for the job. Dr. Sam Parnia is unequivocal in his opinion on the role science can play in exploring the question of what happens to consciousness at the time of death. "I see no reason why a priest should tell us about death," he states, "when we have all this technology available".[30]

However, we should also be careful not to get so carried away with our desire for undeniable evidence that we diminish people's personal opinion or worldview. We all make our best guess at how the world works from the evidence we have at hand – truly, none of us know the ultimate truth. And if there *is* a 'next world', it may well be that our science applies to it as much as it might apply to the 'true world' beyond a virtual reality. All we can do is use science to its limits in order to present ourselves with the best models of reality that we can construct – although perhaps we should be a little more open to integrating that science with the testimony of those that claim to have caught a glimpse from a 'Peak in Darien'.

But you shouldn't need me to tell you this. Some two and a half thousand years ago, the great Greek philosopher Plato illustrated the issue perfectly with his Allegory of the Cave, a fictional dialogue between his mentor Socrates and his brother Glaucon. The former asks the latter to consider the scenario of a group of prisoners held within a cave since childhood, chained so that they cannot move even their heads; they face away from the cave's entrance and can see only a wall before them. Behind them at a distance a fire blazes, and between them and the fire is a raised walkway over which passes a parade of various figures. As such, the prisoners can see only their own shadows and the shadows of those that pass over the walkway behind them; any sounds they hear echo off the wall, and thus appear to come from the shadow of the figure making the sound. "To them", says Socrates, "the truth would be literally nothing but the shadows of the images".

Then Socrates ask Glaucon to consider the scenario where one of the prisoners was released: "At first, when any of them is liberated and compelled suddenly to stand up and turn his neck round and walk and look towards the light, he will suffer sharp pains; the glare will distress him, and he will be unable to see the realities of which in his former state he had seen the shadows; and then conceive someone saying to him, that what he saw before was an illusion, but that now, when he is approaching nearer to being and his eye is turned towards more real existence, he has a clearer vision". Though the objects he now sees are the 'real objects', and not a shadow illusion, Socrates notes that the prisoner might well instead think that what he sees before him is an hallucination, given that they are beyond anything he has previously witnessed.

Led up and out of the cave into the open world beyond, Socrates then notes that though the emancipated prisoner would be initially blinded by the light, he would eventually grow accustomed to the 'upper world', and at some point would witness his own true body and realize he is more than a shadow. He would likely also, says Socrates, now understand that the 'wisdom' of the cave prisoners was clearly flawed and pitiable, and have great disdain for any among them who seemed to be the best at observing and making predictions about the shadows, given their illusory quality.

And if a prisoner were to return to the cave, Socrates notes, his vision would no longer be suited to the land of shadows – so much so that the prisoners still there might mock him: "Men would say of him that up he went and down he came without his eyes; and that it was better not even to think of ascending; and if any one tried to loose another and lead him up to the light, let them only catch the offender, and they would put him to death".

Any one who has common sense will remember that the bewilderments of the eyes are of two kinds, and arise from two causes, either from coming out of the light or from going into the light, which is true of the mind's eye, quite as much as of the bodily eye; and he who remembers this when he sees any one whose vision is perplexed and weak, will not be too ready to laugh; he will first ask whether that soul of man has come out of the brighter light, and is unable to see because unaccustomed to the dark, or having turned from darkness to the day is dazzled by excess of light.

Compare Plato's allegory with the near-death experience – NDErs are taken out of 'the cave', shown things that make no sense to their usual perceptions (consider the reports of 360° vision for example), and upon their return are unable to communicate what they've seen to others in the shadow language of the cave world (the ineffable nature of the experience). All they can say is they *know* what they saw was 'real'...more real than the shadows at least. In the cave, however, they are regarded as "bewildered", and laughed at. I'm sure many near-death experiencers would relate well to this allegory.

In short, the message we should take from Plato's allegorical tale is simple: while we should employ science and critical thinking to get as close as we can to understanding what 'reality' is, we should also always keep in mind that we may still, even in the 21st century, have the barest comprehension of the truth. For as J.B.S. Haldane once remarked, "my own suspicion is that the Universe is not only queerer than we suppose, but queerer than we *can* suppose".

FIVE

Memento Mori

I'll tell you a secret. Something they don't teach you in your temple. The gods envy us. They envy us because we're mortal, because any moment might be our last. Everything is more beautiful because we're doomed. You will never be lovelier than you are now. We will never be here again.

Achilles, in the movie *Troy*

On December 29th, 2012, during the writing of this book, I had my own brush with death. Out in the garden with my son, I was stung on the ear by a wasp that took exception to me getting too close to its nest. No stranger to the occasional wasp sting, I went inside our house to grab some ice to put on the minor wound, but thought little more about it. Around five minutes later, however, I noticed a darkening around the edges of my vision, followed by the odd taste of metal in my mouth, as if I was chewing on a handful of rusted nails. Under the assumption that it was connected to the wasp sting, I walked to the computer and typed "wasp sting metallic taste" into Google, and was faced with a barrage of results that nearly all mentioned "allergy" and "anaphylaxis". I immediately went to tell my wife, making sure

I looked completely calm when I told her "honey, I think I'm having reaction to a wasp sting"...before immediately collapsing into unconsciousness, going into seizures and vomiting up pretty much the entire contents of my digestive system.

My wife called for an ambulance (we got two for our trouble), which arrived some fifteen minutes later. Finding my pulse to be under 40 beats per minute and my blood pressure sitting at around 45/25, the situation at that stage – as the attending paramedics told me later – was "pretty dire". But through the administration of various procedures, including injections of epinephrine and atropine, they revived me to a (barely) conscious state, to a point where I was stable enough to be transferred to hospital. Though my pulse stayed low for most of the night, within twelve hours I was for the most part back to normal everyday health...a rather surreal adventure.

So what amazing experience did I undergo during my excursion to the boundary of life and death? The answer, unfortunately, is absolutely nothing. I remember thinking to myself as I was slipping into unconsciousness "we haven't even called an ambulance yet...I'm not going to survive this"; the very next thing I remember (groggily) is a paramedic cutting my shirt open and asking me questions, some 15 to 20 minutes later. As much as I would have loved to have come back with the perfect anecdote to round out the book I was writing, I didn't. No out-of-body experience, no tunnel, no gates of heaven, no deceased loved ones. Just a quarter of an hour of 'lost time'.

This is par for the course for me though – despite my interest in these topics, my own life has been about as un-paranormal as anyone's could be. But I'm not foolish enough to conclude from my own experiences (or more accurately, lack of them) that these things don't happen to others. For beyond all the accounts that I've come across in my research, there is also no shortage of anecdotes that I've heard directly from family members, people whose honesty I don't doubt. My father, as the progression of

Alzheimer's Disease began to seriously affect his neural processes, reported to us that he had experienced visions of two close friends who had died, who were inviting him to come with them. One of my aunts, fighting for her life due to a problem with her heart, lay in bed grasping desperately at what she said was a rope being thrown to her by her brother, who had died about a year previously, and who she said was at that moment standing at the foot of her bed. My paternal grandmother, a straight-laced woman from Northern Ireland, almost died in hospital at one point from an abscess on her pancreas, the situation being so desperate that the doctor slept on a bed beside her for two nights. The morning after, she said that a black coach pulled by six black horses had come to a halt beside her, with the request that she hop aboard – a request that she refused. My maternal grandmother, after losing a lot of blood during childbirth, told how a man in a white suit, with white hair and beard, had appeared asking her to go with him – she also refused. Decades later, after the death of her husband, she reported seeing and interacting with an apparition of him at their family home some 18 months after he had passed away; he told her not to worry because everything was okay, that she couldn't go with him yet as she had a purpose to fulfil and wouldn't die for quite some time yet (she lived for another 35 years). And a medium was once telling my younger sister about a number of things still to happen in her future, when she suddenly changed track midway through the reading to say that, as they spoke, a woman in my sister's life "with dark or black hair" was crying. The only person matching that description to my sister was our mother, though she told the medium that she doubted very much that would be the case (our mother, being a stockwoman in northern Australia, is not the crying type, so this seemed unlikely). But when my sister laughed to Mum about it later, making fun of the fact that the medium had suggested this, she was surprised to find that our mother actually had been crying and very upset at that exact time, as she had just been told that her brother-in-law was terminally ill. Combined with a number of other stresses, she had collapsed into tears at the exact time (2.30pm) that the medium had told my sister that she could see this happening.

As you can see, even in my own family there have been numerous experiences similar to the ones we've covered in this book. Furthermore, when I announced that I was writing this book, readers of my website emailed me from around the globe, sharing their own personal accounts. And this is a point worth making: despite being considered a fringe topic to science, everyday people from all over the world have these types of experiences *regularly*. In each chapter of this book I've mentioned just a few interesting cases, but if you delve into the literature the number is overwhelming, and it is difficult to transmit the convincing effect that taking in all of this information through years of reading has on an individual. And those researchers who have taken the time to consider all this evidence, generally come to the same view. "None of these stories about NDEs are controlled studies, they're all just anecdotes," Dr. Bruce Greyson has noted, "but I would say that if you combine all the phenomena from NDEs, with all the data from mediumship cases...and put all these things together, the most parsimonious explanation is that some aspect of the human body survives death". Likewise, Julie Beischel told me that "if you consider the numerous modes of studying the afterlife – near death experiences, children who remember past lives, mediumship, etc. – and the body of data collected, it is difficult to claim that nothing is going on". Dr. Sam Parnia, who is usually extremely careful not to commit to any particular conclusion, says that "all we can say now is that the data suggests that consciousness is not annihilated [at the time of death]".[1] In the Australian study of palliative care nurses, all of those interviewed spoke of becoming convinced by these cases of "something else that happens" beyond death; that there is "more out there than any of us really understand".[2] As noted earlier, Edmund Gurney felt it was impossible to transmit in print form the convincing nature of talking directly to those who had experienced 'coincidental' visions of the dying. Janice Holden, after surveying cases of veridical perception during NDEs, gave her opinion that "the cumulative weight of these narratives" should be enough to "convince most skeptics that these reports are something more than than mere hallucinations on the patient's part". William James, in a letter to an old friend of his father discussing his mediumship research, conveyed the profound and disorienting change in perspective that can take place once we engage with the actual evidence:

> I have hitherto felt as if the wondermongers and magnetic physicians and seventh sons of seventh daughters and those who gravitated towards them by mental affinity were a sort of intellectual vermin. I now begin to believe that that type of mind takes hold of a range of truths to which the other kind is stone blind. The consequence is that I am all at sea, with my old compass lost, and no new one, and the stars invisible through the fog.[3]

It certainly does seem that plenty of people who have engaged with the topic enough to gain an appreciation of the evidence, both for and against, lean toward the 'survival of consciousness' conclusion. Your mileage, of course, may vary. We all come to the topic with our own data, with our own biases, and our own desires. And that is absolutely fine. I think as long as we truly look at the evidence, and try to be as honest with ourselves as possible, then whatever conclusion we come to has to be respected. Though hopefully, as I said at the beginning of this book, any conclusions will always be tentative and amenable to being revised.

As for those who have actually undergone what seems to be a genuine paranormal experience, it's difficult to sway them away from the conviction that there is some sort of afterlife –

for example, in a survey of all the cases they have on hand, the Division of Perceptual Studies at the University of Virginia found that 82% of NDErs said that their experience had *convinced* them of survival after death.[4] Given the nature of their experience, to tell them otherwise seems akin to telling Jodie Foster's character Ellie Arroway in the movie *Contact* that what she witnessed was an hallucination, based on the contradiction between the duration of what she claimed to have experienced, and the split-second of time that elapsed to external observers.

But perhaps, by studying certain elements of these experiences in a scientific manner, we *can* somehow get a feel for where the truth may lie – to continue with the *Contact* analogy, such efforts might include studying the length of the video recorded *within* Ellie's capsule. In research into the afterlife hypothesis, we have studies such as the AWARE program's attempt to verify the accounts of out-of-body experiences, and scientific investigation into the validity of the information provided by mediums to sitters. But looking at the entire field of study, we cannot ignore that we have multiple areas concerning death where there seems to be evidence pointing to the same thing. People dying see deceased loved ones appearing at their death-bed, while carers and family often report strange phenomena including lights, sounds, and visions of the dead; people returning from the threshold of death report an afterlife realm; and communication through mediums also offers suggestions of the same post-death destination. Within these individual fields we find further evidence that the mind (or soul, if you like) is a separate entity to our physical body: Peak-in-Darien cases, accounts of veridical OBEs, multiple witnesses of strange phenomena at the death-bed, crisis apparitions coinciding with the time of death, and mediums reporting similar elements to the dying process as those reported during NDEs. Taking all these in total, it seems it would be an amazing coincidence that all of these strange elements just happen to point to the same thing. Skeptics often put forward Occam's Razor – commonly paraphrased as 'the simplest explanation is often the correct one' – as a good tool for getting at the truth of the matter. When taking in total all the evidence from these various fields, it's worth contemplating that the afterlife solution may be the most simplest to explain it all. However at this point there is no unimpeachable evidence to tell us either way whether consciousness survives death – and there may never be. Perhaps we do live in a Total Perspective Vortex, and physical death truly is the end of us – though again, we have no authoritative evidence for that conclusion either. When it comes to trying to find evidence for a world beyond our own – a world which, if it even exists, may not play by the same scientific rules as the physical world – we may be taking part in an unwinnable game. Perhaps, then, we need to let go of this at times debilitating need for certainty, and just have to make our best call based on the evidence at hand.

Regardless of our view though, I think it's important that we recognise the profound effects of the strange experiences we've discussed in this book, and that they are a legitimate, and quite often helpful, part of the dying process. As one NDEr wrote, "It is outside my domain to discuss something that can only be proven by death. However, for me personally this experience was decisive in convincing me that consciousness endures beyond the grave. Death turned out to be not death, but another form of life".[5] Peter Fenwick found that those who had a death-bed experience while dying "underwent a change of mood from agitation and distress to peaceful acceptance".[6] A woman who was part of a Peak-in-Darien experience noted:

> I rarely tell this story, but it feels as if I went from a medical nightmare to the universe stepping in, allowing Mom and Dad to pass away peacefully with each other. I admit that it's beyond my understanding, but I believe that I had a special glimpse into a world rarely seen.[7]

Given the profound nature of these experiences, there should be far less taboo and ridicule associated with research and debate about them, and more importantly, with the personal nature of the experience. And yet, in so many NDE accounts we hear that the experiencer didn't initially share their story with anyone, for fear of being labeled as crazy. In one survey, an incredible 57% of NDErs said that they had been afraid or reluctant to talk about their experience, while more than one in every four didn't tell a single soul about it until *more than a year* had passed![8] Similarly, Peter Fenwick has noted that many carers who recounted witnessing end-of-life experiences in the dying said that it was the first time they had "admitted" it to anyone, as they had previously feared ridicule or even dismissal from their job.[9] For a profound death-bed vision or NDE to not be shared among family members for fear of being considered 'woo-woo' should not be an option, and for a dying person to be treated with less respect for reporting what may be the most fulfilling and important event in their life is almost criminal. Palliative care expert Deborah O'Connor has noted that when palliative care nurses are comfortable with the idea that 'paranormal phenomena' are occurring, it "assisted them to respond to patient reports and to communicate them positively to family and friends of the dying person, normalising the experience within the palliative care setting". Regardless of our views on what these experiences might mean, it is far past time to bring them into the open and regard them as normal, and common, human experiences.

Death is the Road to Awe

Whether you believe in a life after death or not, we all should acknowledge death, and what it brings to life. As palliative care physician Michael Barbato wrote in his book *Reflections of a Setting Sun*, "it may seem hard to believe but the people I care for and their families are more attuned to life than most others. Every moment of a dying person's life is priceless and they endeavour to use this time fruitfully and fully. Because they are dying, they see life and death as never before...in the words of Henry Thoreau, 'darkness reveals the heavenly lights'".

The common thread that should unite all of us, regardless of our belief, is that this life is very likely the only time that you – at least, as 'you' – will experience this Earth and the singular joys it brings. We should therefore cherish every day alive on Earth as a gift. Ann Druyan wrote of the death of her husband, the great science communicator Carl Sagan, in the following words:

> I don't ever expect to be reunited with Carl. But, the great thing is that when we were together, for nearly twenty years, we lived with a vivid appreciation of how brief and precious life is. We never trivialized the meaning of death by pretending it was anything other than a final parting. Every single moment that we were alive and we were together was miraculous...We knew we were beneficiaries of chance. That pure chance could be so generous and so kind... That we could find each other, in the vastness of space and the immensity of time... I don't think I'll ever see Carl again. But I saw him. We saw each other. We found each other in the cosmos, and that was wonderful.[10]

Scientists tell us we are all "made of star dust", while Christian funeral liturgies exhort us to remember that "you are dust, and to dust you shall return". Both statements are worth contemplating: our bodies are a miraculous assembly of molecules born from dying suns, infused with the mystery of life and consciousness for the blink of an eye in the cosmic scale of things, before dissipating back into the universe once more. Regardless of our model of reality we should all recognize, and embrace, how truly magical our conscious existence is.

Steve Jobs said that remembering he would one day die was "the most important tool I've ever encountered to help me make the big choices in life. Because almost everything – all external expectations, all pride, all fear of embarrassment or failure – these things just fall away in the face of death, leaving only what is truly important. Remembering that you are going to die is the best way I know to avoid the trap of thinking you have something to lose. You are already naked. There is no reason not to follow your heart".[11]

'Death makes life possible', was the message that Jobs wanted to convey. "No one wants to die. Even people who want to go to heaven don't want to die to get there. And yet death is the destination we all share. No one has ever escaped it. And that is as it should be, because death is very likely the single best invention of life. It is life's change agent. It clears out the old to make way for the new".

If we give credence to the accounts of near-death experiencers, the message they bring back about the importance of life is clear. Almost without exception, they return with the same conclusion: the 'judgement' they submitted to during the life review stage of their NDE was a personal one, and hinged on two main questions: "What did you do with your life, and how did your actions impact upon others?" The 'being of light' didn't do the judging, instead it offered unconditional love while facilitating the review of one's life. Many NDErs return from this 'judgement' and dedicate their lives to learning, as well as embracing their creative talents. They are also often transformed in their behaviour and attitude towards others; remember the ancient NDE tale of Aridaeus of Soli, who was changed so much that he was given a new name by his community, 'Thespesius', meaning 'divine' or 'wonderful', due to his care and charity toward others. There are certainly worse ways to live your life than through the 'teachings' of the NDE . As one wag once quipped, on the day your life flashes before you, you should make sure it's worth watching...

When I put the question of how we should each approach our own deaths to Michael Barbato – a man who has worked on a daily basis with those doing so – he preaches a similar message. "The best way to prepare for death is to lead a full and self-actualising life", he tells me. "The art of dying well is learnt through the art of living well". As one of his patients told him: "It's not what I did that I regret but the things I didn't do".[12] Also important, Barbato says, are "seeing and accepting death as the natural end to life; bringing death back into the living room (not avoiding the subject when it arises) and preparing for one's own death (taking ownership of it)". In the modern world, he says, medicine struggles to adequately care for the dying. Though doctors have enormous skill and unquestionable dedication to their profession, the simple fact is that their goal is to keep people alive. "If death is seen as the enemy, it will always be met with resistance", Barbato remarks sagely in *Reflections of a Setting Sun.* "If we accept it as the natural end to life then we are more likely to respect its omnipresence and be better prepared when the bell tolls". But today we often sequester the dying in hospitals or palliative care facilities, and as such few people have actually sat through someone else's death. Those who do, such as Michael Barbato, note that the experience brings death 'to life' and allows them to get to know it. "We feel its might – the length, breadth and depth of the emotions that accompany it – and we are overwhelmed by its presence... Death is not the conclusion to a series of medical events but a profound human experience".[13]

Palliative care pioneer Elizabeth Kubler-Ross wisely noted that a fear of death does not prevent death; instead, it prevents living. While we should take the time to consider our own mortality, we should not dwell on it or fear the moment. Instead, we must seize hold of each day and embrace every moment that we are given on this mortal plane, while knowing and graciously accepting that the next moment could be our last.

Michael Barbato sums it up beautifully: "Life is a precious gift that must one day be returned". Regardless of what we believe about the survival of consciousness after death, we should all remember that.

"Let us, at least, not clamour for immortality, not pledge our hearts to it. If the end is sleep, well, when we are tired, sleep is the final bliss.

And yet perhaps what dies is only the dear trivial familiar self of each. Perhaps in our annihilation some vital and eternal thing does break wing, fly free. We cannot know.

But this we know: whether we are annihilated or attain in some strange way eternal life, to have loved is good."

– Olaf Stapledon

NOTES

Preface: Exit Music.

1. http://goo.gl/1hseKy
2. Robert Maio, quoted in documentary series *Matters of Life and Death*

Introduction: Ghosts in the Machine?

1. Ritchie, George G., and Elizabeth Sherrill. *Return from tomorrow.* Revell, 1978.
2. Ibid.
3. Haisch, Bernard. *The God theory: universes, zero-point fields, and what's behind it all.* Weiser Books, 2006.
4. Devoto, Bernard, ed. *Mark Twain: Letters from the Earth.* Harper & Row, 1962.
5. Quoted in Deutsch, David. *The fabric of reality.* Penguin UK, 2011.
6. Crick, Francis. *Astonishing hypothesis: The scientific search for the soul.* Scribner, 1995.
7. Cited in Gardner, James N. *The intelligent universe: AI, ET, and the emerging mind of the cosmos.* Career Press, 2006.
8. Davies, Paul CW. "Life, Mind, and Culture as Fundamental Properties." *Cosmos & Culture: Cultural Evolution in a Cosmic Context* 4802 (2010): 383.
9. Ibid.
10. Nagel, Thomas. *Mind and cosmos: why the materialist neo-Darwinian conception of nature is almost certainly false.* Oxford University Press, 2012.
11. Rosenblum, Bruce, and Fred Kuttner. *Quantum enigma: Physics encounters consciousness.* Oxford University Press, 2011.
12. Stapp, Henry P. *Mindful universe: Quantum mechanics and the participating observer.* Springer, 2011.

13. Van Lommel, Pim. *Consciousness beyond life: The science of the near-death experience.* HarperCollins, 2010.

14. Greyson, Bruce. "Seeing dead people not known to have died:"Peak in Darien" experiences." *Anthropology and Humanism* 35, no. 2 (2010): 159-171.

15. Ibid.

Chapter 1: No One Dies Alone.

1. http://goo.gl/VxWK32

2. Fenwick, Peter, Hilary Lovelace, and Sue Brayne. "Comfort for the dying: five year retrospective and one year prospective studies of end of life experiences." *Archives of gerontology and geriatrics* 51, no. 2 (2010): 173-179.

3. Ibid.

4. MacConville, Una, and Regina McQuillan "Capturing the Invisible: exploring deathbed experiences in Irish Palliative Care", unpublished conference paper.

5. Kelly, Edward F., and Emily Williams Kelly. *Irreducible mind: Toward a psychology for the 21st century.* Rowman & Littlefield, 2007.

6. "Palliative Care Nurses' Experiences of Paranormal Phenomena and Their Influence on Nursing Practice", Deborah O'Connor, unpublished conference paper.

7. Cited in Kelly, Edward F., and Emily Williams Kelly. *Irreducible mind: Toward a psychology for the 21st century.* Rowman & Littlefield, 2007.

8. Barbato, Michael. *Reflections of a Setting Sun: Healing Experiences Around Death.* Michael Barbato, 2009.

9, Giovetti, P. "Visions of the dead, death-bed visions and near-death experiences in Italy." *Human Nature* 1, no. 1 (1999): 38-41.

10. Barbato, Michael. *Reflections of a Setting Sun: Healing Experiences Around Death.* Michael Barbato, 2009.

11. Clarke, Edward Hammond. *Visions: a study of false sight (pseudopia).* Houghton, Osgood, 1880.

12. Cobbe, Frances Power. *The Peak in Darien: With Some Other Inquiries Touching Concerns of the Soul and the Body.* Williams and Norgate, 1882.

13. Ibid.

14. Ibid.

15. Ibid.

16. Miller, Francis Trevelyan. *Thomas A. Edison: Benefactor of Mankind*. (1931).

17. Barrett, Sir William. *Death-bed visions*. London, England: Methuen, 1926.

18. Cobbe, Frances Power. *The Peak in Darien: With Some Other Inquiries Touching Concerns of the Soul and the Body*. Williams and Norgate, 1882.

19. Barrett, W. F. *On the Threshold of the Unseen: Spiritualism & Evidence for Survival After Death*. 1917.

20. Kalmus, Natalie M., 1949 "Doorway to Another World". Coronet 25(6):29–31, cited in Greyson, Bruce. "Seeing dead people not known to have died:"Peak in Darien" experiences." *Anthropology and Humanism* 35, no. 2 (2010): 159-171.

21. Barbato, Michael. *Reflections of a Setting Sun: Healing Experiences Around Death*. Michael Barbato, 2009.

22. Ibid.

23. Barbato, Michael, Cathy Blunden, Kerry Reid, Harvey Irwin, and Paul Rodriguez. "Parapsychological phenomena near the time of death." *Journal of palliative care* 15, no. 2 (1999): 30.

24. Barbato, Michael. *Reflections of a Setting Sun: Healing Experiences Around Death*. Michael Barbato, 2009.

25. Ibid.

26. Ibid.

27. Ibid.

28. Roy, Archie E. *The Eager Dead: A Study in Haunting*. Book Guild Limited, 2008.

29. Fenwick, Peter. "Dying: A Spiritual Experience as Shown by Near Death Experiences and Deathbed Visions". http://goo.gl/YcmzuQ.

30. Fenwick, Peter. "Non Local Effects in The Process of Dying: Can Quantum Mechanics Help?." *NeuroQuantology* 8, no. 2 (2010).

31. O'Connor, Deborah. "Palliative Care Nurses' Experiences of Paranormal Phenomena and Their Influence on Nursing Practice", unpublished conference paper.

32. At the time of publication, Deborah O'Connor (see previous note).

33. 'The Death Whisperers", *The Weekend Australian,* http://goo.gl/JXNjrs

34. Fenwick, Peter. "Non Local Effects in The Process of Dying: Can Quantum Mechanics Help?." *NeuroQuantology* 8, no. 2 (2010).

35. Cited in Moody, Raymond. *Glimpses of Eternity: An Investigation Into Shared Death Experiences.* Random House, 2011.

36. Fenwick, Peter. "Non Local Effects in The Process of Dying: Can Quantum Mechanics Help?." *NeuroQuantology* 8, no. 2 (2010).

37. Cited in Howarth, Glennys, and Allan Kellehear. "Shared near-death and related illness experiences: Steps on an unscheduled journey." *Journal of Near-Death Studies* 20, no. 2 (2001): 71-85.

38. Burgess, OO (1908). "Hallucinations experienced in connection with dying persons". *Journal of the Society for Psychical Research,* 13, 308–311. Dale, LA (1952).

39. Ibid.

40. Santos, Franklin Santana, and Peter Fenwick. "Death, End of Life Experiences, and Their Theoretical and Clinical Implications for the Mind–Brain Relationship." In *Exploring Frontiers of the Mind-Brain Relationship,* pp. 165-189. Springer New York, 2012.

41. Fenwick, P. B. C., and Elizabeth Fenwick. *The art of dying.* Bloomsbury Academic, 2008.

42. Rogo, D. Scott. *A psychic study of the music of the spheres.* Anomalist Books, 2005.

43. Rogo, D. Scott. *A casebook of otherworldly music.* Anomalist Books, 2005, and Rogo, D. Scott. *A psychic study of the music of the spheres.* Anomalist Books, 2005.

44. Rogo, D. Scott. *A psychic study of the music of the spheres.* Anomalist Books, 2005.

45. Cited in Rogo, D. Scott. *A casebook of otherworldly music.* Anomalist Books, 2005.

46. Barrett, Sir William. *Death-bed visions.* London, England: Methuen, 1926.

47. Ibid.

48. Fenwick, P. B. C., and Elizabeth Fenwick. *The art of dying.* Bloomsbury Academic, 2008.

49. Fenwick, Peter, Hilary Lovelace, and Sue Brayne. "Comfort for the

dying: five year retrospective and one year prospective studies of end of life experiences." *Archives of gerontology and geriatrics* 51, no. 2 (2010): 173-179.

50. Splittgerber (1881), cited in Nahm, Michael. "Terminal lucidity in people with mental illness and other mental disability: An overview and implications for possible explanatory models." *Journal of Near-Death Studies* 28, no. 2 (2009): 87.

51. Fenwick, P. B. C., and Elizabeth Fenwick. *The art of dying.* Bloomsbury Academic, 2008.

52. Barbato, Michael. *Reflections of a Setting Sun: Healing Experiences Around Death.* Michael Barbato, 2009.

53. Gauld, Alan. *The founders of psychical research.* Routledge & K. Paul, 1968.

54. Ibid.

55. Gurney, Edmund, Frederic WH Myers, and Frank Podmore. *Phantasms of the living* (2 vols.). London: Trubner (1886).

56. http://archive.org/details/phantasmsoflivin02gurniala

57. Fenwick, Peter, Hilary Lovelace, and Sue Brayne. "Comfort for the dying: five year retrospective and one year prospective studies of end of life experiences." *Archives of gerontology and geriatrics* 51, no. 2 (2010): 173-179.

58. Gauld, Alan. *The founders of psychical research.* Routledge & K. Paul, 1968.

59. Cited in Gauld, Alan. *The founders of psychical research.* Routledge & K. Paul, 1968.

60. Fenwick, P. B. C., and Elizabeth Fenwick. *The truth in the light: An investigation of over 300 near-death experiences.* Berkley Books, 1997.

61. Fenwick, P. B. C., and Elizabeth Fenwick. *The art of dying.* Bloomsbury Academic, 2008.

62. Kelly, Edward F., and Emily Williams Kelly. *Irreducible mind: Toward a psychology for the 21st century.* Rowman & Littlefield, 2007.

63. Fenwick, P. B. C., and Elizabeth Fenwick. *The art of dying.* Bloomsbury Academic, 2008.

64. Though, as with many other people of this time, Happich certainly had some ideas that most today would find abhorrent, such as forced sterilisation.

65. Nahm, Michael. "Terminal lucidity in people with mental illness and other mental disability: An overview and implications for possible

explanatory models." *Journal of Near-Death Studies* 28, no. 2 (2009): 87.

66. Cited in Nahm, Michael. "Terminal lucidity in people with mental illness and other mental disability: An overview and implications for possible explanatory models." *Journal of Near-Death Studies* 28, no. 2 (2009): 87.

67. Nahm, Michael. "Terminal lucidity in people with mental illness and other mental disability: An overview and implications for possible explanatory models." *Journal of Near-Death Studies* 28, no. 2 (2009): 87.

68. Ibid.

69. Ibid.

70. Rogo, D. Scott. *Nad.* University Books, 1972.

71. Nahm, Michael. "Terminal lucidity in people with mental illness and other mental disability: An overview and implications for possible explanatory models." *Journal of Near-Death Studies* 28, no. 2 (2009): 87.

72. Fenwick, Peter, Hilary Lovelace, and Sue Brayne. "Comfort for the dying: five year retrospective and one year prospective studies of end of life experiences." *Archives of gerontology and geriatrics* 51, no. 2 (2010): 173-179.

73. MacConville, Una, and Regina McQuillan "Capturing the Invisible: exploring deathbed experiences in Irish Palliative Care", unpublished conference paper.

74. O'Connor, Deborah. "Palliative Care Nurses' Experiences of Paranormal Phenomena and Their Influence on Nursing Practice", unpublished conference paper.

75. Kelly, Edward F., and Emily Williams Kelly. *Irreducible mind: Toward a psychology for the 21st century.* Rowman & Littlefield, 2007.

76. Cited in Kelly, Edward F., and Emily Williams Kelly. *Irreducible mind: Toward a psychology for the 21st century.* Rowman & Littlefield, 2007.

Chapter 2: A Glimpse Behind the Veil

1. http://www.dailygrail.com/Spirit-World/2012/1/is-Bens-Story

2. http://youtu.be/GEhAtP2Fnb8

3. http://youtu.be/GEhAtP2Fnb8

4. Van Lommel, Pirn, Ruud van Wees, Vincent Meyers, and Ingrid Elfferich. "Near-death experience in survivors of cardiac arrest: a prospective

study in the Netherlands." *The Lancet* 358, no. 9298 (2001): 2039-2045.

5. Van Lommel, P. (2013) "Non-local Consciousness". *Journal of Consciousness Studies*, Volume 20, No. 1-2, pp. 7 – 48.

6. Carter, Chris. *Science and the near-death experience: How consciousness survives death.* Inner Traditions/Bear & Co, 2010.

7. Gabbard, G. O., & Twemlow, S. W. (1984). *With the Eyes of the Mind: An Empirical Analysis of Out-of-Body States.* New York: Praeger.

8. Morse, Melvin, and Paul Perry. *Parting visions: Uses and meanings of pre-death, psychic, and spiritual experiences.* Villard Books, 1994.

9. van Lommel P, van Wees R, Meyers V, Elfferich I. (2001) "Near-Death Experience in Survivors of Cardiac Arrest: A prospective Study in the Netherlands", *The Lancet,* 358(9298):2039–45

10. Van Lommel, P. (2013) "Non-local Consciousness". *Journal of Consciousness Studies*, Volume 20, No. 1-2, pp. 7 – 48. r

11. Long, Jeffrey, and Paul Perry. *Evidence of the afterlife: The science of near-death experiences.* HarperCollins, 2010.

12. Van Lommel, Pim. *Consciousness beyond life: The science of the near-death experience.* HarperCollins, 2010.

13. Greyson, Bruce, "Science and Postmortem Survival", lecture at the Society for Scientific Exploration, http://goo.gl/j0Sgjq

14. Ibid.

15. Greyson, Bruce, Emily Williams Kelly, and Edward F. Kelly. "Explanatory models for near-death experiences." (2009).

16. Ibid.

17. Parnia, Sam, and Peter Fenwick. "Near death experiences in cardiac arrest: visions of a dying brain or visions of a new science of consciousness." *Resuscitation* 52, no. 1 (2002): 5-11.

18. Greyson, Bruce, Emily Williams Kelly, and Edward F. Kelly. "Explanatory models for near-death experiences." (2009).

19. Bruce Greyson told me that "Morse at el (1985) and Klemenc-Ketis et al (2010) found no association between blood oxygen and NDEs; Sabom (1982) found INCREASED arterial oxygen associated with NDEs rather than decreased; and Parnia et al (2001) found that oxygen levels in resuscitated patients who reported NDEs were TWICE those of resuscitated patients who did not report NDEs. NO STUDY has even found decreased oxygen levels to any degree associated with NDEs, as

Braithwaite presupposes."

20. Greyson, Bruce, "Science and Postmortem Survival", lecture at the Society for Scientific Exploration, http://goo.gl/j0Sgjq

21. Cook, Emily Williams, Bruce Greyson, and Ian Stevenson. "Do any near-death experiences provide evidence for the survival of human personality after death? Relevant features and illustrative case reports." *Journal of Scientific Exploration* 12, no. 3 (1998): 377-406.

22. Ibid.

23. Ibid.

24. Ibid.

25. Smit, Rudolf H. "Corroboration of the dentures anecdote involving veridical perception in a near-death experience." *Journal of Near-Death Studies* 27, no. 1 (2008): 47-61.

26. Van Lommel, Pirn, Ruud van Wees, Vincent Meyers, and Ingrid Elfferich. "Near-death experience in survivors of cardiac arrest: a prospective study in the Netherlands." *The Lancet* 358, no. 9298 (2001): 2039-2045.

27. Smit, Rudolf H. "Corroboration of the dentures anecdote involving veridical perception in a near-death experience." *Journal of Near-Death Studies* 27, no. 1 (2008): 47-61.

28. Sartori, P., P. Badham, and P. Fenwick. "A prospectively studied near-death experience with corroborated out of body perception and unexplained healing." *Journal of Near-Death Studies* 25, no. 2 (2006): 69-84.

29. Ibid.

30. Ibid.

31. Ibid.

32. Beauregard, Mario, Évelyne Landry St-Pierre, Gabrielle Rayburn, and Philippe Demers. "Conscious mental activity during a deep hypothermic cardiocirculatory arrest?." *Resuscitation* 83, no. 1 (2012): e19.

33. Holden, Janice Miner. "Veridical perception in near-death experiences," in *The Handbook of Near-Death Experiences*. Praeger, 2009.

34. Ibid.

35. Kelly, Edward F., and Emily Williams Kelly. *Irreducible mind: Toward a psychology for the 21st century.* Rowman & Littlefield, 2007.

36. BBC documentary "The Day I Died", cited in Carter, Chris. *Science and the near-death experience: How consciousness survives death.* Inner Traditions/Bear & Co, 2010

37. http://youtu.be/JL1oDuvQR08

38. Tyrell, George NM. *Apparitions*. 1953.

39. Ring, Kenneth, and R. N. Madelaine Lawrence. "Further evidence for veridical perception during near-death experiences." *Journal of Near-Death Studies* 11, no. 4 (1993): 223-229.

40. Kelly, Edward F., and Emily Williams Kelly. *Irreducible mind: Toward a psychology for the 21st century*. Rowman & Littlefield, 2007.

41. Cited in Cook, Emily Williams, Bruce Greyson, and Ian Stevenson. "Do any near-death experiences provide evidence for the survival of human personality after death? Relevant features and illustrative case reports." *Journal of Scientific Exploration* 12, no. 3 (1998): 377-406.

42. Holden, Janice Miner. "Veridical perception in near-death experiences," in *The Handbook of Near-Death Experiences*.

43. Kelly, Edward F., and Emily Williams Kelly. *Irreducible mind: Toward a psychology for the 21st century*. Rowman & Littlefield, 2007.

44. Parnia, Sam, and Josh Young. *Erasing death: The science that is rewriting the boundaries between life and death*. HarperCollins, 2013.

45. http://www.horizonresearch.org/main_page.php?cat_id=38

46. Tart, Charles T. "Six studies of out-of-body experiences." *Journal of Near-Death Studies* 17, no. 2 (1998): 73-99.

47. Parnia, Sam, and Josh Young. *Erasing death: The science that is rewriting the boundaries between life and death*. HarperCollins, 2013.

48. Ibid.

49. Ibid.

50. Ibid.

51. Ibid.

52. Ibid.

53. Ibid.

54. Ibid.

55. Greyson, Bruce. "Seeing dead people not known to have died:"Peak in Darien" experiences." *Anthropology and Humanism* 35, no. 2 (2010): 159-171.

56. Greyson, Bruce, "Science and Postmortem Survival", lecture at the Society for Scientific Exploration, http://goo.gl/j0Sgjq

57. Greyson, Bruce. "Seeing dead people not known to have died:"Peak in Darien" experiences." *Anthropology and Humanism* 35, no. 2 (2010): 159-171.

58. Crookall, Robert. *The study and practice of astral projection*. New

York: University Books, 1966.

59. Van Lommel, Pim. *Consciousness beyond life: The science of the near-death experience.* HarperCollins, 2010.

60. Ibid.

61. Cited in De Morgan, Sophia Elizabeth Frend, and Augustus De Morgan. *From matter to spirit: The result of ten years' experience in spirit manifestations. Intended as a guide to enquirers.* London, Longman, Green, Longman, Roberts, & Green, 1863.

Chapter 3: Voices From Beyond?

1. Hodgson, Richard. "A further record of observations of certain phenomena of trance." In *Proceedings of the Society for Psychical Research*, vol. 13, pp. 284-582. 1898.

2. Piper, Alta L. *The life and work of Mrs. Piper.* K. Paul, Trench, Trubner & Company, Limited, 1929.

3. Ibid.

4. Blum, Deborah. *Ghost hunters: William James and the search for scientific proof of life after death.* Penguin, 2007.

5. Spence, Lewis. *Encyclopedia of occultism & parapsychology.* Kessinger Publishing, LLC, 2003.

6. Robbins, Anne Manning. *Both sides of the veil: a personal experience.* Sherman, French & Company, 1909.

7. Hodgson, Richard. "A record of observations of certain phenomena of trance." In *Proceedings of the Society for Psychical Research*, 8, 1-167. 1892

8. Ibid.

9. Blum, Deborah. *Ghost hunters: William James and the search for scientific proof of life after death.* Penguin, 2007.

10. Cited in Simon, Linda. *Genuine reality: A life of William James.* University of Chicago Press, 1999.

11. Robbins, Anne Manning. *Both sides of the veil: a personal experience.* Sherman, French & Company, 1909.

12. Lodge, Oliver. *The survival of man.* Methuen, 1909.

13. Simon, Linda. *Genuine reality: A life of William James.* University of Chicago Press, 1999.

14. Ibid.

15. Ibid.

16. Richardson, Robert D. *William James: In the maelstrom of American modernism*. Mariner Books, 2007.

17. Simon, Linda. *Genuine reality: A life of William James*. University of Chicago Press, 1999.

18. Ibid.

19. Ibid.

20. Ibid.

21. Sage, Michel. *Mrs. Piper & the Society for psychical research*. Scott-Thaw co., 1904.

22. Blum, Deborah. *Ghost hunters: William James and the search for scientific proof of life after death*. Penguin, 2007.

23. James, W. (1886). "Report of the Committee on Mediumistic Phenomena". *Proceedings of the American Society for Psychical Research*, 1, 102-106.

24. Hamilton, Trevor. *Immortal longings: FWH Myers and the Victorian search for life after death*. Imprint Academic, 2009.

25. Melton, J. G. "Spiritualism." *Encyclopedia of American Religions*, Volume 2. Wilmington, NC: McGrath Publishing Company. 1978

26. Chan. M. (2009). "Warrior gods incarnate of Chinese popular religion". Unpublished manuscript., cited in Graham, F. "Vessels for the gods: tang-ki spirit-mediums in Chinese popular religion" (forthcoming)

27. Gauld, Alan. *Mediumship and survival: A century of investigations*. Academy Chicago Publishersm, 1984.

28. Ibid.

29. Cited in Grosso, Michael. *Experiencing the next world now*. Simon and Schuster. 2004.

30. Case notes taken from Grosso, Michael. *Experiencing the next world now*. Simon and Schuster. 2004.

31. Hamilton, Trevor. *Tell My Mother I'm Not Dead: A Case Study in Mediumship Research*. Imprint Academic, 2012.

32. Grosso, Michael. *Experiencing the next world now*. Simon and Schuster. 2004.

33. Gauld, Alan. *Mediumship and survival: A century of investigations*. Academy Chicago Publishersm, 1984.

34. Ibid.

35. Cited in Grosso, Michael. *Experiencing the next world now.* Simon and Schuster. 2004.

36. Johnson, Alice. "On the automatic writing of Mrs. Holland." In *Proceedings of the Society for Psychical Research,* vol. 21, pp. 166-391. 1908.

37. Hamilton, Trevor. *Tell My Mother I'm Not Dead: A Case Study in Mediumship Research.* Imprint Academic, 2012.

38. Ibid.

39. Ibid.

40. Ibid.

41. Kelly, Emily Williams, and Dianne Arcangel. "An investigation of mediums who claim to give information about deceased persons." *The Journal of nervous and mental disease* 199, no. 1 (2011): 11-17.

42. Ibid.

43. Beischel, Julie. *Among Mediums: A Scientist's Quest for Answers.* Windbridge Institute, 2013.

44. Ibid.

45. "Research Brief: Proof-Focused Research: Gathering evidence to address anomalous information reception (AIR) by mediums", 2012. Accessed 10th August, 2013. http://www.windbridge.org/papers/ResearchBrief_Proof.pdf

46. http://www.afterlifescience.com

47. Kelly, Emily Williams, and Dianne Arcangel. "An investigation of mediums who claim to give information about deceased persons." *The Journal of nervous and mental disease* 199, no. 1 (2011): 11-17.

Chapter 4: Broadening Our Horizons.

1. http://goo.gl/XBhUKQ

2. Haraldsson, Erlendur. *Departed among the Living. An investigative study of afterlife encounters.* White Crow Books, 2012.

3. Kelly, Edward F., and Emily Williams Kelly. *Irreducible mind: Toward a psychology for the 21st century.* Rowman & Littlefield, 2007.

4. Bell & Karnosh, 1949; Choi, 2007, cited in Nahm, Michael. "Terminal lucidity in people with mental illness and other mental disability: An overview and implications for possible explanatory models." *Journal of Near-Death Studies* 28, no. 2 (2009): 87.

5. Lewin, 1980; Lorber, 1983, cited in Nahm, Michael. "Terminal

lucidity in people with mental illness and other mental disability: An overview and implications for possible explanatory models." *Journal of Near-Death Studies* 28, no. 2 (2009): 87.

6. http://goo.gl/mx5NVD

7. Linde, Andrei. "Inflation, quantum cosmology and the anthropic principle." *Science and ultimate reality* (2003): 426-458.

8. Ibid.

9. Ibid.

10. Rosenblum, Bruce, and Fred Kuttner. *Quantum enigma: Physics encounters consciousness.* Oxford University Press, 2011.

11. Ibid.

12. Ibid.

13. Zeilinger, Anton. "Why the quantum? 'It' from 'bit'? A participatory universe? Three far-reaching challenges from John Archibald Wheeler and their relation to experiment." *Science and Ultimate Reality: Quantum Theory, Cosmology and Computation* (2004): 201-20.

14. Cited in Kafatos, M., and Robert Nadeau. *The Non-Local Universe: the New Physics and Matters of the Mind.* 1999.

15. Quoted in *The Observer*, 25 January 1931

16. Stapp, Henry P. *Mindful universe: Quantum mechanics and the participating observer.* Springer, 2011.

17. Ibid.

18. Ibid.

19. Carter, Chris. *Science and the near-death experience: How consciousness survives death.* Inner Traditions/Bear & Co, 2010.

20. http://www-physics.lbl.gov/~stapp/stappeditedversion.pdf

21. Ibid.

22. Stapp, Henry P. "Compatibility of Contemporary Physical Theory with Personality Survival".

23. http://www-physics.lbl.gov/~stapp/stappeditedversion.pdf

24. Sahu, Satyajit, Subrata Ghosh, Batu Ghosh, Krishna Aswani, Kazuto Hirata, Daisuke Fujita, and Anirban Bandyopadhyay. "Atomic water channel controlling remarkable properties of a single brain microtubule: correlating single protein to its supramolecular assembly." *Biosensors and Bioelectronics* (2013).

25. Emerson, Daniel J., Brian P. Weiser, John Psonis, Zhengzheng

Liao, Olena Taratula, Ashley Fiamengo, Xiaozhao Wang et al. "Direct Modulation of Microtubule Stability Contributes to Anthracene General Anesthesia." *Journal of the American Chemical Society* 135, no. 14 (2013): 5389-5398.

26. Kelly, Edward F., and Emily Williams Kelly. *Irreducible mind: Toward a psychology for the 21st century.* Rowman & Littlefield, 2007.

27. Ibid.

28. http://www.nytimes.com/2007/08/14/science/14tier.html

29. Tipler, Frank J. *The physics of immortality: modern cosmology, God and the resurrection of the dead.* Random House Digital, Inc., 1994.

30. Appleyard, Bryan. "The Living Dead", in *The Times Online* (December 14, 2008).

Chapter 5: Memento Mori.

1. http://www.wired.com/wiredscience/2013/04/consciousness-after-death/2/

2. O'Connor, Deborah. "Palliative Care Nurses' Experiences of Paranormal Phenomena and Their Influence on Nursing Practice", unpublished conference paper.

3. Richardson, Robert D. *William James: In the maelstrom of American modernism.* Mariner Books, 2007.

4. Kelly, Edward F., and Emily Williams Kelly. *Irreducible mind: Toward a psychology for the 21st century.* Rowman & Littlefield, 2007.

5. Van Lommel, Pim. *Consciousness beyond life: The science of the near-death experience.* HarperCollins, 2010.

6. Fenwick, Peter, Hilary Lovelace, and Sue Brayne. "Comfort for the dying: five year retrospective and one year prospective studies of end of life experiences." *Archives of gerontology and geriatrics* 51, no. 2 (2010): 173-179.

7. Kessler, David. *Visions, Trips, and Crowded Rooms.* Hay House, Inc, 2010.

8. Kelly, Edward F., and Emily Williams Kelly. *Irreducible mind: Toward a psychology for the 21st century.* Rowman & Littlefield, 2007.

9. Brayne, Sue and Peter Fenwick. *End of Life Experiences: A guide for carers of the dying.* http://goo.gl/0VffBV

10. Druyan, Ann. "Ann Druyan Talks About Science, Religion, Wonder, Awe... and Carl Sagan." *Skeptical Inquirer* 27, no. 6 (2003): 25-30.

11. Steve Jobs, commencement address to graduating students at

Stanford University, 12 June 2005

12. Barbato, Michael. *Reflections of a Setting Sun: Healing Experiences Around Death.* Michael Barbato, 2009.

13. Ibid.

ACKNOWLEDGEMENTS

This book wouldn't have been possible without the contributions and friendship of a large number of wonderful people. They did more than simply support this work, they were instrumental in its creation. First off, I must give my sincere thanks to all the fantastic people who contributed to the crowd-funding campaign that 'kick-started' the entire project, regardless of the pledge – this book would not exist without your help. The following 'Gold' and 'Platinum' sponsors are owed a special mention and thank you:

Platinum sponsor: A. Goodrum.

Gold sponsors: Natalie Kerslake, L. van Veen, Michael Tymn, Bryan Colgur, Jeff Gardiner, Matt Cumberland, Gareth Pashley, N.J. Muse, Simon Green, Michael Prescott, G. Calof, Kevin Wright, Steve Thornton, Simon Nugent, Jamie Folse, Bobby Jones, Paul D. Condon, Luis Balaguer, Keith Ellis, Gene Semel, Ryan Weeks, Lars Henrik Laustsen, Frode, Pete Lyon, Tim Binnall, Gary Billingsley, Rick Petes and Michael Moulton.

Thanks also to those researchers and experiencers who graciously gave their time to answer my questions, including Bruce Greyson, Julie Beischel, Michael Barbato, Trevor Hamilton, Deborah Morris, Emily Kelly, Stuart Hameroff, A-J Charron and Kevin Wright. Michael Prescott offered feedback on an early draft of the book, as well as some much-needed positivity during the editing process!

Over the years I have also received much support from a number of friends, including David Pickworth, Rick Gned, Kat Lowry, James Kennedy, Miguel Romero, Richard Andrews, Grant Calof, Cat Vincent, David Metcalfe, Blair MacKenzie Blake, Luke and Graham Hancock, Matt Staggs, Steve Volk, Alan Boyle, David Pescovitz, Tim Binnall, Paul Kimball, John Higgs, John Reppion, Mark Staufer, Alex Tsakiris, Robert McLuhan, Dean Radin, Rupert Sheldrake, Michael Prescott, Paul Devereux, Jacques Vallee, Charles Laughlin, Loren Coleman, Andrew Gough, Mark Pilkington, David Luke, Jack Hunter, all the folks at The Anomalist, Mysterious Universe and Who Forted, Michael Scott, Mitch Horowitz, and Bill Block. Mark James Foster and Christopher Butler deserve a special mention for their fantastic work on the cover of this book, as well as their friendship and support. And of course, thanks to all those readers and supporters of The Daily Grail throughout the years for your contributions, from financial to moral support.

Last but certainly not least, overwhelming thanks and love to my family, who have had to endure a very long writing and editing process which has no doubt tested their patience to the limit. The sacrifices they made allowed me to create something that I am extremely proud of, and for that I owe them a great debt. All my love to Tonita, Isis, Phoenix and Maya, as well as Mum, Dad, Leanne, Natalie and the rest of my extended family.

If I have omitted anybody's name from the above list, the fault lies entirely with me. If you have helped me at some point on my journey, my unreserved thanks goes to you for the contribution you have made, and you have my sincere apologies for not including you above.

CPSIA information can be obtained at www.ICGtesting.com
Printed in the USA
BVOW05s1005311214

381543BV00002B/78/P

9 780987 422439